D0931593

A Catechism of the Catholic Church
2,000 Years of Faith and Tradition

A Catechism of the Catholic Church
2,000 Years of Faith and Tradition
by
Father Robert J. Fox

Franciscan Herald Press
1434 West 51st Street
Chicago, IL 60609

A *Catechism of the Catholic Church* by Father Robert J. Fox.
Copyright © 1979 by Franciscan Herald Press, 1434 West 51st Street, Chicago, IL, 60609. All rights reserved.

Second Printing

Library of Congress Cataloging in Publication Data

Fox, Robert Joseph, 1927–
  A Catechism of the Catholic Church.

    1. Catholic Church—History. 2. Church history.
I. Title.
BX945.2.F69   282   79-1120
ISBN 0-8199-0758-8

MADE IN THE UNITED STATES OF AMERICA

Contents

Introduction

This book on the Catholic Church is more than a history book. It contains much of the faith and traditions of the Church during its 2,000-year history. It was felt that such a book is needed for modern Catholic youth, and today's adults in the post-Vatican II Church. In this way one could be assisted in understanding his or her Catholic identity with the faith of our fathers, with the faith of the centuries, and recognize one's Catholic youth.

Occasionally, during the book, traditions have been incorporated which have been part of our Catholic heritage during its 2,000 years. It is true that not every tradition is the same as defined divine faith, but the mode in which the faith has often been handed down is tied up in customs and traditions very dear to Christians through the centuries.

For instance, while it is not defined as divine faith that St. James came as the apostle to Spain, yet the legends and traditions handed down for centuries, and the practices approved yet today, such as venerating his relics in Santiago and the granting of the Jubilee Indulgence whenever the Feast of St. James falls on a Sunday, which makes the entire year a Holy Year in Spain, with millions of pilgrims passing through the Holy Door of the Basilica—all this is part of the Catholic tradition and has a basis in defined faith. History verifies the devotion and celebrations of the people for centuries in such observances. The Church itself has approved and encouraged them. The same is true, for example, of Our Lady of Guadalupe in Mexico and Our Lady of Lourdes in France.

The author has made an effort to make the history of our Catholic faith during its 2,000 years a living reality, identified with the present. Rather than by the study of dry, abstract statistics, the story of our faith should come *alive* in this book for youthful readers. Aid is given to interpret some modern-day problems in the Church in relationship to the past. One can discover through the story of the faith in the lives of Christian people for 2,000 years that, after all, "nothing is new under the sun."

This story of the faith, lived for 2,000 years, offers the Catholic student not only a review of his basic Catholic faith but some apologetics as well, while relating Church history. A study of history will reveal to youth interested in mysticism that the Catholic Church has long been the home to great mystics.

Suggestions to Teachers Who Use This Catechism of Church History in the Classroom

Teaching from this book should be greatly facilitated by the format of questions and answers, which gives you the opportunity to approach definite topics under the general subject of each chapter. The history book could have been written without the questions and simply have had the answers form a continuous flow, one into the other, without the need to answer specific questions. Still, the author, who has taught grade and high school students for a quarter of a century, has learned by experience that the mind of youth is best recollected and their attention gained when specific questions are to be answered.

The method of questioning offers a valuable method of teaching. While the student may not have knowledge of the various subjects, yet, when a question is asked, it is human nature—and especially when the teacher has motivated his or her students—to *want* to discover the answer.

Teachers are cautioned against having students memorize specifics such as precise dates, which are soon forgotten by most. What is more important are the major *trends* of the Church's life during its 2,000-year history. This history book contains the story of the life of the Church. The teacher who *motivates* will make the life of Christ Jesus in his Church come alive, and students will thrill to discover their Catholic identity with 2,000 years of Christians who have gone before them but are united with them in the Communion of Saints.

The author of this history book has worked to create a balance so that students are not impressed only with the weaknesses of humanity in the Church but see the divine quality of Christ's Church shine through in the Church traditions and in the holiness of the saints, and even the common members. It is suggested, therefore, that the book *Saints and Heroes Speak* be a counterpart of this history book. The author has remained realistic in facing human weaknesses but always balances them with the qualities of holiness, catholicity, oneness and apostolicity so that the student can discover his or her *Catholic identity* and rightly conclude, in the objective facts of history, "This is indeed the Church of Jesus Christ."

The "points for discussion" at the end of each chapter will enable the teacher to give the student three opportunities to cover the subject matter. It can be accomplished in this way. The teacher may dedicate part of each class to presenting in his/her own style, but *without* questions, the part of the text which the student is to study at home. This is preparation (motivation) for home study.

The first part of the next class can be used for discussion and questioning the class on the assignment. The teacher then discusses twice in class, in a style different from the book itself, the various subjects of the book, while the student has read and studied the various questions at home, as well as sought the answers for the points of discussion at home.

The teacher with an imaginative mind will create a different style of questions from those explicitly asked in the book, to enable the student to digest and comprehend the matter more fully. As the teacher tells the story of the Church in his/her own words, preparing for home study, the class can be greatly motivated to seek fuller information.

What the teacher should especially endeavor to do is aid the student to understand and appreciate his/her *Catholic identity* while appealing to the *idealism* which is always a part of youth, without denying that at times, Christ's members have become spotted and the robe of Christ torn, but always the divinity of the Church protects, preserves, rebuilds, without the true Church being universally destroyed, because Christ promised otherwise.

A teacher may seek other background resource materials so as to comprehend the subject more fully, as those who teach generally need to know more than those they teach. Hopefully, the mistake will not be made—to pile so much upon students from all the resource materials available that students become discouraged or confused, when they do not yet have the maturity to judge or the capacity to sort out and remember every detail of history; and, as a result, little is accomplished.

The author has felt that the content in this book is sufficient challenge for students to gain a basic understanding of the history of the Church, without overwhelming them in the attempt to accomplish in one book or one year what scholars present in many volumes in several years.

Chapter 1
The Advent of the Church

1. What is the Catholic Church?

The Catholic Church is a community of faith, shared by people of all nations, united in Christ Jesus. The Church has both visible and invisible qualities.

2. What are some of the "invisible" qualities of the Catholic Church?

The invisible qualities of the Catholic Church are, first of all, Christ Jesus as head, keeping it in truth through the power of the Holy Spirit. The Holy Spirit, as the soul of the Church, dwells in the hearts of the faithful as in a temple. Invisible also are the acts of Christ, present in the Church's sacraments, which give glory to God and grace to men. Also invisible is the spiritual unity of the people in Christ, who form his Mystical Body, which is the Church.

3. What are the "visible" qualities of the Catholic Church?

The Catholic Church is a visible society of believers in one faith. The Pope, the head of the Church on earth, is visible, as are the bishops who form the organs of special authority, representative of Christ, and all the bishops, priests, deacons, religious, and laity, all of whom form the one, same Church. Also visible are the "signs" of the seven sacraments, which contain the power of Christ Jesus.

4. When did the Catholic Church begin?

The Catholic Church, as we know it, began almost 2,000 years ago, and was founded by our Lord and Savior, Jesus Christ. The Church was present "in figure" even at the beginning of the world. The Church was prepared in marvelous fashion in the history of the people of Israel and in the "old alliance."

Jesus Christ founded the Church so that the fruits of his redemption could be available for all times and for all nations. He founded the Church upon Peter, the Prince of the apostles, and promised that the Church would continue until the end of the world (Mt 28:13).

5. What is the sole Church of Christ, which in the Creed we profess to be one, holy, catholic, and apostolic?

According to Vatican Council II and the constant teaching of the Church, "This Church, constituted and organized as a society in the present world, subsists in the Catholic Church, which is governed by the successor of Peter and by the bishops in communion with him."

6. Does any religious truth and sanctity exist outside the Catholic Church?

Yes. Vatican II said: "Nevertheless, many elements of sanctification and of truth are found outside its visible confines. Since these are gifts belonging to the Church of Christ, they are forces impelling toward Catholic unity." The Catholic Church possesses the fullness of divine revelation from Christ, although not all its members live that truth to the full, as is shown by its history. Failure to live the true faith in holiness leads to disunity among Christ's members.

7. What was the greatest event in the history of salvation?

The greatest event in the history of salvation was when the Son of God, the Second Person of the Most Blessed Trinity, as the Word of God, was made flesh in the womb of the Virgin Mother Mary by the "overshadowing" of the Holy Spirit, so as to accomplish the redemption of the world by his death on the cross.

8. Was the Redemption foretold?

The promise of the Redeemer was made by God to our first parents, Adam and Eve, after their fall into sin. This promise of redemption was kept constantly alive in the souls of men by the patriarchs and prophets God sent his chosen people, as recorded in the Old Testament.

9. Did the hope of the Redeemer remain alive among people other than God's special chosen people of the Old Testament?

Yes, but only in a vague and corrupt manner. The heathen nations, or the Gentiles, which became separated from divine revelation as given by the one true God, fell into idolatry.

10. What historical incidents indicate that distorted traditions about a promised Redeemer remained even in heathen nations?

Seutonius and Tacitus, who wrote for ancient pagan Rome, are recorded as saying that the world was full of rumors about a mysterious power at the time of Christ, which was to come out of Palestine and rule the whole world according to ancient traditions. The Greeks had a legend that the son of their highest god would become man and be born of a virgin mother in order to redeem our fallen race. The emperor Mingdi of China in the year A.D. 64 sent ambassadors to the West to search for the divine teacher who was foretold in ancient books of China. They arrived at India, discovered the religion of Buddha, and embraced this religion, thinking it to be true. Many confused ancient pagans beliefs of pagan gods who appear in human form.

11. What role did God give the people of Israel in the history of salvation?

God chose the people of Israel, in spite of their being a small nation and their sinfulness, to keep alive the hope of the coming of the Redeemer of the world. These chosen people would foreshadow, in their history, the future kingdom of God on earth—the coming of the Savior who would establish the Church. The Redeemer was to come from their people, according to the divine promise.

12. What was significant about the location of the people of Israel?

These chosen people of God were established by divine power in Palestine, in the midst of great and ancient nations. To the east and north were the kingdoms of Babylonia, Assyria, and Persia. To the south was Egypt. To the west were the Macedonian and Roman empires. The prophet Ezekiel could therefore call Jerusalem the "gate of the nations." Palestine was the gateway from Africa to Asia. It had a waterway to India through the Red Sea.

God's chosen people, who retained the hope of the Messiah, spread into all great lands, and this prepared the way for the apostles of Christ Jesus to set forth from Jerusalem to take the Good News of Christ to the entire world.

13. Did God give special help to the people of Israel for their great mission to the world?

Yes. God frequently sent them prophets to keep them mindful of him. God guided this nation as his very own people, with divine protection.

14. How did God fulfill his promise of a Redeemer?

God kept his promise of a Redeemer, which he made in the Bible (Gn 3:15), by sending his only begotten Son, the Second Person of the Blessed Trinity, made Man. Jesus Christ was conceived in Mary by the power of the Holy Spirit and then was born of the same Virgin Mary. The birth of Jesus Christ was the beginning of the fulfillment of the great promise of God, first made to Adam and Eve.

15. How did Jesus Christ redeem the world?

Jesus Christ, true God and true Man, redeemed the entire world by his life, death, resurrection, and ascension into heaven, after which he, together with God the Father, sent the Holy Spirit upon the Church on Pentecost Sunday. This gave birth to the Church, which is the "people of God," the Mystical Body of Christ in the world. The Church, through the centuries, will always have the powers to continue the very same work that Jesus came to earth to accomplish.

16. What are the chief powers that Jesus Christ gave his Church to continue his work—to apply the fruits of his Redemption to all men?

The powers that Jesus Christ shares with his Church are:

1. To *teach* all nations of the world the Good News of the gospel and to keep it in the divine truth until the end of the world, through the power of the Holy Spirit (Mt 28:19-20, Jn 16:13).
2. To *sanctify* souls. This is done especially through the sacrifice of the Mass and the sacraments (Jn 20:23, Lk 22:19, Mt 28:19).
3. To *govern* the members of the Church in spiritual matters for their salvation (Mt 16:18-19, Jn 21:23).

17. How is the inner nature of the Church made known to us?

Vatican Council II answered this question in the following manner: "The inner nature of the Church is now made known to us in various images. Taken either from the life of the shepherd or from cultivation of the land, from the art of building or from family life and marriage, these images have their preparation in the books of the prophets.

"The Church is, accordingly, a sheepfold, the sole and necessary gateway to which is Christ (Jn 10:1-10). It is also the shepherd (cf. Is 40:11, Ex 34:11ff.), and whose sheep, although watched over by human shepherds, are nevertheless at all times led and brought to pasture by Christ himself, the Good Shepherd and Prince of shepherds (cf. Jn 10:11, 1 Pt 5:4), who gave his life for his sheep (cf. Jn 10:11-16).

"The Church is a cultivated field, the tillage of God. . . . Often, too, the Church is called the 'building of God' " (1 Cor 3:9). The Church, further, which is called "that Jerusalem which is above" and "our Mother" (Gal 4:26; cf. Rv 12:17), is described as the spotless spouse of the spotless lamb (Rv 19:7, 21:2, 9, 22:17)" (*Dogmatic Constitution on the Church*, Vatican II).

Jesus Christ, our Lord, called it his Church and said that the gates of hell shall not prevail against it (Mt 16:18). He spoke of the Church as one fold under one shepherd (Jn 10:16). Jesus spoke of the light of the world, the city on a mountain which cannot be hid (Mt 5:14), and he spoke of inaugurating the kingdom of heaven on earth, to be brought to its glorious completion at the end of time.

In the Bible the missionary apostle, St. Paul, calls the Church the ground and pillar of truth (1 Tm 3:15), the flock of Christ over which the bishops rule by the power of the Holy Spirit (Acts 20, 28).

Through the centuries, the Church has meditated on her inner nature, which is essentially divine but also has human elements. The fruit of almost 2,000 years of meditation on the nature of the Church is revealed in the *Dogmatic Constitution on the Church,* issued by the Ecumenical Council of the Church on November 21, 1964 (known as Vatican Council II).

18. In what condition was the world when Jesus came to found the Church?

The world was in the darkness of sin. The nations of the world were adoring false gods, idols—things of creation. In this worship of false gods, crimes were sometimes committed. Immorality was widespread and there was little respect for the rights of God or man. God's chosen people, the Jews, especially protected and guided by God, continued to worship the one true God. In spite of the evils of the world, God judged it was the "fullness of time" when he sent his only begotten Son into the world to redeem it.

19. What are some examples of false worship that prevailed when the Church was founded?

Greece and Rome, ruling nations with highly developed culture; nonetheless had false gods that their people worshiped. Venus was worshiped by impurity, Bacchus by drunkenness, Mars by bloody revenge. There was little respect for the unity of family life. The family was downgraded by divorce and women were degraded. Over two-thirds of the world's population was held in slavery. People, who considered themselves cultured, even questioned whether slaves were human beings. It took some time for Christianity to take root in the hearts of some and to accept that slaves have immortal souls. There were public games of gladiators in the circus, where they and captives were forced to kill one another to amuse the crowds.

20. Did God's chosen people, the Jews, accept Christ Jesus as the promised Messiah?

Some did. The apostles and our Blessed Mother were among this number. But as holy scripture testified, Jerusalem did not recognize God's moment when it came (cf. Lk 19:42). Jews for the most part did not accept the gospel; on the contrary, many opposed it (cf. Rom 11:28). Even so, the apostle Paul maintains that the Jews remain very dear to God for the sake of the patriarchs, since God does not take back the gifts he bestowed or the choice he made. Together with the prophets and that same apostle, the Church awaits the day, known to God alone, when all peoples will call on God with one voice and "serve him shoulder to shoulder" (Soh 3:9; cf. Is 66:23, Ps 65:4, Rom 11:11–32) (*Declaration on the Relation of the Church to Non-Christian Religions,* Vatican II).

21. What is the attitude of the Catholic Church toward the Jews who rejected Christ?

Vatican Council II spoke as follows about the Jews: "The Church of Christ acknowledges that in God's plan of salvation, the beginning of her faith and election is to be found in the patriarchs, Moses and the prophets. She professes that all Christ's faithful, who as men of faith are sons of Abraham (cf. Gal 3:7), are included in the same partriarch's call and that the salvation of the Church is mystically prefigured in the exodus of God's chosen people from the land of bondage. On this account the Church cannot forget that she received the revelation of the Old Testament by way of that people with whom God in his inexpressible mercy established the ancient covenant. Nor can she forget that she draws nourishment from that good olive tree onto which the wild olive branches of the Gentiles have been grafted (cf. Rom 11:17-24). The Church believes that Christ who is our peace has through his cross reconciled Jews and Gentiles and made them one in himself (cf. Eph 2:14-16).

"Even though the Jewish authorities and those who followed their lead pressed for the death of Christ (cf. Jn 19:6), neither all Jews indiscriminately at that time, nor Jews today, can be charged with the crimes committed during his passion. It is true that the Church is the new people of God, yet the Jews should not be spoken of as rejected or accursed as if this followed from holy Scripture. Consequently, all must take care, lest in catechizing or in preaching the Word of God they teach anything which is not in accord with the truth of the Gospel message or the spirit of Christ" (*Declaration on the Relation of the Church to Non-Christian Religions*, Vatican II).

22. What happened to the Jews who did not accept Christ after the birth of Christianity?

They continued to believe in the one true God but did not believe that the Son of God had become Man in Christ Jesus. They continued to accept the true faith of the old covenant, which we often speak of as the Old Testament of the Bible. They remain our ancestors in faith, under the one Fatherhood of God, with whom we have much in common. Unfortunately, they have not accepted Jesus Christ as the fulfillment of the Old Testament.

Summary

Immediately after Adam sinned entrance to the eternal life of Heaven was closed to him and his descendants. Man lost friendship with God through separation from sharing in the life of God, called sanctifying grace. Henceforth every child would be conceived with sin on its soul. Mankind fell into the depths of sin and suffering, and his body would undergo death. While sin was added to sin, man faced the prospect of eternal separation from the God who made him. Man was powerless to raise himself from his great misery of slavery to sin, or ever regain the beauty of God's life in his soul through his own power.

God, however, had promised our first parents a Redeemer, a Savior, who would in some way reopen the gates of heaven for mankind and make it possible for man to live in the hope of eternal life. God knew, in the divine plan which included the creation of man, that man would fall. From all eternity, then, it was in the mind and will of the all-holy God that the Second Person of God would become Man in Christ Jesus, born of the Virgin through her cooperation, and thus would the God-Man merit man's redemption.

Vatican Council II (in its first paragraphs in *Dogmatic Constitution on the Church*) said: "Already present in figure at the beginning of the world, this Church was prepared in marvelous fashion in the history of the people of Israel and in the old alliance. Established in this last age of the world, and made manifest in the outpouring of the Spirit, it will be brought to glorious completion at the end of time."

To Abraham, the father of the chosen people, whose story is told in the Book of Genesis, God promised: "In thy seed shall all the nations of the earth be blessed." During thousands of years of waiting and hoping for the Redeemer's coming, mankind offered sacrifice upon sacrifice, holocaust upon holocaust to its God. None is sufficient to appease God so as to lift man from sin and misery.

A thousand years after Abraham, God revealed to King David through the prophet Nathan that the throne of the Messiah would be forever: "I will be to him a father and he shall be to me a son."

Then 300 years pass, and God sends the prophet Isaiah. This prophet declares: "Behold, a virgin shall conceive and bear a son, and his name shall be called Emmanuel." That Son was Jesus Christ, who fulfilled all the Old Testament promises in establishing the Church.

Questions for Discussion

1. When did the Catholic Church begin?
2. What is meant by visible and invisible qualities of the Church?
3. When did God first foretell the redemption?
4. Did any peoples of the world besides the people of Israel have traces in their religions of the original promise made to our first parents? Explain your answer.
5. Explain how the insignificant nation and people of Israel were used by God to accomplish his plan for the establishment of the Church.
6. Were the Jews the only people who put Jesus Christ to death? Explain your answer.

Chapter 2
The Church of the First Century

1. Do any writers besides Christian writers speak of Jesus Christ in the first century?

Yes, non-Christian writers described the belief of Christians in the Christ whom they believed to be God made Man. The Jewish historian Josephus writes of Christ in this manner. Pliny, governor of Bithynia, sent a report to the emperor Trajan telling how Christians "honor Christ, their God."

2. At the coming of Jesus Christ, what was the world of Jewry like?

The Jewish people were no longer fully established in Palestine, the land which God had assigned to them. Many of their sons and daughters were dispersed throughout the world. Jesus did not preach the Good News to these dispersed Jews, nor to the pagans, Judea was subject to many rulers but the Roman power was dominant. The various rulers, Roman and Herodian, and Jewish high priests overlapped in authority. At the same time, the different peoples who had occupied the country, one after another, had each imposed some of its cults and civilization upon the Jews.

Many souls were "hard soil" and the faith could not take deep root in them. Nevertheless, there were Israelites, such as Nathanael, "in whom there was no guile" (Jn 1:47). There were among these chosen people the apostles, even if one, Judas, betrayed Jesus. There was Mary of Bethany, who broke the alabaster box to pour the most precious perfumes generously upon his head. There was, of course, their most noble member, the Mother of Jesus, the woman of faith.

Unfortunately, the pride of race, which perverts true religion, was operative, so that John the Baptist had warned: "Think not to say within yourselves, 'We have Abraham for our father,' for I tell you that God is able of these stones to raise up children to Abraham" (Mt 3:9–10). The apostles, finally, had to go to the Gentiles to preach the gospel and spread the Church when the majority of God's first chosen people rejected them.

3. When did the Church begin to convert many souls?

After Jesus ascended into heaven to be with his heavenly Father, Jesus kept his promise to send the Paraclete, the Spirit. On Pentecost Sunday the apostles were filled with the Holy Spirit as they prayed in the "upper room" with the Mother of Jesus. Pentecost is often called the "birthday of the Church," for then the Holy Spirit, the soul of the Church and the spirit of truth, empowered the apostles in a special way, with truth and courage, to profess the divine faith in Jesus Christ. With the special assistance and power of the Holy Spirit, thousands were soon converted. Believers in Christ Jesus increased daily. The Church spread over Judea, Galilee, Samaria, and into all the surrounding countries. It was at Antioch, the capital of Syria, that the faithful were first called Christians, because they were believers in Christ, sealed in him as their Lord and master.

4. To whom did Jesus Christ command the Apostles to preach the gospel?

Christ commanded the apostles to preach the Good News to all nations, Jews and Gentiles alike. Beginning at Pentecost, they were gifted to preach in tongues so that people of different nations understood them, each in his own language. At first it was difficult for the apostles (in some cases) to understand the command to preach to non-Jews. St. Peter had a heavenly vision to baptize Cornelius, a Gentile. The apostles called a council at Jerusalem among themselves, about the year 51, and decided that converted Gentiles did not have to observe the Mosaic rites but were nonetheless fully Christian. From the very beginning, then, the mark of Catholicity was to characterize the Church of Christ for all the nations.

5. Where did the Apostles preach when they went to the nations to carry out the command of Christ?

St. Peter first preached in Palestine, Syria, and Asia Minor. The other apostles immediately recognized that Peter had been placed as their head by Christ Jesus, and, therefore, he was in charge of the election to fill the vacancy left by Judas, when Matthias succeeded the traitor apostle. St. Peter also presided over the first council at Jerusalem. He established his see of authority at Antioch but went to Rome about A.D. 42. Rome, the capital of the world, seemed the best place to establish the chief see of authority for the Church which Christ had established for all the nations.

According to traditions (with many reliable proofs), St. John, the "beloved apostle" of the Lord, became the bishop of Ephesus and was in charge of the local churches of Asia Minor. Also, according to tradition, St. James, the brother of St. John, first preached in Judea and finally went to Spain. At

Santiago, to the present day, Spanish people come from all over the world to pay reverence to his bodily remains at the Cathedral of St. James, where they believe his relics lie in a silver casket.

St. James the Less became bishop of Jerusalem. He is also called St. James the Just because of his holiness.

St. Andrew went to southern Russia to preach, and to the coast of the Black Sea.

St. Philip died at Hierapolis in Phrygia, Asia Minor, and St. Bartholomew went to Armenia. St. Thomas is believed to have gone to India to spread the faith of Christ Jesus. St. Simon went to Egypt, North Africa, and Babylon. St. Jude Thaddeus went to Syria, Mesopotamia, and Persia. St. Matthias is believed to have gone into countries south of the Caucasus, and St. Matthew to countries south of the Caspian Sea.

6. Were the Apostles well received wherever they preached the Gospel?

Just as Jesus Christ was crucified and put to death for preaching the gospel, the apostles of Jesus were persecuted and put to death. St. John alone, to whom Jesus entrusted the Blessed Virgin Mary, died a natural death about 100, although attempts were made on his life.

7. Did St. Paul have great success in preaching the Gospel?

Yes. This saint, formerly called Saul, was not one of the original twelve Apostles. He wrote many of the New Testament epistles of the Bible and is known as the Apostle of the Gentiles. He was born around A.D. 5–10 at Tarsus in Cilicia, a Roman colony in Asia Minor. By trade, he was a tent maker. He studied in Jerusalem at the rabbinical school of Hillel.

About the year 36 he stood by at the stoning to death of the deacon Stephen, the first martyr of the Church. After this, on the road to Damascus, Saul was converted as a dazzling light blinded him and he heard the voice of Jesus: "Saul, Saul, why do you persecute me?" (cf. Acts 9:3–9).

After his conversion, St. Paul went on three famous missionary journeys, in 45–49, 50–52, and 53–58. He thereby established local churches throughout Asia Minor.

This man, called an apostle because he too had seen the Lord, wrote fourteen epistles. He was beheaded in Rome in the year 67.

8. Did Jesus help the apostles in any special way to establish the Church?

Yes. As mentioned, he instigated the gift of tongues on Pentecost. The preaching of the apostles was also testified as true by miracles that accompanied the Good News. The holiness of the apostles, as the Holy Spirit worked in them to witness Christ, had a great effect on conversions, and the shedding of their blood in martyrdom became the seed for more conversions.

9. Did the Apostles preach to the Jews?

Yes, but for the most part they were not accepted. It was the will of God that the gospel first be preached to God's chosen people, as Christ Jesus himself did. Many Jews were converted but usually not from the leaders, who persecuted the Christians (as Saul did before his conversion). Christ had foretold the destruction of Jerusalem, and the Roman army, under Titus, in the year 70 destroyed Jerusalem. The destruction of the temple, the center of God's worship in the old covenant, signified the end of both the old law and the unity of the chosen people who did not accept Christ.

10. Did the Apostles offer the divine liturgy of the Mass and the sacraments?

Yes. The Acts of the Apostles in the Bible gives us a short view of the first establishment of the Christian Church. Acts is a history of the early Church, although it does not tell us what was done by all the apostles. We are told that the essentials of the Mass and the sacraments were present and were essential to early Christian life.

Acts 2:42 says: "They were persevering in the doctrines of the apostles and in the communication of the breaking of bread and in prayers."

Acts 8:17 and 19:6 tell us that after baptism the sacrament of confirmation was administered by imposing an Apostle's hands and invoking the Holy Spirit, as St. Peter and St. John did in Samaria and St. Paul in Ephesus.

Acts 19:18 says: "Many of them that believed came confessing and declaring their deeds."

Acts 13:3 says: "One day while they were offering worship to the Lord and keeping a fast, the Holy Spirit said, 'I want Barnabas and Saul set apart for the work to which I have called them.' So it was that after fasting and prayer they laid their hands on them and sent them off." (This formula is still used in the rite of ordination.)

Ephesians 5:32 speaks of the mystery (sacrament) of matrimony.

Some books of the Bible are historical books, as well as the word of God, and give testimony to the various sacraments, such as the anointing of the sick (Jas 5:14) and penance (Jn 20:21–23).

11. Did the early Church have a hierarchy of authority?

Yes. The Bible clearly—in more than one way—signals the special authority of St. Peter, the first pope. Peter presided over special functions of the apostles. The early Church had deacons, priests, and bishops, as well as the pope as visible head.

St. Ignatius, writing in 107, said: "Let all be obedient to the bishop as Jesus to the Father, to the priests as to the apostles, and to the deacons as God's law." Writing just after the close of the first century, he looks to the Church at Rome as the head of the whole Church. St. Ignatius said to the Philadelphians: "Partake of the one Eucharist; for one is the body of the Lord Jesus Christ and one is the chalice of his blood, one altar and one bishop with the priests and the deacons."

12. Do we have any writings from the immediate disciples of the apostles?

Yes. St. Clement of Rome, who was the third successor of St. Peter and fourth Pope (88–97), wrote a letter to the Corinthians. St. Ignatius was a disciple of the apostle John and bishop of Antioch, and history records seven of his letters. Another disciple of John, St. Polycarp, bishop of Smyrna, wrote a letter. St. Barnabas, early companion of St. Paul, left a letter that is recorded in history.

St. Barnabus wrote about changing the Lord's day from Saturday to Sunday: "But we celebrate with festive joy the eighth day on which Jesus rose from the dead."

St. Ignatius wrote further about Sunday: "They [the Christians] have the new hope and do not keep the Sabbath. but regulate their lives according to the Lord's day."

13. Did all twelve apostles leave sacred writings of the Bible?

Not all of them. Jesus commanded the apostles to go forth and preach to all nations, but did not command them to write a book (or any writings) as such. However, these apostles wrote: Saints Peter and Paul, John, Matthew, James, and Jude Thaddeus. Also the two evangelists who were disciples of the apostles, viz., St. Luke and St. Mark.

The writings of these apostles and evangelists make up the New Testament of the Bible. The authority of the Catholic Church has declared their writings the inspired word of God. Their writings form the books of the "canon" of the New Testament.

The New Testament of the Bible is a Church book, written by churchmen under the inspiration of the Holy Spirit for the Church's use, to assist it in its duty of preaching God's word.

It was the Church's Council of Carthage (in North Africa) that published a canonical list of the sacred scriptures. The Church existed before the world had the Bible as we know it. The Church was in existence after Pentecost, before the last of the New Testament was written. The Church existed hundreds of years before the world knew the Bible, with its many books, as we do today.

The chief work of the apostles, upon whom Christ built his Church with Peter as the "rock," was to preach and establish the Church throughout the world through the living, spoken word through which faith comes. "Faith comes by hearing."

The Gospel of St. Matthew was not compiled until about the year 50, several years after the Ascension and Pentecost. St. John is credited with having written his gospel about the year 97.

14. Where did the Catholic Church get its canon of Old Testament books?

The Church looked to ancient Jewish tradition for authentic writings before Christ's coming. Jesus Christ himself and his apostles respected the ancient Jewish traditions regarding the scriptures and quoted them. The Septuagint, or Greek translation of the Old Testament, made about 200 years before the coming of Christ, was used by the apostles and the first Christians.

The canon of both the Old and the New Testaments was defined in a council of the Church at Rome under Pope Damasus in 374 and again at the African councils of Hippo in 393 and Carthage in 397.

15. Did the Church make efforts in the first century to translate the Bible?

The Church of the first century did not have a bible with its canons of the Old and New Testaments, as it was near the end of the first century before the last part of the New Testament was written. The canons of these two testaments had not yet been clearly defined by the Church.

Once the authority of the Church had more clearly defined the texts which were truly the inspired word of God (spurious writings, claiming to be inspired, also circulated in the early Christian world), the Catholic Church authorized translations from the original Hebrew and Greek texts.

A Latin translation was made for the Christians of the Roman Empire, called Itala. An Egyptian or Coptic translation was in use as early as the second century, even though the canon was not yet clearly determined. By the fourth and fifth centuries, Ethiopian and Armenian translations of the Bible were in use.

Partial or total translations were made following the conversion of the barbarian nations of Europe. Bishop Ulfila, who invented the Gothic alphabet, made a Gothic translation about 360. The Bible was translated into Slavic by Saints Methodius and Cyril, apostles of the Slavs, for whom they invented the alphabet. Venerable Bede, a Benedictine monk in England, finished an Anglo-Saxon translation of the Gospel of St. John on his deathbed in 735.

16. Did the Apostles have to struggle against false teachers within the Church?

Yes. Christ promised the Holy Spirit to keep the Church one in divine truth in faith and morals; but individual teachers, not teaching in harmony with the pope, can go astray. St. John wrote his gospel because Corinth and other localities were attacking the divinity of Jesus Christ. St. Peter condemned the teaching and practices of Simon Magus, who is called the Father of Heresy. The term "simony" comes from Simon, who offered money to St. Peter to obtain the power of imparting the gifts of the Holy Spirit. He was told: "Keep your money to yourself to perish with you." St. Paul also had to warn against false teachers.

Christ had predicted that false teachers would arise. At the Last Supper, Jesus prayed for unity in his Church.

17. Was the primacy of Peter's authority recognized in the first century?

Yes, and by the apostles as well as by the Christians of the first and succeeding centuries. Peter was the first apostle publicly to profess his faith in Jesus Christ, and Jesus promised Peter the primacy in the Church (Mt 16:16-19). After the resurrection of Jesus from the dead, this promise was fulfilled when Peter made his threefold profession of love for Jesus (Jn 21:15 ff.).

Peter acted as the leader of the first Christian community after Jesus ascended into heaven. He presided at the election of Matthias, and gave the first sermon on Pentecost as chief spokesman for the new Church. He was the first apostle to perform a miracle. Peter also pronounced the sentence on Anania and Sapphira and Simon Magus.

Peter and Paul had their differences over methods of evangelizing but they did not disagree on doctrine, as Paul too recognized the primacy of Peter in teaching. Paul referred to Peter as *Kephas*, "rock," which indicates that this great missionary-apostle accepted Peter as the foundation stone or rock of the Church.

18. Did the persecutions of the Roman emperors against the spread of Christianity begin when the Apostles were still alive?

Yes. Peter had left Jerusalem and begun his apostolic journeys, which finally took him to Rome. The first persecution was under Nero, beginning about the year 64. It was during the persecution under Nero that Peter, the first pope, was crucified. Peter, according to tradition, was buried at the foot of Vatican Hill. Constantine built a basilica over the site, which was replaced by the present St. Peter's Basilica at Vatican City in Rome.

It was in Rome that St. Peter wrote his two epistles, addressing them to new converts in Asia Minor. Through these epistles the first pope sought to strengthen the faith of the Christians and to encourage them in the practice of virtue. Christ had given Peter the command to strengthen the faith of his brethren.

St. Paul also died in the persecution under Nero. Nero set Rome afire and blamed the Christians for it. Christians were killed by the thousands in the streets and others were tortured in various ways, such as being covered with pitch and burned alive to entertain Nero at his nightly garden feasts.

St. John, the beloved apostle of Christ, was the youngest of the apostles when he was chosen. He grew to an old age, and according to tradition was cast into a caldron of boiling oil in the second persecution under the emperor Domitian. Miraculously, John was saved from death. He was then sent in exile to the island of Patmos, where he received divine revelations about the future of the Church and the glory of eternal life in heaven. He then wrote the Book of Revelation (the Apocalypse).

St. James the Greater was beheaded under King Herod Agrippa in 43. St. James the Less, according to tradition, was cast from the wall of the temple in Jerusalem and killed with a club in the year 63. St. Andrew was crucified at Patras in Greece. St. Philip died at Hierapolis in Phrygia, Asia Minor. St. Bartholomew was flayed alive in Armenia.

19. Is there evidence in modern times that St. Peter was actually buried at Vatican Hill, where the Basilica now stands in his honor?

Yes. Pope Pius XII ordered excavations by archeologists under the high altar of St. Peter's Basilica. Scientists, after much study, agree that there is sufficient evidence in the archeological findings to point to this site as the burial place of St. Peter's body, over which the largest church building in Christendom was built. Archeologists in the twentieth century uncovered evidence that St. Peter in fact went to Rome and was buried on Vatican Hill.

Summary

By the year 150 St. Justin could write: "There is no people, neither among the barbarians, nor the Greeks, nor any known tribe, where prayers and thanksgivings are not offered to God in the name of Christ crucified." By the end of the first century the Church was already called "catholic."

Preaching Christ crucified appeared as foolishness to the proud and immoral pagans, and even the Jews of the dispersion were not in most cases willing to accept the Redeemer. On their journeys, the apostles of Christ everywhere found racial brethren who should have been the first disciples of the Messiah. But few disciples were found among them—in fact, many enemies. But those who received the faith were often heroic and suffered for it, and the blood of the martyrs became the seed of Christianity. How else can one explain the rapid spread of the Church to the nations of the world, when everything natural and the civil powers were opposed?

There is a lesson in this for our modern materialistic, pleasure-saturated society. For example, St. Paul, when invited to preach the faith before Felix, pagan governor of Syria, chose to treat of justice and chastity and the judgment to come. The governor was frightened at such teachings and ordered him away. Without openness to humility, purity, and Christian morality without compromise—regardless of what age or century—Christ and his church, which is his Mystical Body, will not be welcomed and embraced.

Christ Jesus came to establish the kingdom of God on earth and to bring it to its completion in heaven. The apostles, and the Church today, continue the mission of Christ. As many did not welcome Christ or his apostles and disciples, the same struggle goes on. The cross is a mystery of faith, and it is perpetuated in

Catholic worship in the Mass. It is carried in our daily lives as we witness for Christ Jesus.

The apostolic age of the first century left the mark of apostolicity upon the Church. The four marks of the true Church have long been listed as (1) one, (2) holy, (3) catholic, and (4) apostolic. The Catholic Church is truly apostolic, for its history reaches back to the original apostles upon whom Christ founded his Church, with Peter, the rock, primary in teaching and ruling authority.

Questions for Discussion

1. Describe the world into which Jesus was born and in which he taught.
2. Why do you think many of the chosen people could not accept Jesus as the promised Messiah?
3. Did Jesus establish the Bible as the foundation of his Church? Explain your answer.
4. Which came first, the Bible or the Church? Explain your answer.
5. Show how the Church of the first century had a hierarchical structure of authority, much as we know today.
6. What evidence do we have that the primacy of Peter was recognized from the days of Christ Jesus?
7. To what would you attribute the success of the early Church, in spite of all natural obstacles?
8. What evidence exists, even today, that the first pope, Peter, went to Rome and taught and died there?
9. What are some of the special, supernatural helps the apostles received in spreading the true faith?
10. Did the Church encourage use of the Bible in the first centuries? Indicate how.
11. Can the Bible itself be considered a history book?

Chapter 3
The Church Persecuted and Defended

1. How long did the pagan Roman Empire wage war on the Church?

For 300 years the powerful Roman Empire waged an almost uninterrupted war of persecution on the early Church of Christ. Christians were always under suspicion and in danger of being arrested and put to death.

2. Why did the powerful Roman Empire fear the humility of Jesus Christ and hate his followers?

The Romans were not interested in eternal spiritual life but put all their emphasis on happiness in worldly power and possessions, comforts, and pleasures. They recognized no authority above the state, no power above the emperor. They considered the state divine and the emperor was looked upon as a god.

Christians could not accept these teachings, or that the state could do no wrong. Christians were taught by their faith to obey the state only when its laws were not against the supreme laws of God. They respected the authority of the state and its laws when they did not interfere with the right of the individual citizen to have a union with God and be worthy of eternal life.

Consequently, the Romans could not understand how Christians could be good citizens. To profess and practice the true Christian faith was therefore regarded as treason against the empire. While claiming to be tolerant of all religions, the Romans made exception to the Christian religion.

3. How did leaders of pagan religions regard the Christians?

Those attached to pagan temples, who made their living from pagan worship, hated the Christians. Also, those who made pagan idols or provided meat and

17

material for pagan sacrifices did not want to see the spread of Christianity, as it threatened their means of existence and mode of worship. They therefore supported movements to destroy Christians.

4. What kind of charges were made against the Christians?

False accusations, appealling to ignorance and the passions of the mob spirit, were used against the Christians. False rumors were spread, whereby they were accused of immorality, since they met in secret. It was said that they had a sacrifice in which little children were killed and eaten. Ignorance and hatred caused the pagans to spread vicious lies.

Christians were also accused of plotting to overthrow the empire. When problems arose in society, such as a pestilence or hard times, the Christians were blamed, as pagans said the gods were angry because the Christians refused to worship them.

5. What were the chief persecutions decreed by the Roman emperors against the Christians?

There were ten great persecutions.

The first was under Nero, about the year 64.

The second was under Domitian, about 95.

The third was under Trajan, about 107. One of its first victims was Pope St. Clement. Simeon, second bishop of Jerusalem, was crucified, and St. Ignatius, the bishop of Antioch, was cast to lions in the amphitheater in Rome. The same persecution continued under Hadrian, who condemned St. Symphorosa and her seven sons to death. Holy places in Jerusalem were profaned and statues to false gods were placed on Mt. Calvary and over the holy sepulchre of Jesus, the Lord.

The fourth was under Marcus Aurelius, about 167. St. Polycarp, 86 years old, was killed at the stake. In Lyons and Vienne, in France, St. Pothinus, first bishop of Lyons, and Blandina, a heroic young slave, were martyred.

The fifth was under Septimius Severus, about 202. Even though cured by the prayers of a Christian, he turned against them. Of this persecution St. Clement of Alexandria wrote: "We see daily many martyrs burned and crucified before our eyes." Also martyred were St. Irenaeus at Lyons and St. Perpetua and St. Felicitas at Carthage.

The sixth was under Maximus Thrax, about 236. Popes Pontian and Anterus were martyrs in this persecution. Repeated earthquakes were considered by the heathens to be due to the neglect of their gods, and so they cried: "The Christians to the lions!"

The seventh was under Decius, about 250. This persecution was especially directed against the bishops and priests of the Church. Decius said that Christianity and the Roman Empire could never be reconciled. St. Agatha and St. Apollonia were martyred at this time.

The eighth was under Valerian, about 258. Pope Sixtus II and the deacon St. Lawrence were martyred.

The ninth was under Emperor Aurelian. This persecution of the Christians did not last long, for the emperor soon met a violent death.

The tenth was under Diocletian, about 303. This was the most violent of the persecutions. Diocletian even had a coin struck which read "Diocletian, emperor, who destroyed the Christian name." Martyrs under Diocletian were St. Sebastian, tribune of the imperial guard, who was shot with arrows and left to die a lingering death. Also, St. Anastasia, the youth; St. Agnes of Rome; St. Lucia of Syracuse; and many others were martyred who had consecrated their virginity to Christ.

6. Summarize the persecutions of the early Christians as they became more general.

Persecutions of the Christians became general under the reign of Emperor Decius (A.D. 250) as the Roman Empire everywhere began an organized effort to destroy the Church. Before his time, persecutions were frequent but limited to certain provinces. Nero had struck out at Christians in the city of Rome. Domitian was concerned because so many of the higher classes of citizens, leading men of the state, were turning to the faith of Christ Jesus. He even banished his own wife to a lonely island and put his cousin to death because of this. What must have been the strong witness of the early Christians to make such converts under such conditions?

For fifty years after the time of Septimius Severus, Christians had considerable freedom, since the emperor had many things to be concerned with. There was much unrest throughout the empire. The emperor had to obey the military leaders, who controlled the state. The government changed frequently. The Roman Senate lost its power.

During this time Christians could own their own property and build churches. However, under affluence, some Christians became worldly and less fervent and their faith was weakened. Is there not a lesson in this for modern Christians, who may become too comfortable in the world?

The brief period of freedom for the early Christians ended, as indicated, under Decius, who was determined to destroy Christianity entirely. A person who was even suspected of being a Christian was arrested and tortured until he died or gave up the faith.

There was no limit, it seemed, to the persecutions. Christians were cast before wild beasts for entertainment, scourged, put to the rack, burned at a stake, crucified, and tortured in many other ways to satisfy the cruel customs of the pagans.

If the shepherd is struck down, the flock is scattered and disunited. The emperor Decius realized this when his persecution of Christians was aimed primarily against the bishops and priests of the Church. Without men of holy orders, the Church cannot exist or function as Christ intends. The Church needs valid bishops to ordain other bishops and priests and to pass on the power which Jesus gave the first priests in the persons of the apostles. Without a valid priesthood, there can be no sacrifice of the Mass, which perpetuates the worship of Jesus Christ on the cross and brings his resurrected body in the sacrament of the Holy Eucharist. Also, there can be no sacrament of penance for the forgiveness of sin; no confirmation for the special coming of the Holy Spirit to souls and sealing them in Christ Jesus to complete baptism.

Many Christians, not strong in the faith, became apostates and offered sacrifices to pagan gods. Others, while not offering sacrifices, used bribery to obtain certificates saying they had offered pagan sacrificial worship. Even some bishops and priests were among those who thus denied Christ Jesus.

When the persecution was over, some held that the apostates should not be forgiven. The debate ended with the Church receiving the apostates back into the true fold, but they were punished by having to do penance for the rest of their lives.

During the persecutions the popes remained strong and firm in the faith, dying as true shepherds in imitation of Christ Jesus. Governing the Church was very difficult during the persecutions, but historical records attest that the chief pontiffs of the Church used their authority well, watching for wolves.

7. Did the persecutions bring happiness and satisfaction to the persecuting emperors?

On the contrary. Nero stabbed himself to death as his people revolted against him. Domitian was assassinated. Hadrian went insane in despair. Marcus Aurelius starved himself to death, heartbroken over the ingratitude of his only son, Commodus. Septimius Severus died in despair, as his life had been attempted by his son. Decius, in a battle with the Goths, was killed in a swamp. Valerian was flayed alive, having been taken prisoner by Sapor, the king of Persia. Maxentius was drowned in the Tiber. Diocletian starved himself to death.

8. What are the Roman catacombs?

The catacombs are underground tunnels that were bored through soft rock. They are long, narrow, winding corridors. The dead were buried in the walls on either side. From time to time, going through these corridors, one comes to a wider space, like a room. In these rooms the Christians would gather for the sacrifice of the Mass, so as to worship free from the pagans' persecutions.

Burial in the catacombs stopped when the barbarians plundered Rome. The popes removed the relics of the saints and martyrs from the catacombs to the Roman churches in the seventh and eighth centuries. The catacombs, once abandoned, were gradually forgotten and not discovered again until the end of the sixteenth century. Most famous of the catacombs is that of St. Callistus, where many of the popes were buried after they were martyred for the faith.

9. How do the catacombs bear witness to the true Catholic faith even today?

An authentic Catholic catechism, containing to true Catholic teachings, could be composed from the pictures and inscriptions on the tombs and walls of the ancient catacombs of the first centuries. Pictures, medals, and inscriptions in the catacombs identify the faith of the early Christians with the Catholic faith.

The catacombs prove that the first Christians believed that Jesus Christ is true God and true Man. They also believed in the real presence of Jesus in the holy Eucharist, the divine institution of the papacy, the dignity of the Mother of God, the intercession of the saints, purgatory, and prayers for the deceased.

The emblem of the fish, *ichthys,* was frequently used in the catacombs. It is a symbol of the Lord Jesus, for the Greek word *ichthys* means "fish" and its letters are the initials for "Jesus Christ, God's Son, Savior." When the Christians spoke of "receiving the fish," they meant to receive Jesus in holy Communion.

Frequently, pictures of our Savior in the catacombs reveal him as the Good Shepherd, carrying the lost sheep on his shoulders. This is the ancient biblical form which reveals the same message as our modern devotion to the Sacred Heart of Jesus. A number of people are pictured sitting around a table on which are bread and fish.

Death and resurrection were often in the minds of the early Christians, as indicated by pictures of Noe and the ark, Jonah and the whale, Daniel in the lions' den, and the raising of Lazarus. Their faith in resurrection and eternal life gave them courage in facing death under persecution. There is also the famous account of Tarsicius being martyred as he took the holy Eucharist, the bread of life, to Christian prisoners.

The eucharistic sacrifice of the Mass was offered in the catacombs on altars under which rested the bodies of martyrs. Catholic altars even today have "altar stones" in which relics of saints and martyrs were placed by bishops when they consecrated the altar stones.

10. What role did Tertullian play in the early Church?

The apologist Tertullian, born in Carthage about 160, was a scholar of Greek and Latin literature. He was also a lawyer. Practicing in the city of Rome, he became a Christian around the year 193. Returning to Carthage, he became a great defender of the faith.

His original style was imitated by others. As a layman, he wrote in Latin. He is called the Father of Ecclesiastical Latin. His most famous work is the *Apologeticus,* in which he answers charges against the Christians and shows how the Christian religion and its teachings are superior to all others, and the emptiness of paganism.

Tertullian, while very gifted, became too "rigorous." His severity led to a fanaticism in which he did not believe that certain sins could be forgiven. He held that all kinds of amusements are sinful.

While Tertullian went too far, and beyond the teaching of Christ and his Church, his apologetical writings were valuable to history as records of certain basic beliefs of the early Christian Church.

11. Who was the apologist Origen?

From 203 until 230, Origen was in charge of one of the earliest educational institutions in the Church of which we have historical records, the catechetical school in the city of Alexandria. Instruction was given in the scriptures and Christian doctrine, and also in the Greek sciences. Of great intellectual ability, Origen began teaching when he was only 17 years old. He wrote many books, although we have only remnants of his writings. He wrote a book, *On Prayer*, a commentary on the Lord's Prayer.

When Origen was ordained a priest without the knowledge of his bishop, he was removed from the catechetical school. He went to Caesarea and opened another school, which became as famous as that at Alexandria.

Arrested under Emperor Decius, he was tortured in every imaginable way, but Origen held fast to the faith. Sixty-seven years old and subjected to great torture, he held to the faith. After two years he was given freedom, but, badly injured and in broken health, he lived only two more years.

12. Who are meant by the "apologists" of the Church?

Apologists are the great writers who in the second century defended and explained the doctrines of Christianity. They proved how false and contrary to reason were the arguments of those who attacked the Church. Many of their works have been lost, but we have some of them in part or in whole. Sometimes other ancient writers quoted them, although their original work is lost.

13. What is significant about the apologist St. Justin Martyr?

St. Justin Martyr was born in Sichem, in Palestine, of Roman parents shortly after A.D. 100. Hungry for truth, he studied all pagan teachings, but his soul was not satisfied. Meeting an aged Christian, he heard for the first time the message of Jesus the Savior. He felt he had found the truth.

St. Justin then made a deeper study of Christianity and became a master of its doctrines. Going to Rome, he opened a school of Christian philosophy. He wrote *Dialogue with Trypho*, a defense against the Jews' position. He wrote two *Apologies* to the emperor, the Senate, and the Roman people. The second of these apologies merited his martyrdom under Emperor Marcus Aurelius.

14. What did St. Irenaeus do as an apologist?

St. Irenaeus was the bishop of Lyons. He came from Syria and Asia Minor, and was a disciple of St. Polycarp. He was concerned not only with attacks of pagans but with errors and heresies seeping into the Church among her own members.

Some of the learned Christians, studying religions that had their origin in eastern countries such as Persia, confused these religious beliefs in attempting to explain the Christian mysteries, but their explanations had nothing to do with divine revelation. St. Irenaeus wrote *Against the Heresies* to correct these mistakes.

The oldest catechism in existence was written by St. Irenaeus and is called *The Proof of the Apostolic Teaching.* In it, St. Irenaeus clearly states the fundamental truths of the Church. Even a child can understand his basic explanations.

15. Who is St. Cyprian of Carthage?

St. Cyprian was the son of a wealthy patrician family of Carthage. Well educated, he became a teacher of rhetoric. Around the year 245 he converted to Chrisitanity and followed the advice of Jesus to give his wealth to the poor. He worked to promote the true teachings of the Church. Within four years, in 249, he was ordained bishop of Carthage.

Tertullian was a guide to St. Cyprian in the art of expression, and so St. Cyprian called him his "master." St. Cyprian wrote *On the Unity of the Catholic Church.* In this famous work he says: "Outside the Church there is no salvation. He cannot have God as his Father who has not the Church for his Mother." He likened the Church to the seamless robe of Christ.

St. Cyprian was martyred in 258.

Summary

St. Irenaeus, bishop of Lyons, who left us a list of the popes of the first and second centuries and who wrote about the year 200, said: "With the Church of Rome all churches must agree on account of her higher rank" (*Adv. Haereses* 3,3).

Writings by non-Christians have come down to us which testify to the continuity of the faith of the early Christians with ours today. Pliny, the governor of Bethynia, wrote to the pagan emperor Trajan, giving a remarkable report about the Christians: "They assemble on certain days before sunrise to sing hymns of praise in honor of Christ, their God; they take an oath to abstain from certain crimes and partake of a common but blameless meal" (the holy Eucharist).

The Christian influence of St. Polycarp, disciple of St. John the Apostle, won the reluctant admiration of the pagans and Jewish accusers, who wrote: "He is the teacher of Asia, father of the Christians and destroyer of our gods." When he was commanded to deny Christ, St. Polycarp replied: "I have served Christ for six and eighty years, and never has he done me evil. How, then, can I blaspheme my King and Savior?"

St. Cyprian gave testimony to the fear of the pagans for the papacy when he wrote, during the seventh persecution: "Emperor Decius had become so jealous of papal authority that he said: 'I will rather have a rival in my empire, than to hear of the election of the priest of God [Pope Cornelius] in Rome.'"

St. Lawrence, a deacon under Pope Sixtus II in the eighth persecution, gave us a marvelous manifestation of the values of many early Christians who were persecuted. Commanded to turn over the treasures of the Church, St. Lawrence gathered the poor in assembly and showed them to his persecutor with these words: "Behold the treasures of the Church."

During the tenth persecution, Bishop Felix was commanded to turn over the sacred books of the Church. As he was led to his execution, he said: "It is better that I be cast into the fire, than the sacred volumes. I thank you, O Lord, for fifty-six years of my life were spent in your service. I have preserved sacerdotal chastity, have guarded the holy gospels, and preached your truth. For You, O Jesus, God of heaven and earth, I offer myself as victim."

The apologists of the first centuries, who defended the true doctrines of the Church, are as valuable today as they were in the very first centuries. Not only did they need to explain and defend the faith for the sake of guiding the Christians but to defend themselves from the pagans who sought falsely to accuse and destroy them.

Questions for Discussion

1. Why was the Church of Christ such a threat to the Roman Empire?
2. What was the attitude of Christians toward the state?
3. Why did the emperor Decius strike out, especially against bishops and priests, in his effort to destroy Christianity?
4. Why did promoters of pagan religions want to destroy the Christians?
5. Does it seem that the persecuting emperors were dealt justice even in this world? Explain.
6. What are the Roman catacombs?
7. What is meant by apologetics?
8. Why are the Roman catacombs a valuable instrument for teaching apologetics today?
9. Who wrote the oldest Catholic catechism in existence and what is significant about it?
10. Give examples of some of the false accusations against the early Christians.
11. What happened during the period when the persecutions of the first centuries were interrupted?
12. What lesson can be learned by modern-day Christians from the reaction of early Christians when the practice of their faith was made easy?

Chapter 4
Church and State: Fathers of the Church and Heresies

1. Who was Constantine?

Constantine was born in Serbia and was 32 years old when he became emperor of the Roman Empire. Maxentius had made himself ruler of Italy and Africa. Constantine led his army into Italy, to defeat Maxentius in two battles, and finally came to the city of Rome, where Maxentius took a final stand. The night before the battle, according to the first historian of the Church, Eusebius, Emperor Constantine saw a cross of light in the sky, surrounded by the words: "*In hoc signo vincis* (In this sign thou shalt conquer)." A voice from heaven told Constantine to adopt the cross as his standard, rather than the Roman eagle. This he did, while marching against the pagan emperor Maxentius, and so Constantine became the sole Christian emperor of the world. Constantine built an arch of victory in the city and erected a statue of himself, holding the cross as a standard.

2. What was the Edict of Milan?

Issued in 313 at Milan by Constantine (together with Licinius, who fought for freedom of religion for Christians in the East), it was an edict of toleration, granting religious tolerance to pagans and Christians alike. It abolished all laws against the Christian religion, granted liberty of worship, restored confiscated property to the Church, and entitled the Church to acquire property and accept testamentary bequests. It made Sunday a day of rest, and forbade public business and servile work on the Lord's day.

3. Did Constantine do anything else for the Christians, besides give them religious fredom?

Constantine also built many churches. In Rome, he built the magnificent basilica over the tomb of St. Peter, the apostle and first pope. This church lasted until the Middle Ages, when it was rebuilt. He also built a church at the tomb of St. Paul and the noble Lateran basilica. He presented the pope the imperial palace that stood nearby. He also built churches at Nicomedia, Antioch, Tyre, and Jerusalem.

Constantine delayed his official entrance into the Church. He died in 337, receiving baptism on his deathbed.

4. What religion became the chief religion of the Roman Empire after Constantine?

The Christian religion became the chief religion of the Roman Empire, as Constantine gave the Church full liberty and honored popes and bishops. St. Helena, the mother of Constantine, brought the holy cross and many sacred relics to Rome from Jerusalem.

5. Did Constantine always live at Rome after his sudden conversion?

No. Constantine decided that the East was to be the center of his empire. He founded the city of Constantinople on the site of the ancient Greek town of Byzantium. Ancient culture and civilization were thereby taken from Rome, which might have been destroyed when barbarians from the north overran Italy.

This removal of political power to the East had advantages by allowing the Church in the West greater liberty to grow spiritually without too much interference from the state. In the East, however, the Church became too identified with the empire, and as history developed, it was too far removed from influence of the Roman See, where the pope, visible head of the Church, resided.

6. Did the problems of the Church cease with the defeat of its pagan enemies?

No. Christ foretold false prophets and inner conflicts but promised that the Church, built upon Peter, would never be destroyed. Internal conflicts developed in the Church, tending to lead many into heresy. Nevertheless, even these heresies had a good effect, for God can draw good out of all things, even evil. They caused the Church to define her teachings of faith. As the Church continued to grow it became necessary to perfect her organization to exist in the changing world while preserving the true faith. Popes had to defend divine truth against heresies. God raised up great saints and teachers in his Church to teach the truth and overcome false teachings.

7. What were the chief heresies the Catholic Church had to combat after it won freedom?

The chief heresies during this time were Arianism, Macedonianism, Pelagianism, Nestorianism, and those of the Monophysites, Monothelites, and Iconoclasts.

8. What was the heresy of Arianism?

An apostate priest, Arius of Libya, in 318 began to preach a false doctrine about the Son of God. Arius denied the divinity of the Son, the Second Person of the Trinity. He taught the blasphemy that Christ Jesus is only the first and highest creature of God. Considering Christ only a creature, he denied that the Son is co-eternal and of the same divine substance as God the Father.

His bishop condemned this teaching of Arius and excommunicated him and his followers. The error nonetheless spread widely and Arians appeared in every part of the Christian world as a threat to true Catholic doctrine. The heresy of Arianism lasted until the seventh century.

9. What did the Church do about the heresy of Arianism?

With the consent of Pope Sylvester, the emperor called all the bishops of the Church together in 325 at Nicaea. Three hundred bishops held a general council. (A general or ecumenical council is a meeting of all the bishops of the world, under the authority of the pope, to define the teachings of the Church or to adopt better measures for its government and further the cause of Christ's teaching.)

The Council of Nicaea drew up a profession of faith, which we still call the Nicene Creed and which Catholics still recite at Mass. It proclaims the true Catholic doctrine: Christ Jesus is true God and true Man. "We believe in one Lord, Jesus Christ, the only Son of God, eternally begotten of the Father, God from God, light from light, true God from true God, begotten, not made, one in being with the Father ... by the power of the Holy Spirit he was born of the Virgin Mary, and became Man ..."

10. What was the heresy of Macedonianism?

This heresy is named after Macedonius, the bishop of Constantinople, who denied the divinity of the Holy Spirit, the Third Person of the Trinity. This heresy was condemned by the Council of Constantinope (381), which affirmed the divinity of the Holy Spirit.

11. What was the heresy of Pelagianism?

Pelagius was a British monk who (about the year 400) denied original sin and the necessity of grace. This heresy, if accepted, would have destroyed many divine truths. It said that natural goodness is sufficient to save man—which is false because man is born into a fallen human race, in the state of sin inherited from Adam and Eve. Man is helpless of and by himself, but is saved only through the one Savior and Mediator, Jesus Christ.

Natural goodness is not sufficient for salvation. The grace of Jesus Christ must be added, a participation in his divine life, which supernaturalizes and elevates man to a participation in the divine nature.

The heresy of Pelagius was condemned by the provincial Council of Carthage and by Pope Innocent I (417).

12. What is Nestorianism?

It is a heresy, named after Nestorius (patriarch of Constantinople), that taught the existence of two persons in Christ, one divine and one human. A false consequence of this would be that Mary would not be the true Mother of God. This heresy, which said that no human person could be the Mother of God, was preached during Advent, 428.

The love of the faithful for Mary as the Mother of God, very early in Christian history, is shown by the reaction of the people to Nestorianism. When he preached from the pulpit, Nestorius was forced to leave the church. The false doctrine of Nestorius was opposed on every side, and the Church called a general council in 431.

St. Cyril, the patriarch of Alexandria, represented the pope at the council and the doctrine of Nestorius was condemned. When it was announced to the common faithful waiting outside the council hall that the position of the Church was that Mary is truly the Mother of God, great joy and festivity and rejoicing broke out among the people, manifesting their love for the Mother of God.

Nestorius died in exile, excommunicated from the Church for refusing to accept the Church's official position that our Lady is truly God's Mother.

13. What was the heresy of the Monophysites?

Eutyches, abbot of a convent near Constantinople, taught that there was only a divine nature in Christ, no human nature. One false teaching can lead to many others, and a consequence of this would be that Jesus Christ, having no human nature, could not have died on the cross to redeem us. There could then have been no historical Resurrection of the crucified Christ.

The heresy of Eutyches was condemned by the Council of Chalcedon in 451. This council declared that there are two natures in Christ, one human and one divine. Both the human and the divine nature exist in the one person of Jesus Christ.

When the letter of Pope Leo I was read at this council, the assembled bishops declared: "St. Peter has spoken through Leo." They accepted the decision of the chief vicar of Jesus Christ.

14. What was the heresy of the Monothelites?

Sergius, who was patriarch of Constantinople, together with his followers taught the false doctrine that there was only one will in Christ—the divine, and not the human will. This was contrary to the mystery of the redemption. Scripture says that Jesus Christ was a man in all things except sin.

The Monothelite heresy was condemned by the Council of Constantinople (called the "Trullanum" from the church where it was held) in 680. This council declared that there are two wills in Christ, the divine and the human. Both wills are under the control of the one divine person of Jesus Christ.

This Third Council of Constantinople answered Pope Agatho's letter with these words: "We have received your letter as if written by the Prince of the Apostles under divine inspiration, and instructed by it have condemned error."

15. What were the Iconoclasts?

They attacked the veneration of holy images. Leo the Isaurian, emperor of Constantinople, and his followers were called Iconoclasts or "image breakers."

Pope St. Gregory II condemned Iconoclasm. Nevertheless, fanatic emperors caused a bloody persecution in which sacred images were destroyed. Many defenders of the use of sacred images were put to death. Pope Hadrian convened the Second Council of Nice in 787, during the reign of the pious Empress Irene. The heresy was silenced.

16. Who were the chief opponents of heresies in the first centuries of the Church?

Learned and holy men, called fathers of the Church, led the combat against heresy in protecting the purity of the faith of Christians in the first centuries. Their writings have become standard witnesses of the true Catholic faith. The great books which the fathers of the East and West wrote against the various heresies helped bring about a clearer definition of the truths of the Catholic Church.

Jesus Christ left his Church in the world to teach the true faith until the very end of time. He sent the Holy Spirit to keep the Church in the truth. He knew that errors would arise, misinterpreting his teachings, and so he established the apostles as bishops with Peter as Prince of the Apostles, to whom he said: "He who hears you, hears me." The Church through its chief teachers—the bishops with the pope as chief bishop—soon found it necessary, beginning with the Council at Jerusalem in the year 51 and the twenty-one councils which have followed, to oppose false teachings and define true doctrines.

To assist the chief teachers, the bishops and pope, in their first duty, God gave the Church great teachers in both the East and the West.

17. Who are the great fathers of the Church of the East and the West?

Most noteworthy among the Greek fathers are St. Athanasius, St. Basil, St. Gregory of Nazianzum, and St. John Chrysostom. Among the Latin or Western fathers are St. Ambrose, St. Augustine, St. Jerome, and St. Gregory the Great.

18. What is the significance of St. Athanasius?

St. Athanasius the Great lived from 296 to 373 and was bishop of Alexandria. He was only 30 years old when, at the Council of Nicaea, he defended the true doctrine of the Church against Arianism. His life was a continuous battle against the Arian heresy. He debated the apostate priest Arius at the council and proved him wrong. But the Arian rulers concocted false charges against Athanasius and five times had him sent into exile. This great confessor of the true faith never wavered.

Finally the people rose to the defense of the saint and threatened to bring him back by force. In 367 Bishop Athanasius finally came home to stay and spent his remaining six years in the midst of his flock.

By the time of his death, Arianism was dying all over the Roman Empire, even though many bishops had embraced the falsehood of Arianism.

19. What were the high points in the life of the great Eastern teacher, St. Basil?

St. Basil was born about 330 at Caesarea, in Cappadocia. In 357 he opened a school of rhetoric in Caesarea, which became popular. Though at first he was not deeply religious, he was gradually converted to more holy ways. He spent some time with monks in the Syrian Desert, in Palestine and Egypt. Returning to Caesarea, he retired into solitude but was soon joined by disciples whom he organized into a religious community. He drew up two rules which are still followed by monks in the Eastern Church.

In 364 he began preaching every day to great crowds in Caesarea, and the poor especially flocked to hear him. Ordained its bishop in 370, he proved a real father and shepherd to his people.

St. Basil refused to bend to the emperor Valens in compromising with the Arians. He defeated Arianism in the greater portion of Asia Minor. Cultured and of great mind, he was ascetic and frail in body.

20. What about St. Gregory of Nazianzum, a father of the East?

St. Gregory of Nazianzum lived from 330 to 390. He was a friend of St. Basil. He is noted for his writings in which he defended the truths of the Catholic Church. The historian Rufinus wrote: "It is the general verdict, that whosoever does not agree with St. Gregory cannot be right in his faith."

21. For what was the Eastern father of the Church, St. John Chrysostom, known?

St. John Chrysostum, who lived from 344 to 407, was known for his wonderful eloquence and was called the Golden Mouthed. He became patriarch of Constantinople.

St. John Chrysostom spent six years in the desert with monks, and two years alone in a cave to purify himself by prayer and penance. Returning to Antioch in 386, he hesitated a long time about being ordained a priest, considering himself unworthy for such a great calling. While debating the question with himself, he wrote the book *On the Priesthood*.

Zeal for holiness and against the vices of the time brought St. John Chrysostom persecution and banishment. The people rose to the defense of St. John, their bishop, but the emperor prevailed. He died in exile in 407.

Thirty years after the death of the emperor Theodosius, his son brought the body of St. John Chrysostom back to Constantinople amid great rejoicing of the people. The new emperor, with his face upon the coffin, prayed God to forgive his parents for having persecuted the holy man unjustly.

22. Give a brief history of the Latin father, St. Ambrose.

St. Ambrose, bishop of Milan, was born at Treves in 340. He studied law and became governor of northern Italy. When the bishop of Milan, who was an Arian, died, a quarrel broke out between Catholics and Arians for a successor. St. Ambrose gave a speech to restore peace. When he finished, a child in the crowd called out: "Let Ambrose be our bishop!" The multitude, Arians and Catholics alike, took up the call.

Ambrose was still a catechumen, studying the faith, and was not yet baptized. He tried to escape the demand that he be ordained bishop. Within eight days after baptism, he was ordained a priest and then was consecrated bishop.

He immediately devoted himself to a deep study of the Bible and Christian writings. Being of practical mind, he worked for ways and means to make the faith applicable in the daily lives of the faithful.

Ambrose's hard work removed the last traces of paganism and Arianism from the people in Italy. When the emperor Valentinian demanded a church for the Arians of Milan, St. Ambrose replied: "I cannot yield; the emperor is in the Church, but not above the Church." When the emperor Theodosius the Great ordered an unjust massacre at Thessalonica, Ambrose refused to allow him to step across the threshold of the church until he had done public penance. The emperor submitted to the just demand of the holy bishop, who died in 397.

23. For what is St. Jerome of the West known?

St. Jerome (331–420), a personal friend of Pope Damasus, was a man of great learning and devoted to sacred scripture. He translated the scriptures from Hebrew and Greek into Latin. The translation, called the Vulgate, became the official and standard biblical textbook of the Church, even into modern times.

24. Briefly tell the life of the Western father, St. Augustine.

St. Augustine was born on November 13, 354, at Tagaste, a small town in Numidia, Northern Africa. His father, a pagan, converted to Christianity only shortly before his death. His mother, St. Monica, worked from the beginning to prepare her son's heart for the true faith. The poor example of his father and his own resistance to his mother's efforts caused him to give his youth up to vanity and sensuality.

Augustine became a teacher of literature at Tagaste; later he taught law at Carthage, then at Rome and Milan. His mother, Monica, continued to pray for him. Studying the philosophy of Plato did not satisfy him but it brought him closer to Christian teaching. He kept looking for a religion with idealism and authority.

St. Ambrose was at this time bishop of Milan and his sermons were attracting great crowds. Augustine went to listen to him and, for the first time, heard the true faith explained in a way he could accept. Reading the epistles of St. Paul, he decided to become a catechumen. Augustine was able to take his final step and be baptized after reading the life of St. Anthony, the hermit, by St. Athanasius.

When 37 years old, Augustine visited the city of Hippo, where the bishop insisted he become a priest. He was educated for the priesthood, and shortly afterward Augustine became bishop of Hippo. For thirty-five years St. Augustine was the leader of the Church in Africa. Through his writings his name became known throughout the Christian world.

He wrote fifteen essays against the Pelagians which dealt with the fall of our first parents, the necessity of baptism, the free will of man, and the nature of the divine life of grace. Because of these essays (and sermons on the same subject) he is called the Doctor of Grace.

St. Augustine wrote a book, *Confessions,* in which he tells the story of his life from childhood and through his sinful youth, showing how divine grace led him from error to truth itself. It is one of the greatest spiritual classics of all time.

St. Augustine wrote: "Our hearts have been made for you, O God, and they can find no rest until they rest in you."

The many books dealing with the faith and written by St. Augustine did much to determine Catholic expressions of the faith for the next 800 years.

25. Briefly relate the history of the Western father, St. Gregory the Great.

St. Gregory the Great (540–604) is one of the greatest popes to occupy the see of St. Peter. He was a true reformer of Church discipline. He is the father of plain chant, named after him "Gregorian chant." He was pope from 590 to 604. He sent St. Augustine of Canterbury with forty Benedictine monks to convert England. His activity in establishing Church discipline and order was exerted in all parts of the world. His leadership did much to shape the form of the papacy and make Western Christian doctrine the official doctrinal form for the Western Church.

As pope, St. Gregory I gave himself the title "the Servant of the Servants of God."

Summary

Even though the cultural center of Christianity shifted to the Eastern empire in the early centuries, Western Christendom had its centers of learning and influence. Cities along the northern coast of Africa (Roman Africa), united to Italy by commerce, government, and culture, were intellectual centers of Christianity in the West. The Western schools of theology were more "practical" and the Eastern schools were more concerned with mysticism.

Western theology, usually written and preached in Latin, and influenced by Roman traditions of practical government, meant that efforts were channeled into changing men's lives, into dealing with the problems of the world so as to Christianize it. The period of the Western fathers of the Church was about one century later than the period of the Eastern fathers.

The greatest of the Western fathers was St. Augustine of Hippo. His ideals were greatly influential in shaping Western Christian civilization. Most of his writings are still in existence, including 232 books, more than 350 sermons on the faith, and 260 long letters. He wrote 93 major works, which include *On the Trinity, On Teaching Christian Doctrine,* and *On the Faith and the Creed.* He wrote commentaries on the epistles of St. Paul and the Gospel of St. John. His *Confessions* is considered the most famous and greatest autobiography ever written. In *The City of God* he gives his idea of the destiny of the world.

St. Augustine was an intellectual and spiritual giant whose Christian theology dominated the West for 800 years, until the time of St. Thomas Aquinas.

Never in the history of the world has a religion caused so many people to surrender to its idealism as the religion of Jesus Christ. Truly, Christ came "in the fullness of time." There was the opposition of the Jewish religious leaders to begin with, then of the pagan Roman world. On the natural level, the odds were stacked high against this new, Christian religion surviving.

The Church of these early centuries was very conscious of the divine commission to carry the gospel to "all nations," even though its members were but vaguely informed of the vast numbers of people who lived on the fringes of the Roman Empire. They were not aware of the cultures in India, China, and Japan and had no idea of the existence of the Americas.

Questions for Discussion

1. Explain how the Edict of Milan was a turning point in history for the early Christian Church.
2. What problems did the Church continue to have with the end of the pagan persecutions?
3. What is meant by Arianism in the early Church?
4. How did the early Church handle the problems and questions of faith which tended to undermine the faith of the followers of Christ?
5. Whom did God raise up to defend the teachings of Christ in the early Church, when its faith was under attack?

6. Who were the great teachers of the Church in the East? In the West?
7. What was significant about St. Ambrose's sudden rise to a teaching position in the early Church?
8. Relate the significance of St. Augustine in the life of the Church and how he affected the Western Church for centuries.
9. How did the theology of the East and the West take a different tone, while still promoting the one true faith?

Chapter 5
The Early Constitution of the Church

1. What kind of constitution or structure of authority did Jesus give his Church?

The Lord Jesus built his Church upon the original apostles with Peter as the "rock" or chief, in authority over the other bishop-apostles. The original apostles, chosen and ordained by Jesus Christ, were all bishops with the fullness of priestly powers for the glory of God and the salvation of souls. Christ commissioned the original apostles to go forth and teach all nations, baptizing them in the name of the Father, Son, and Holy Spirit. He gave the apostles their chief power of offering the sacrifice of the Mass at the Last Supper, the night before he died. On the evening of Easter Sunday, the day he arose from the dead, Jesus Christ gave the apostles the power to forgive sin in his name through the power of the Holy Spirit.

The constitution of the Church, as it came from the hands of its divine founder, was very simple in structure, with pope, bishops, and the faithful who entered the Church (known as the Body of Christ) through the sacrament of baptism.

2. What was a Christian community like in the beginning years of Christianity?

Each Christian community had its bishop, who tended to the spiritual needs of the people. These communities were small, usually restricted to one city and the neighborhood around it. As the number of Christians grew, bishops appointed deacons to assist them. Deacons took care of the poor, assisted the bishop at Mass, and brought Holy Communion to the sick and to those in prison. The Bible indicates that the first apostles judged they had the power to appoint some men as deacons (Acts 6).

3. When did bishops ordain some men as priests who did not have the fullness of the priesthood, as bishops do?

When the Christian faith began to spread into outlying districts of key cities where bishops presided, it was found necessary to ordain priests who would not have all the powers of a bishop. The priests could offer Mass and forgive sins in Jesus' name. At first these priests lived with the bishop but went out from the bishop's house to administer to the needs of the faithful in the outlying districts. (Only the bishop had the right to offer Mass in his city.) The priests were subject to the authority of the bishop and represented him in whichever areas they were assigned. As the church continued to grow, it became the custom to assign a priest to a definite territory, where he would live, still subject to the bishop in the city. The first bishops of the Church understood that they had the authority from Christ not only to ordain bishops with the *fullness* of priestly powers, as successors to themselves, but to ordain certain men who participated in various orders or by degree in the authority and obligations given the original apostles. Thus, even today, we still have the three orders of deacon, priest, and bishop.

4. When did the early Christians recognize the special authority of the Pope?

From the time of the very first apostles and other followers of Christ, the position given to St. Peter was recognized. The New Testament itself testifies repeatedly to the special role of Peter.

5. How were bishops chosen by the early Christians?

The popes claimed from the beginning the right to appoint bishops. For a time, however, the clergy and people of a diocese were permitted to elect their own bishop. Until the time of the Council of Nicaea (325), laymen could participate in the election of a bishop, either by proposing a candidate to the clergy or by approving a choice made by the clergy.

By the end of the fourth century, the election of bishops was placed entirely in the hands of the clergy, who acted with the neighboring bishops and archbishop.

Our Catholic faith informs us that it is not merely a matter of "electing" someone to the office of a bishop, but the one who is chosen (by whatever process) must be validly ordained by an authentic bishop who is a successor of the original apostles.

6. Did the first popes exercise all their powers?

While the early popes did not always exercise all the powers of their sublime office, the authority was invested in them by Christ in the person of Peter. In the days of the persecutions, conditions kept the popes from exercising their authority fully and it was necessary for bishops to control their local churches without much communication with the papacy. Nevertheless, historical records prove that the popes knew they had the authority to teach and govern the faithful in every diocese or local church. The faithful everywhere respected this right.

7. Name some of these records which show that early Christians recognized papal authority.

In the year 96, when the evangelist St. John was still alive, St. Clement, who was the fourth pope, wrote a letter to the Christians at Corinth. This early pope writes in Christ's name, as one who had authority over them.

St. Ignatius, the martyr, wrote of the church of Rome as "the President of Charity," meaning that it was the chief church of Christendom.

St. Polycarp went to Rome in 154 to speak with the pope on the observance of Easter.

Historical records show that many appeals were made to Rome in the third century, and often by men who were disobedient to their bishops. There is no record of these bishops' protesting the right of men to appeal to the authority of the pope, showing they recognized that the pope had the right of authority in final decisions.

Both St. Athanasius and St. John Chrysostom, driven into exile, appealed to the authority of the pope of Rome.

St. Augustine is recorded as having given a sermon to his people after Pope Innocent approved the Council of Carthage against the heresy of the Pelagians in 416. St. Augustine joyfully announced that the case was finished, now that Rome had spoken.

Even after the political power moved to the East, when Constantinople became the capital of the Roman Empire and no strong government remained in the West, people turned for help to the spiritual power of the papacy. The popes were even called upon to give material help to poor people.

The sermons of Pope Leo the Great (440–461) have come down to us, indicating his great humility, learning, and holiness, and showing that he had constant contact with the Church in every part of the world.

8. How did the Church develop titles among its hierarchy such as "patriarch" and "archbishop" and "metropolitan," when Jesus simply ordained the apostles with episcopal powers?

As already indicated, the Church, as it came from the hands of its divine founder, Jesus Christ, was very simple in structure. Our Lord left it to his Church to develop a structure whereby it could keep the same faith, morals, and authority which he had given his Church. The Church must live in each era of time, with different social problems and civil governments. It must preach the one true faith, and bring the divine saving and healing powers without alteration. To accomplish this, the Church must use the most effective structure to glorify God and save souls, while administering to the needs of people without in any way changing divine truth.

The "deposit of faith" ended with the death of the last apostle. Conveying that deposit may vary in method but never in content. Thus it developed in the early centuries that in every political division of the empire there was one bishop of superior position to the others. He was called a metropolitan or archbishop in the West and (as is still the practice) he had a number of "suffragan" dioceses under him. In the East, a number of provinces, with their metropolitans, were placed under the authority of a bishop called a patriarch.

9. What were some of the chief patriarchates of the early Church?

The chief patriarchates of the East were Alexandria, Antioch, Constantinople, and Jerusalem. The pope was the only patriarch in the West, although the bishops of Carthage, Milan, and Arles had great influence in the Church. *The pope was supreme patriarch of the entire world.*

10. What was the life style of early priests and bishops?

Married men were allowed to become priests at first, but very early, men were not allowed to marry after they had been ordained. The life style of priests who lived with their bishop had to change as the Church grew. Even the apostles who were married gave up that form of life for full-time commitment to Christ and his Church.

Large numbers of the baptized laity chose to live a more perfect Christian life and remained unmarried, as scripture praised the single life—*if it were to dedicate oneself more fully to union with Christ and for the service of souls.*

Bishops were inclined to choose their priests from the single and more zealous members of the Christian community rather than from the married, who had many other cares. It gradually became the general rule, and toward the end of the third century it became the law, in several dioceses in the West, that only unmarried men could be ordained priests.

11. What special form of Christian life began in the third century?

Monastic life started during the third century. This meant a life lived away from the world, devoted to working for higher Christian perfection. "Monastic" is taken from the Greek word *monos*, which is translated "alone."

Monastic life had for its inspiration the three evangelical counsels as preached by Jesus Christ himself and as our divine Lord himself lived. From the time of the apostles, Christians attempted to live these counsels, which are not commanded of every Christian but presented as the more perfect Christian life if lived for a truly supernatural reason.

12. What are the three evangelical counsels which became the focus of monastic life at this time in the Church?

The evangelical counsels are (1) voluntary poverty, (2) chastity, and (3) obedience to a religious superior.

Many early Christians practiced virginity and had this state consecrated before the altar, with the bishop placing a veil upon their head as a sign of consecrated virginity and with a prayer and laying on of hands.

Many Christians of both sexes, called "ascetics," practiced voluntary poverty, continency, and prayer and fasting. "Widows" were of apostolic institution, and were employed by the Church in ecclesiastical and charitable works.

13. Give a summary of the development of monastic life.

During the persecution of Decius in 250, hermits left the world and retired to the desert to live the Christian life in solitude. The hermits began to form communities or congregations around themselves. Though they lived separately in their cells, they would elect a common spiritual father or director, called an abbot. St. Anthony of Egypt, a very holy father of the desert, was a chief promoter of this form of monastic life.

It next developed that monasteries were founded with a common rule of religious life. St. Hilarion established one in Palestine, St. Pachomius in Egypt, St. Basil in Asia Minor. For women, monasteries of nuns were founded by St. Anthony and St. Pachomius, whose sisters were appointed the first superiors.

Monastic life found its chief promoters in the West in St. Ambrose, St. Martin of Tours, St. Augustine, St. Patrick, and St. Columba, as well as other holy bishops.

St. Martin founded a large monastery near Tours, and when he died, 2,000 monks and many consecrated virgins attended his funeral (in the year 400).

At Bangor, Ireland, it is recorded that 3,000 monks sang the canonical hours without intermission in seven divisions.

In the West and in the East, monks were originally laymen, although their superior was a priest who had the power to offer the sacrifice of the Mass. The monks arose at dawn and sang hymns of praise to God. Then they meditated on the holy scriptures. They would come together for special prayers at nine o'clock, at noon, and at three.

The monks of the early centuries dedicated the remainder of their time to work, tilling the soil, administering to the needs of the poor, taking care of the sick, and protecting those persecuted by the civil government.

14. What special role did St. Benedict have in Western monasticism?

St. Benedict (d. 543) founded the Benedictine Order. He wrote the famous rule blending prayer, study, work, silence, and mortification. It soon spread over Europe, and 37,000 convents developed the Benedictine way of Christian life.

St. Benedict (born in 480) led a life of prayer and penance in the solitude of Subiaco. Many disciples were attracted by his holiness, and he established a monastery at Monte Casino which became the "motherhouse" of his order.

Due to harshness of climate and other circumstances, some monks in the West made their rule easier to live by, so that gradually in many places the monks began living a Christian life little different from people in the world. It was the role of St. Benedict to lead the monks back to their first spirit. St. Benedict is therefore known as the Father of Monasticism in the West.

The Benedictine Order produced many hundreds of canonized saints.

15. How did the Church of the early centuries reconcile her fallen children to God and the Church?

Holiness is the second characteristic mark of the true Church. Christ knew that his members would not always persevere and so he established the sacrament of penance in his Church for the forgiveness of sins for those who are truly repentant (Jn 20:19-23). Early Christians often looked upon this sacrament (received from the bishop) as a second baptism.

The early Church also developed a well-organized system of public penance of four degrees, instituted for certain sins of a *public* nature:

1. *Weeping*—those who had to remain outside the church. 2. *Hearing*—those who could assist at Mass only until the Gospel and sermon. 3. *Kneeling* and 4. *Standing*—these two degrees were permitted to remain until the end of the Mass, but were separated from the rest of the faithful and could not receive Holy Communion until they were completely reconciled to Christ and his Church.

Forms of early Church penance may seem severe and humiliating to us today, but through these penitential stages the faithful who had seriously fallen were led back to a pure and holy life in Christ.

Even such men as Theodosius the Great, Charlemagne, Otto I of Germany, St. Louis of France, and Philip II of Spain (as well as others) so accepted the ascetic spirit of the Church that they used the hairshirt and the scourge.

16. What is meant by the "oneness' which Jesus gave his Church?

Jesus commanded that "one Lord, one faith, one baptism" be taken to "all nations." Truth does not vary with geographical location. Jesus taught clearly and with authority. He founded one Church, not many. He spoke of building one Church upon Peter.

"Truth is one" means, when speaking of true faith, that there can be no contradictions in the same tenet of faith. True faith and morals must be the same throughout the world.

17. What is meant by "holiness," which Jesus required for his Church?

Holiness is found in the Catholic Church (which Jesus established) because God is holy and the founder is both God and Man. The Church teaches a holy doctrine and gives its members all that is needed for a holy life, and its history bears evidence from its earliest years to holiness in many of its members.

Most popes of the first centuries are honored as martyrs for the faith. The holiness of many early Christians is testified by their martyrdom.

Holiness is seen in the early Church as many Christians gave up all things for the love of God, some even the right to marriage, so as to give full time to Christ and the service of his Church.

The monastic life of the ascetics, who lived the evangelical counsels of Christ and drew thousands of followers, bears testimony to holiness in the early Church.

18. What is meant by the "catholicity" of the Church, as Christ established it?

The word "catholic" means universal. Jesus gave the command, "Go, therefore, and make disciples of all nations" (Mt 28:19).

Jesus is the universal Savior who brought us "one Lord, one faith, one baptism" for "all nations."

History, even the brief history in this manual, verifies that the one faith of Jesus began to spread to "all nations" from the first century.

19. What is meant by the "apostolicity" which Jesus gave to the Church he established?

That the Church is apostolic means that Jesus built his Church upon the original apostles, as stated in the Bible, and with Peter as head.

Only the Catholic Church has a history, almost 2,000 years old, extending back to Jesus Christ and his first apostles.

20. Did the Church from the first century mandate only one form of ceremonial worship?

No. Jesus gave the command, when he instituted the holy Eucharist, "Do this in commemoration of me." Jesus did not command only one manner of offering the Eucharist, which Catholics came to call in later centuries "the sacrifice of the Mass."

From the early centuries there were various rites in the Church, as it spread throughout the world. From the first, the Church of Jesus preserved unity in diversity, even in the form of celebrating the eucharistic mysteries.

While the Church of apostolic succession always retains the internal mystery of Christ (really present and perpetuating his sacrifice of the cross and giving his risen body, blood, soul, and divinity in sacramental form), the external form, from apostolic days on, took forms with different aspects, according to the different languages, customs, and cultures of the worshipers.

21. Did the early Church celebrate many liturgical feasts?

No. The Christians at first knew only one feast, Easter. They were "sons of the Resurrection," and every Sunday was a "little Easter." In the early Church there was no feast of Christmas.

Very early, the commemoration of Christ's birth was observed on the feast of the Epiphany, when the Savior is manifested to the nations.

St. Clement of Alexandria first mentions the feast of Christmas around the year 200. The Western Church, about 300, began celebrating it on December 25, to replace a pagan feast of lights in the darkness of winter.

The Church, through her feasts, was able to Christianize pagan customs and fulfill the needs of the people in a manner which protected their new faith in Jesus Christ.

22. Did Catholic devotion to God's Mother exist in the early Church?

There is sufficient evidence that it began with the apostles, although the early Church was more concerned with establishing faith in Jesus Christ as Lord, God, and Savior.

From sacred scripture we know that Jesus gave his Mother into the care of John, the youngest apostle. As best as scholars can determine, Mary was about 49 when Jesus left this earth and John became her protector and guardian. She left this world about sixteen years later, at the age of 64, according to tradition.

There is an account by St. Juvenal, bishop of Jerusalem, at the Council of Chalcedon in 451, and repeated by St. John Dasmascene in 780, that tells of Mary's death, although it is not defined that Mary died physically, only that she was taken into heaven, body and soul.

This is the early account: "Mary died near the Coenaculum in Jerusalem and was buried at Gethsemane, where Sts. Joachim and Anna and Joseph were buried. At her death, after three days the song of the angels came to an end. Thomas, the only apostle then absent, arrived and desired to see and venerate the body in which God had dwelt. The apostles opened the tomb but did not find the sacred deposit. Seeing only the linen which had enveloped the body of Mary, and from which a sweet odor arose, they closed the sepulchre. Astonished at the miracle, they could have but one thought: that he who has been pleased to become incarnate in the chaste womb of the Virgin Mary and to be born of her, being the Word of God and the Lord of glory and having already preserved the virginity of his mother, had also willed to preserve from corruption her immaculate body after death, and to translate it to heaven before the general and universal resurrection."

Such details are not defined doctrines but give evidence of the constant faith of the Church in Mary's bodily assumption.

Historical records show that Mary's Feast of the Assumption was celebrated as early as 400 (Epiphanius). The day of liturgical celebrations in its honor was called Mary's Dormitio or Transition, which means Mary's "going to sleep," her "passing over."

In modern times, there has been renewed interest in Ephesus in relationship to the Mother of Jesus. Recent studies at Ephesus seem to verify the discovery of Mary's house, where she lived with St. John after the death of Jesus Christ. The ruins of the oldest church built in honor of Mary, the Basilica of St. Mary, where the famous Council of Ephesus was held in 431, are believed to remain to the present day. There are also the ruins of St. John's Basilica, where, scholars are convinced, they recently discovered the body of St. John the Apostle.

Early Christians prayed the rosary, but not in the form known today. While priests prayed the 150 psalms of David, the faithful from very early times sought some form of substitute in prayer. Their love for God's Mother, as demonstrated at the time of the Council of Ephesus, which declared Mary truly the Mother of God and which brought such rejoicing from the baptized, found expressions of faith in Christ joined to the love of his Mother. The educated religious prayed 150 psalms, and the common faithful found a substitute in 150 Hail Marys.

The history of the rosary reaches back to the days of early Christianity and the monks in the desert. A devout ascetic who desired to say a certain number of prayers (usually Our Fathers) would gather a hundred or more pebbles or seeds into a basket and place them, one at a time, in another container as he said his prayers.

It was often customary to make a genuflexion with each prayer. In some Eastern rites these customs are retained, with prayers being recited upon knotted cords or strings of beads. In the Western Church, the Hail Mary came into general use about the middle of the twelfth century. Hail Marys and Our Fathers were used in reciting the rosary, especially in monasteries by lay brothers and sisters who could not read the 150 psalms or the Divine Office.

The laity in large numbers gradually took to praying the rosary. Hail Marys were substituted for the psalms, bringing the number to 150 when all the chief fifteen mysteries were meditated upon while saying these prayers. The rosary, as a form of Marian devotion, from its inception was Christ-centered and scriptural.

Summary

Jesus Christ established his Church with a very simple structure, yet with potential for adaptation to meet the needs of every age. While every mode of operation of the Church did not take shape immediately upon the ascension of our Lord into heaven, Jesus so constituted his Church that it could adapt itself to every part of the world, to every culture, and Jesus, living in the history of the world through his Church, could become "all things to all men."

Adaptations of government of the Church and changes in the divine liturgy, which comprises the worship of the Church, do not mean that true faith changes with time and location. Jesus gave his Church the power to teach, to rule, and to sanctify. He established his Church with characteristics of oneness, holiness, catholicity, and apostolicity. Such authority and such characteristics exist in the Catholic Church until the present day.

The Church is one and it is different. It is one in its Lord, faith, and baptism. It is diverse in its mode of expression to meet the needs of every tribe and culture. The infinite God desires to manifest his unchangeable divine truth to the souls of all and his Son, Jesus Christ, established his Church in such a manner as to accomplish that purpose.

Questions for Discussion

1. Describe a church community in the early years of Christianity.
2. Did the popes of the first centuries exercise their God-given authority to the fullest capacity? Explain.
3. When and how did the tradition of priests' not marrying develop in the Roman Catholic Church?
4. Explain what special Christian communities, which developed in the life of the Church in the third century, were like.
5. How did the monastic communities start?
6. Give some evidence that early Christians recognized the special authority of Peter's successor in the see of Rome.
7. How did the concepts of archbishop, patriarch, and metropolitan develop in the Church?
8. What are the four marks of the Church? Indicate how each of them is manifested in the history of the Catholic Church.
9. Do we have evidence from history that modern-day Catholic practices, such as celebrating the assumption of the body of God's Mother into heaven, reached back to the early centuries? Explain.
10. Explain how the rosary devotion, as we have it today, began to form in the early centuries.
11. Did the Christians of the early centuries observe the great variety of liturgical feasts that we do in the Church today? Explain.

Chapter 6
The Barbarian Invasions and the Downfall of the Roman Empire

1. What was the origin of the barbarian invasions?

Fifty years before Jesus Christ was born, far away in the East, the "migration of nations" had its origin. The Chinese Empire expelled a people known as the Huns, who turned to the West and conquered the nations along the way, scattering them as they moved forward. These scattered nations in turn conquered other nations. Within 500 years the face of Europe was changed.

2. What happened to the once mighty Roman Empire of the West?

The Roman Empire of the West fell before the invading nations in the year 475 and the barbarian Goths, Franks, Vandals, Sueves, Lombards, Saxons, and various German tribes established new states on the ruins. When the invasions were over, only a small territory remained, in the vicinity of Constantinople, of what was once the proud Roman Empire. All of the Western world was composed of new nations. There was a Lombard kingdom in Italy, a Gothic kingdom in Spain, a Frankish kingdom in Gaul, and seven Anglo-Saxon kingdoms in Britain.

3. Were the barbarians complete savages?

No. They had a culture of their own, but not as advanced as that of the Romans or Greeks. There was much that was noble and beautiful in their culture, and they were more like tribes than nations. While these peoples had warriors, most of the tribes were agricultural and pastoral.

The barbarians' tribes, which formed the new nations, had high ideals of self-respect and personal liberty. The barbarians were loyal to their tribe, to their relatives. They had great respect for womanhood. Their nobility of spirit lent itself to eventual conversion as Christians.

4. How did the Church react to the invading barbarians?

The pope and the bishops were great leaders of the people in the West in the last days of the Roman Empire. They were leaders in defending the cities from the invasions and made treaties with the invaders. The king of the Huns, Atilla, who called himself the Scourge of God, had taken Germany and France with force. When he entered Italy, Pope Leo the Great went to meet him. Atilla was greatly impressed by the pope and felt that he was a ruler with greater authority than his own. Atilla was persuaded by Pope Leo to leave Italy, return to Hungary, and live in peace with Rome.

When the Vandals came into Italy by way of the sea, Pope Leo again went to meet their leader, Genseric. Genseric took the city of Rome, but in respect for the pope he did not massacre the inhabitants or plunder the churches.

The pope and bishops sent priests and missionaries to work among the new people to convert them to Christ. The Church, ever conscious that her mission was above that of nations, became their teacher and spiritual mother, to form these people in the knowledge and love of Christ Jesus. Churches and schools were established in the midst of the new peoples.

5. Did St. Benedict have a special role in Christianizing these barbarian nations?

Yes. While the rule of St. Benedict was a masterpiece, and aimed primarily at the sanctification of the Benedictine community, with its motto *Ora et labora* ("Pray and Work"), the monks were also interested in the world outside their monasteries. They did much to help the people around them.

The holy monks established monasteries in the forests and cleared and cultivated the land, while teaching others how to do the same. They taught the people faith and morals, established schools for their education, and instructed them in the trades and arts as well as agriculture.

6. What role did St. Patrick have in Christianizing the nations?

St. Patrick converted Ireland around the year 432. According to tradition, when only 17 years old Patrick was carried to Ireland by pirates and made a slave. His time of slavery was an opportunity to meditate on the Christian faith, and after his escape he longed to return to be the Apostle of Christianity to Ireland.

St. Patrick went to France to prepare himself. He studied at a monastery and for fifteen years labored as a deacon in northern Gaul. In 432 Patrick was consecrated bishop of Ireland. He knew the Irish language and customs and the political organization of the country. He directed his attention to converting people who had great influence over the populace (e.g., chieftains, lawyers, poets). He built up a native clergy and established monasteries. Within a generation after St. Patrick, the monasteries of Ireland were considered the greatest in Europe.

St. Patrick left behind him ardent missionaries, and within two centuries Ireland was completely Christianized. Ireland developed the greatest religious communities in the world and had famous schools attached to her monasteries. From these went forth missionaries to distant lands to establish other monasteries and schools and set an Irish influence on every nation of Europe.

7. Who are some of the other great missionaries who helped in this task?

There were many. Scotland was converted by St. Ninian and St. Columba. St. Ninian, a friend of St. Martin of Tours and the son of a British king, studied at Rome, where Pope Siricius consecrated him bishop for Scotland. He taught the southern part of Scotland and founded the great monastery of Withern. St. Ninian died in 430.

St. Columba was an Irish monk who evangelized northern Scotland. He established the famous monastery of Iona in the Hebrides, and for many centuries it produced apostolic men for the northern countries. St. Columba died in 597.

8. How was England converted?

England, or Britain, began to receive the Christian faith toward the beginning of the second century. The invasion of the pagan Anglo-Saxons in A.D. 448 almost destroyed Christianity in England, as it destroyed the Roman civilization on the island. Bishops and priests were driven out; churches were destroyed or converted into pagan temples. The country became known as England, which means Land of the Angles.

Pope St. Gregory the Great had longed to be a missionary to the Anglo-Saxons in Britain when he was still a monk. One day he saw some people he considered beautiful in the marketplace as he was passing through the streets of Rome. He asked who these captives were, who had such noble bearing and natural dignity. Informed that they were Angles, he answered: "They are not Angles, but angels."

Pope Gregory chose forty monks from his own monastery, placed Augustine at their head, and sent them to preach the gospel to the people of England. In 597 they landed in England and met with great success.

The king of Kent, Ethelbert, was married to a Frankish princess who was a Christian. This queen persuaded the king to meet the missionaries, and they were given liberty to preach the gospel. The king himself, with many of his people, was soon baptized.

When Augustine died in 605, the faith had deep roots in England.

Monasteries sprang up over the island. Great monks came forth from them, such as Willibrod and Winifred (later known as Boniface).

9. Tell about the conversion and reconversion of France.

France (in ancient times "Gaul") was converted very early—according to tradition, by Lazarus, Martha, Magdalen, Dionysius, and various disciples of the original apostles. The faith was destroyed, however, with the migration of the pagan Franks.

France was brought into the Church again when King Clovis was influenced by his holy wife Clotilda. Almost defeated in the battle with the Allemanni, Clovis called upon Christ, the God of his wife. He gained victory. He was baptized by St. Remigius in 496 and was influential in bringing the people of France into the Church.

10. What influence did Boniface have in Germany?

Southern Germany had been converted by disciples of the apostles who went to the countries along the Rhine and Danube rivers. After the barbarian nations overran Germany, missionaries from England and Ireland brought the faith to them.

The middle and northern parts of Germany were converted in the eighth century by St. Winifred, the English Benedictine monk whom Pope Gregory II named Boniface. Living in the forests, the Germans were great lovers of nature and they practiced nature worship. They reverenced, and held as sacred, a great oak tree in the forest known as the Tree of Thor. It was dedicated to the false god Thor. They said that the God of Boniface was not mighty enough to destroy the Tree of Thor. With an ax, Boniface cut down the famous oak and, according to tradition, out of it built the first Christian church. When nothing happened to him, the faith of the pagans in Thor was shaken and great numbers asked to be baptized.

Boniface then built convents and schools for the education of young men and women.

11. Explain the conversion of the Slavonic nations.

The pope sent St. Cyril and St. Methodius to the Slavonic nations in the year 870, and many were converted through their preaching. St. Adalbert of Prague became the Apostle of Prussia around the year 1000. King Borzivoi and Queen St. Ludmilla were helped by missionaries from Germany in establishing the Christian faith in Bohemia. Poland came to the Christian faith around the year 1000, under the influence of Prince Miesko I. St. Stephen, the king of Hungary, also received help from missionaries from Germany around the year 1000 to bring the faith to his entire country.

12. What about the Scandinavian countries?

Sweden was brought to the Christian faith about 850, when the apostolic St. Ansgar preached there. Queen Emma influenced King Canute to assist in the conversion of Denmark. King Olaf completed the Christianizing of Sweden. King Olaf the Holy in the tenth century saw to the conversion of Norway. By the year 1000, Iceland and Greenland had bishops.

13. Who Christianized Spain?

Tradition has it that Spain first received the Christian faith from St. Paul and St. James and other disciples of the apostles. During the migration of barbarian nations, the Arian Visigoths separated Spain from the Church. Spain was brought back to the Church under Pope Gregory about 595, when King Reccared was converted through the martyrdom of Prince Hermenegild and the apostolic work of St. Leander.

14. When were the Netherlands converted?

The gospel was preached in the Netherlands during the third and fourth centuries by St. Piatus and St. Servatius. Their work was completed by St. Eligius, St. Willibrod, St. Amand, and St. Lambert after the migration of the nations.

15. What happened to the Lombards in Northern Italy?

Although the Lombards destroyed the Christian faith in northern Italy, they were eventually converted through the action of Pope Gregory the Great and Queen Theodolinda, a daughter of the duke of Bavaria.

Summary

During the barbarian invasions, if it had not been for the Catholic Church all of Europe would have fallen in ruin and the ancient Greek and Roman culture would have been lost. The Church, however, rather than simply fight the nations, converted them.

Popes and bishops during these years of crisis, caused by the invasion of the barbarians or the migration of nations (which extended from the fourth to the seventh century, received little help from the empire. Monasticism proved an invaluable help to the Church during these years, with St. Benedict standing tall in history, along with St. Patrick and others. Though the empire fell, Christ's Church increased.

Because the Church was more or less, from a worldly point of view, dependent on the empire, when Western Europe was overrun by the barbarian nations and the collapse of the Roman Empire was inevitable, it seemed as though the Church would end. But as we shall see in our study of the 2,000-year history of the Catholic Church, there will frequently be predictions of its end. In fact, almost every century will bring that prediction, but Christ and his Church are above all nations and dependent on none. The Church is catholic, universal—for *all nations.*

What happened in the reaction of the Church to the migration of the nations was not the destruction of the Church, but many new converts—fulfillment of the command of Jesus to "preach to all the nations"—and thus was laid the foundation of a new Europe.

At this point in Catholic Church history we can see how the modern world is developing and how the Church is a very important part of that development. The civilized and cultured Christian nations of the world today are the descendants of the converted barbarian nations. We can see how much of the greatness of these nations is due to the education given by the Church. The Church is often maligned in her role in history, as she is often misrepresented in our own day, but to the honest historian there is an undeniable influence of the Catholic Church in her saints, monasteries, and schools in building great and civilized nations.

Questions for Discussion

1. Can you see God ultimately as the author of the history of salvation, working in the Huns' being driven from the frontiers of the Chinese Empire fifty years before Christ? Explain.
2. What lesson can be learned from the fact that the Roman Empire fell during the migration of the nations but the Church continued to grow?
3. Name the good qualities of the barbaric tribes and tell how they fit them for conversion to Christianity.
4. How did the Church set itself to convert the barbarian nations, rather than simply resist them?
5. Explain the role of St. Benedict in converting the nations.
6. Explain the role of St. Patrick in converting the nations.
7. How did Pope St. Gregory contribute to the conversion of England?
8. How was St. Boniface fearless in the face of paganism?
9. How did the Catholic Church contribute to creating a new Europe?

Chapter 7
Mohammedanism and the Christian Crusades

1. What is Mohammedanism and how did it originate?

Mohammedanism is a religion, practiced by millions of people in southeastern Europe, Asia Minor, Arabia, Persia, India, North Africa, and parts of Asia. Mohammed, a native of Arabia, became a merchant and began his teaching in pagan Arabia about A.D. 622.

Arabia, though pagan, was also the home of many heretical Christians and numerous Jews. Mohammed claimed he received his new religion in a vision, but in reality it is a mixture of paganism, Christianity, and Judaism. As a merchant, he learned something of the Old Testament as well as the teachings of Christ. He combined his paganism with Judaism and Christianity, and wrote his doctrines on leaves, stones, and leather. These teachings were rewritten after his death and put into one volume, known as the Koran.

2. What did Mohammed teach in his new religion?

Mohammed denied the Trinity but taught there is but one God and Mohammed is his prophet. Each man is predestined by God to reward or punishment in the next world. External observances are emphasized at the expense of self-discipline. The use of pork and wine was forbidden. A man could have any number of wives. One who died in war for his religion would immediately be admitted to heaven. Mohammed's heaven is a place of beautiful trees, filled with fruits, in which there are all the sensual delights. The great tenet of Mohammed's faith is "God alone is God, and Mohammed is his prophet."

51

3. How did Mohammedanism advance?

Mohammedanism spread first through Arabia and then its members organized for a "holy war" against all outsiders. They conquered Arabia, Palestine, Syria, and Egypt within ten years. North Africa and Spain also fell to them, and they reduced Christians to a low condition of poverty and oppression when they later resisted them.

4. How did Mohammed's followers treat the Christians at first?

At first the Mohammedans were easy on the Christians when they conquered a country, and many Christians gave up their faith to win the favor of their conquerors. But later, when books defending Christianity were sent into these countries, the Mohammedans manifested their religious intolerance and forced Christians to become Mohammedans or die.

5. How did the Mohammedans become a new threat to Christians in the eighth century?

In the eighth century they began to use the great libraries of Syria and Egypt, which they had conquered. They became skilled in the sciences and arts and developed scholarship. Traders along the shores of the Mediterranean, they posed a new threat to Christianity since their knowledge of philosophy and the sciences was impressive to many Christians with whom they came into contact, and this caused some Christians to doubt their own faith.

6. Were the Mohammedans known by various names?

The Mohammedans were called Arabs in Arabia. They became known as Saracens when they attacked Africa and Europe. In Spain, they were known as Moors, and in southeast Europe as Turks. Today we frequently call them Moslems.

7. What was the importance of the Battle of Tours for Christendom?

The Mohammedans would have conquered western Europe and affected the future of Christianity had not the Franks, under Charles Martel, defeated their huge army in the Battle of Tours in 732.

The Mohammedans took Constantinople and the Balkan peninsula, and would have defeated Germany, but were overcome by Austria and Poland.

8. How did the conquest of Jerusalem by the Mohammedans cause a good reaction in Christians?

It helped unite the Christian nations of Europe and directed their energies from internal squabbles to uniting in charity and faith to protect their holy religion. The conquest of Jerusalem resulted in the great Crusades, when knighthood was elevated and sanctified by the Church and even war was put to a holy use, as princes and kings united under the leadership of the pope to rescue the holy places in Jerusalem from the Turks.

9. What is meant by the Christian Crusades?

The Crusades were sacred wars, waged by Christian nations to deliver the Holy Land, and the Sepulchre of Jesus Christ, from the oppression of the Mohammedans. "Crusader" is taken from "cross," since the Crusaders wore the cross on their breasts as a sign of their undertaking.

"Chivalry" has been associated with the ideals and principles by which a true knight should live, and the authentic Christian today, of course, should live the nobility to which knights of old aspired. It is sad that sometimes God must permit tragedies to unite Christians in love and common purpose.

In 1095 the Greek emperor appealed to the West for assistance in saving his kingdom from the Turks. Pope Urban II called a council at Clermont for discussion on Church discipline, and also spoke to the assembled crowd of the atrocities in the East. He urged kings and princes and nobles and counts to forget their quarrels and join forces to drive the Turks out of Palestine. All enthusiastically shouted: "God wills it!"

The preaching of the Crusades motivated the people toward a holier life, such as began at the famous monastery of Cluny and was carried to the clergy by Pope Gregory VII. Common Christians saw in the movement a challenge to devote themselves and all their property to the cause of Christ. In sacrificing for Bethlehem, Nazareth, and Jerusalem, they were sacrificing themselves for Jesus.

God does not always grant victory in the way man desires. But God always answers prayers which have a noble intent. God protected his Church through the sacrifices of his people, for the faith was more strongly instilled in the hearts of the people at the time of the Crusades.

10. What were the principal Crusades?

The First Crusade was led by Duke Godfrey of Bouillon, who led an immense army. On July 15, 1099, Jerusalem was delivered from the Turks, to become a Christian kingdom with Godfrey as its king. This First Crusade was preached by Peter the Hermit, who returned from the Holy Land having witnessed the desecration of the holy places where our Lord suffered and died. He rode through Europe on a donkey and preached to the Christians with stirring eloquence. Pope Urban II endorsed this Crusade.

The Second Crusade was led by Emperor Conrad III of Germany and Louis VII of France in 1147. St. Bernard preached this Crusade.

The Third Crusade was led by the emperor Frederick Barbarossa of Germany in 1189. He gained great victories over immense Turkish armies but met his death suddenly when swimming on his horse across a river. The Crusade was continued against Sultan Saladin by Philip Augustus, king of France, and the chivalrous Richard the Lion-hearted, king of England.

The Fourth Crusade was led by Baldwin of Flanders in 1203. It captured Constantinople, and the Latin empire was erected on the Balkan peninsula.

The Fifth Crusade was led by King Andrew II of Hungary and Duke Leopold of Austria in 1217.

The final two crusades were led by St. Louis IX, king of France.

11. What was the Children's Crusade?

It consisted of an army of thousands of children who in 1212 went singing and praying through Europe for the deliverance of the Holy Sepulchre. Most either died of disease or were sold into slavery.

12. Were the Crusades successful from a military point of view?

From a military point of view, the victory consisted in keeping the Turks from attacking Europe. In 1291 the Turks won back control of Palestine. In their chief intention, the Crusades failed.

13. In what way did the Crusades succeed?

Much good was accomplished in other ways. A great religious revival, resulting in Catholic unity, was realized. The ideals of Christian knighthood were elevated. The West became better acquainted with the East and Greek culture was brought back to Italy, Germany, and France. Commerce and navigation developed, and this led to the discovery of America in 1492. The lower and middle classes of society were improved.

14. Relate the foundation of the great orders of Christian knights in the Middle Ages for the defense of the Holy Sepulchre.

Knights of St. John, 1099. They had a history of great faith, bravery, and honor. They wore military cloaks of black with large white crosses. After Jerusalem fell, they moved to the island of Rhodes and then to Malta.

Knights Templars, 1118. They were given this name because their fortified monastery stood on the site of Solomon's temple. They wore white cloaks with red crosses. King Philip the Fair of France urged their abolition, and this was accomplished by the Council of Vienne.

German Knights, 1143. They wore white cloaks and black crosses. These knights moved from Palestine to Prussia in 1226 and defended Christians against the heathens.

15. What was the main purpose of these orders of knights?

The orders of knights defended pilgrims who came to the Holy Land to pay honor to the places made holy by the life, death, and resurrection of our Lord and Savior Jesus Christ. They also fought the Turks in defense of the Holy Sepulchre. They were really monks in armor, and in their ritual of reception they were asked: "Do you solemnly promise, beloved brother, in the name of God and the Blessed Virgin, to practice faithfully a lifelong obedience to your superiors? Do you promise perpetual celibacy and perfect purity of soul and body? Do you pledge yourself to renounce forever all worldly goods, and to serve the Order in poverty and submission, and to risk your life for the deliverance of the Holy Land?"

To these questions the ritual of reception replied: "As you promise each and all of these things we receive you into the holy brotherhood, and promise you bread and water, the simple garb of our monastery, and labor and trials in abundance."

16. Did the Turks continue to threaten Christianity?

Yes. Christianity continued to be threatened by the Turks and therefore Europe itself was in danger. The Turks took Constantinople in 1453 and the Balkan peninsula. Europe was continuously threatened by attacks. The Church introduced the Angelus in memory of God become Man through the instrumentality of Mary. It was introduced to beg God's special help in these wars.

17. How was the Turkish power finally broken?

It was the popes who motivated the Christian nations to break the Turkish power. The popes called the faithful to recite the rosary and the Angelus in all Christian lands for this purpose, and to physical resistance.

Under the efforts of Pope Pius V, Don Juan of Austria formed a mighty fleet and defeated the Turkish navy in the great victory of Lepanto in 1571. On the sea, the Turkish power was finally broken. The combined Christian fleet completely destroyed the invading armada, liberating Christians and thus Europe from being overrun by Moslems. The Christians were inspired in their battle by the image of God's Mother.

The Turkish land army was completely disorganized in 1683 before the city of Vienna by Christian forces made up of Poles under King Sobiesky and of Germans under Charles of Lorraine.

Then, in 1717, Prince Eugene, a Christian general famous in the songs of the people, destroyed the land power of the Turks in the Battle of Belgrade.

The Christians of Spain and Portugal had fought the Mohammedans from the time of their conquest in the eighth century. But in the reign of Ferdinand and Isabella, in 1492, the last Mohammedan ruler was forced to leave the Iberian peninsula.

18. What were the details of the Battle of Lepanto?

When Pope Pius V became the successor of St. Peter in 1566, he found the Church surrounded on all sides by threats of destruction. The Church was ravaged in northern Europe by the Protestant Revolt. In the south, the Albigensians were threatening the Latin countries. The Turkish Empire (the Ottomans) was threatening the East.

The pope, realizing that, in the natural course of things, the Church would be defeated, directed Christians to seek supernatural help. Pope Pius V called for a rosary crusade among all Christians, as he anticipated a decisive battle. The Battle of Lepanto (Nafpactos, which is now the Gulf of Corinth in Greece) ended the threat of Moslem domination of Europe, and in victory for the Christian forces.

The Christian forces were composed of 300 galleys, with naval crews, 3,000 soldiers, and 8 ships of artillery. The Turkish fleet comprised about an equal number of ships. Its commander was Ali Pasha, with ships lined up inside the entrance to the gulf and stretching almost from shore to shore in a crescent. In the center was Ali Pasha; to his north was Mahomet Sirocco, while to his south Uluch Ali was in command.

From the northern side of the gulf, the Christian allies had to come abreast of the Turkish ships, forming into three squadrons. In the center were the Spanish ships, the Venetians to the left, and Andrea Doria commanded a squadron to the right. The full fire of the Turks fell upon the left and center, and the Christians appeared to be suffering a destructive blow. To appreciate the significance of the sudden change of fate for the Christian forces at this time, keep the following points in mind.

Spain had struggled against the Mohammedan power for more than 700 years and became an independent kingdom only in 1492, the year Columbus discovered America. The Ottoman or Turkish Empire in the East was experiencing renewed power and lusted for conquest. It had captured Constantinople in 1453 and was intent on conquering all of Christendom, to bring it into slavery. It had invaded the Balkan peninsula, and all the eastern Mediterranean countries were under its power. By the middle of the sixteenth century its navy had captured Cyprus and was menacing Venice.

The Moslems had a plan to conquer all the European countries bordering the Mediterranean Sea by building the world's greatest naval power. This would enable them to push northward until all of Europe was in their grasp. It was then that Pope Pius V was instrumental in forming the Holy League to resist this force. The pope convinced the Spanish and Italian powers to unite for this purpose.

From Spain came a large naval squadron under the command of the marquis of Santa Cruz. From Venice came another, with Veniero and Barbarigo as admirals. There were smaller squadrons from the Papal States, and Parma and Savoy were joined to Genoese forces under Prince Andrea Doria. Don Juan of Austria, half-brother of King Philip of Spain, had supreme command.

The reader should be mindful that this was not just another of many historical battles. What was involved was the threat of Moslem domination of Europe, the destruction of Christianity itself, and the changing of all future history.

Pope Pius V called for a rosary crusade among all Christians, as he anticipated the conflict. At the same time, the second archbishop of Mexico, Don Fray Alonso de Montufór, had become a devotee of Our Lady of Guadalupe, the miraculous image of the Mother of God given to a humble Indian convert, Juan Diego, on the newly discovered continent. The archbishop had seen evidence of continuous miracles through the intercession of God's Mother, and he was aware of the crisis in Europe. He had a small reproduction of the holy image of Our Lady of Guadalupe made, then touched it to the original and sent it to King Philip of Spain in 1570. Archbishop Montufór expressed the desire that the king would see that this copy of the sacred image of our Lady was placed in a suitable place in the Christian navy when the battle began.

Archbishop Montufór believed that God's Mother would work a miracle for the Holy League which the Pope had organized, just as she had so often done for the Mexicans. The king agreed and had it mounted in the cabin of Admiral Andrea Doria as the Battle of Lepanto approached.

During the battle, Andrea Doria was compelled to separate from the center force of Christians. Uluch Ali then broke through the gap and was prepared to destroy Andrea Doria's fleet. Doria knew he was facing destruction, together with his fleet. His was the ship with the image of Our Lady of Guadalupe in his cabin, and the battle was thus under her intercession.

At this critical moment a tremendous wind came up and blew the Turkish navy into total disorganization. Their squadrons were thrown into panic and, thus stricken, most of their fleet was captured or destroyed.

The historian may record this only as fate, telling us, at the same time, that it was the last sea battle fought with oar-propelled vessels and enormous casualties. About 8,000 Christians were killed and 16,000 wounded. Among the Turkish fleet, about 25,000 were killed, and it is not known how many were wounded. About 15,000 Christians, who had been chained to the oars in the Turkish galleys, were freed. This victory of Lepanto ended the Moslem threat to Christians.

The pope ascribed the victory to the Queen of the Rosary, since he had sponsored the rosary crusade for Victory. He evidently did not know of the miraculous image of Our Lady of Guadalupe. Pope St. Pius V established the Feast of Our Lady of Victory to celebrate the October 7 victory. His successor, Pope Gregory XIII, changed the title of the feast to Our Lady of the Most Holy Rosary and decreed that the month of October should be dedicated to renewing the praying of the rosary.

Our Lady had told Juan Diego and his uncle, Juan Bernardino, that she was the Immaculate Conception. Her image aboard Doria's ship, according to devout Christians, was an instrument of Mary's moral presence as the Warrior Queen and the Mother of the Church, "fair as the moon, bright as the sun, terrible as an army set in battle array."

Until 1811 the small reproduction of the holy image of Guadalupe remained in the Doria family. A descendant, Cardinal Doria, made a present of it to the people of Aveto in Liguria, north of Genoa. There it remains, enshrined to the present day in the Church of San Stefano d'Aveto. Pius VII in 1815 granted that shrine the faculty of a Mass of Our Lady of Guadalupe, as well as indulgences, in answer to the great faith and love inspired by the shrine and the reported miracles. Pope Leo XII granted perpetual privileges to the altar of Our Lady of Guadalupe in San Stefano d'Aveto.

It is little wonder that some devout historians record that after the victory of Lepanto the crews attributed the triumph to Our Lady of Guadalupe. While a secular historian would record such a victory and defeat as the results of chance, the devout Christian will consider the victory due to prayer and divine providence, working in the history of Christianity.

Summary

This chapter relates the high challenges which Christians can meet and the great nobility which can be theirs when the faith is stirred to action in their hearts. Doubtlessly, there were abuses among the Crusaders, as there always is in time of war, but in general these events of history demonstrate that Christians are capable of greatness, of taking up the cross and following the Lord even unto death if need be.

The young man would pray at night before Jesus Christ in the Blessed Sacrament in preparation for knighthood. Before him, as he knelt at the foot of the altar, was the armor that he was to be invested with on the morrow, when he would receive Communion and his sword would be blessed and dedicated to the service of widows and orphans of the Church.

The young knight meant well at the time of his reception, but a life of war sometimes caused him to forget his honor and he became cruel. Chivalry, at this time, produced many noble characters, and even those who were not completely true to their vows doubtlessly felt restraint while engaged in battle.

The rise of Mohammedanism, with Mohammed claiming visions and combining qualities of paganism, Judaism, and Christianity, tells us why the Church is skeptical when anyone claims a vision—even when they finally prove authentic, as in the cases of Guadalupe, Lourdes, and Fatima. Consider the trouble to Christianity that resulted from the enthusiasm generated from the supposed vision of Mohammed.

Study, prayer, and action are the blend of balanced Christianity. One does not simply pray and let the opposition pound one into annihilation. The popes called the Crusades to resist evil forces that threatened destruction of the Christian faith and countries, as well as to defend the places made holy by the life, death, and resurrection of Jesus Christ.

Questions for Discussion

1. How is Mohammedanism a combination of religions?
2. How were the Mohammedans a threat to Christians?

3. How was good among Christians realized as a result of the invading Mohammedans?
4. What is meant by a Crusader, in the strict sense of the word?
5. How were the Crusades a failure?
6. How were the Crusades a success?
7. What did a knight promise upon reception into the order of knighthood?
8. How did the Crusades inspire the laity to live for the highest Christian motives?
9. How did the challenge of the invading Turks and the attempts to rescue the Holy Land inspire people of the time to build a new Christendom?
10. What incidents connect the newly discovered continent of the Americas to the Battle of Lepanto?
11. Give an example (from this chapter) of how a secular historian and a man of devout Christian faith would interpret the events of history, each in a different light.

Chapter 8
The Temporal Power of the Popes:
Church and State in the Middle Ages

1. How did the Church obtain temporal power and possessions among the newly converted nations?

Religious orders had settled among the barbarian nations and provided education, not only in the Christian faith but in agriculture, as the forests were cleared. In gratitude for the civilizing and prosperous influence of the Church, people, as well as their rulers, made gifts of land to missionaries, bishops, or the religious orders for the foundation and endowment of institutions dedicated to religion and education.

People settled around monasteries and cathedrals, forming villages, cities, and counties. These communities requested the temporal government of bishops and abbots, detecting the charity of Christ in their rule. Emperors and kings approved of this, realizing it contributed to the stability and order of society in their realms. They made bishops and abbots feudal lords over their territories of spiritual authority.

2. What is meant by feudalism?

Feudalism was a system which developed during the Middle Ages and consisted of "inferior" lords who inherited their positions and governed lands and provinces received in trust from the prince, to whom they were bound to swear allegiance and render military and other needed services. It was also a system of defense, as otherwise the people in local districts would have no outside help to defend themselves.

Local leaders bound themselves together under a superior who could call on them in case of invasion. They were called dukes or counts, and in time became more powerful than the distant king. The duke demanded that all land be deeded over to him. Those under him could use it on condition they guaranteed the duke military service in time of need. The duke or count, in turn, recognized the king as lord and swore to come to the king's aid in a foreign war.

In the unsettled state of Europe after the migration of nations, feudalism sprang up and became a great instrument for public order. Feudal castles were powerful centers of authority in each district with the passing of Charlemagne's empire.

The strong men in each district, or their fathers before them, had been soldiers under Charlemagne, and these were the men who built the fortresses which later became castles in which the people found refuge in time of danger.

3. What is meant by the Middle Ages?

The Middle Ages was that period of European history that began with the coronation of Charlemagne in 800 and ended with the invasion of Italy by the French in 1494.

The great Benedictine movement spread through Europe during this period. Great missionaries (like Columban, Patrick, Augustine, Boniface, Wilibord) spread the gospel and education as best they could under the circumstances. During that period the Byzantine culture reached its height; but a heresy eventually broke out in the East, causing political problems.

4. What was the heresy that created problems between the pope and Christians in the East?

When Pope Gregory the Great was unable to get the emperor in the East to protect Rome from the invading Lombards, he made a treaty of peace with the Lombards. A split occurred between the pope and the emperor, and widened under Popes Gregory II and III, when a heresy grew in the East which taught that it was sinful to venerate images of our Lord and the saints. Of course, the Catholic Church did not approve the *adoration* of images, but it permitted their use to inspire faith and reverence and to instill love and honor for the persons whom the images represented.

In the East, Emperor Leo the Isaurian promoted the heresy and issued an edict in 726 ordering all images to be destroyed throughout the empire. When Pope Gregory II resisted the edict, the emperor of the East sent his representative (the exarch of Ravenna) with an army to Rome to put the pope to death. The pope won the protection of the Lombards and the exarch was turned back.

When the successor to Pope Gregory called a council at Rome to condemn the emperor for the heresy he was propagating, Leo the Isaurian reacted by taking over Sicily and southern Italy, which belonged to the Holy See, and forced the bishops of these areas to accede to the patriarch of Constantinople.

The pope was in a delicate position, as he could look to the Lombards for protection from the emperor of the East, but the emperor or his exarch of Ravenna would not promise to give help in any trouble with the Lombards. The pope then looked to the Franks and their rulers, who under St. Boniface had returned to fervent practice of the Catholic faith.

5. How did the pope's position become more secure?

The rulers of the Franks were known as "mayors of the palace" (similar to prime ministers in our day). These mayors came from a family known as the Carolingians, and one of them was Charles Martel, who had defeated the Mohammedans at the Battle of Tours. Charles Martel was succeeded by his brothers, Carloman and Pippin. Carloman became a Benedictine monk at Monte Cassino and Pippin became sole ruler of the Franks.

Pope Zachary, who succeeded Gregory III, agreed to the request of Pippin that he be declared king of the Franks. St. Boniface therefore anointed Pippin king on November 11, 751. The Lombards soon returned to their old tricks, threatening Rome, and Pope Stephen II looked to King Pippin for help. Pippin defeated the Lombard king and protected Rome. Then the emperor at Constantinople, through representatives, tried to persuade Pippin to give the empire in the East all the territory he had regained from the Lombards. Pippin refused and renewed his loyalty to the Holy See.

Rather than give this territory to the emperor, Pippin gave it to the apostle St. Peter in his successors, the popes. This is how temporal power came into being for the papacy. The pope ruled not only Rome, Ravenna, and the surrounding territory, but five cities to the southeast.

When Pippin, king of the Franks, died, he left his kingdom to his two sons, Charles and Carloman. When Carloman died, Charles reunited the nation. The Lombards again attempted to take the papal territory, but Charles crossed the Alps and defeated them. Charles gave himself the title King of the Lombards, and Pope Hadrian added Patrician of the Romans. From this time on, Charles was prepared to protect the pope and the papal lands whenever necessary. Any attack on the pope meant war with the Franks. It was under Pope Hadrian's successor, Pope Leo III (795–816), that Charlemagne was crowned emperor of the Romans in the year 800.

Charlemagne, after a few difficulties in understanding a proper separation of Church and state, finally came to a proper agreement. With his help the gospel was preached to the people of the north and to the Slavs. The Saxons were still pagans. Charlemagne's army invaded Saxony and Charlemagne attempted to force its conversion. Alcuin protested this, as being against the manner of Christ. Charlemagne came to understand that patience, preaching, good will, and much work are needed for real conversions.

6. Who was Chalemagne and what is meant by his empire?

Charlemagne is the name given to Charles the Great, the ruler of the Frankish Empire, which comprised the larger portion of western and middle Europe. The Church, among the Franks, had been reorganized by St. Boniface and more closely united with the Holy See at Rome. This great English monk was providential in his work, for it resulted in the crowning of Charlemagne as head of the Holy Roman Empire.

Charlemagne was crowned on Christmas Day, 800, by Pope Leo III as emperor of the West and protector of the Church. Charles had saved the papal territory from the invading Lombards. At first, Charles did not understand his proper relationship to the pope, but when he came to Rome in 800, the pope placed a crown on his head while the people shouted, "To Charles, the Augustus, crowned by God, great and pacific emperor of the Romans, long life and victory!" By allowing himself to be crowned by the pope, the king of the Franks, now the Roman emperor, acknowledged that his authority came from God through the Church.

The pope gave the emperor Charles authority over the city of Rome and the Papal States. The priests and people of Rome had the power of election of the pope, but Pope Leo promised Charlemagne the electors would await the arrival of the emperor's ambassadors before proceeding with the election.

Ambassadors came from Constantinople in 812, and in return for Venice and Dalmatia, which Charles surrendered, they agreed to acknowledge him as the new emperor. The new empire was to be a universal Christian monarchy under the two powers of the emperor and the pope, with each supreme in his own sphere. The pope would be the spiritual ruler and the emperor would rule in temporal affairs. There was harmony in this regard, for the most part, as long as Charles lived.

7. How did Charlemagne rule?

Charlemagne sought the spiritual and temporal welfare of the people in union with the pope as visible head of the Church. Charlemagne gathered holy and learned men around himself. There was much ignorance when Charlemagne rose to power, resulting from confusion during the barbarian invasions.

Sometimes this period is mistakenly called the Dark Ages and is said to have continued until the thirteenth century, with the false implication that "enlightenment" did not come until the Protestant Reformation in the sixteenth century. In reality, the period was an Age of Faith, for it saw the founding of monasticism and the spread of the Benedictine monasteries. Rather than retrogression, it was a period of realignment and Christian advances in conversion and education. During the invasions, the monks preserved many of the works of the great Latin and Greek writers.

Charlemagne proved to be a student. His favorite book was St. Augustine's *City of God,* on which he dreamed to model his empire. Charlemagne searched Europe for the best scholars. The emperor placed the English Benedictine and famous scholar Alcuin over the palace school, and Alcuin and the emperor labored for fifteen years to create schools everywhere to revive learning and scholarship. He was the adviser to Charlemagne until the former's death in 804.

Charlemagne desired that even the poorest of his people should have the best education. Had the successors of Charlemagne followed his example, the great revivals of learning in the twelfth and thirteenth centuries would have come soon after the days of Charlemagne.

Charlemagne died in 814 and is called the founder of the modern world. He sought to bring together the old and the new, the Romans and the barbarians, the Church and the state, and thus create a unity and the beginnings of the Europe with which we are familiar today.

8. What happened to the empire founded by Charlemagne after his death?

Charlemagne was not succeeded by great men. His empire was divided into three parts among his grandsons. There were rulers in France, Germany, Burgundy, and Italy, and each claimed kinship with Charlemagne. By the tenth century, the title Emperor meant no more than King of Northern Italy. Even before Charlemagne's death there were threats from the Vikings, the Scandinavian raiders, falling upon the cities of northern Europe, the seacoasts, and making their way (as they did after his death) up all the rivers of Europe. They overcame Ireland, England, Iceland, Greenland, and captured Sicily and southern Italy.

At this same time the Sacracens invaded and laid waste the coast of the Mediterranean, landed at the mouth of the Tiber, and sacked the churches of Rome.

Charlemagne's empire had broken into parts, and there was no central power to organize them and resist. One raid after another was carried into the very heart of Germany and France. Although the invaders were driven out, no leader was strong enough to put an end to the invasions. As a consequence, the feudal system arose.

9. How did the clergy become feudal lords?

A duke or count who headed a feudal castle and its territories was required to kneel before the king and take an oath pledging fealty, placing his hands within the hands of the king. A clod of earth or a twig was given him as a sign that he was given local authority. This was the act of investiture, and by it the manor lord became a vassal of the king. The vassal had to pay the king a certain amount of money, and they promised mutual protection.

As the kings claimed the authority to invest the lords of the manor, they also claimed that the bishop had his power and authority by the king's handing over the crosier. The bishop was expected to take an oath of fealty and present the king a sum of money, just like the lay lords. This had the effect of making the bishop a vassal of the king. It put the bishop under the king's authority, not only in civil matters, but invited interference in the spiritual government of the local church (diocese). Bishops, becoming feudal lords over temporal possessions as vassals, gave the state far more than the Church got in return from the state.

Many evils were brought upon the Church by princes and kings who, by their feudal authority, interfered with the appointment of bishops and abbots so as to obtain their favorites. This opened the door to the appointment of men in Church positions who were more interested in worldly than spiritual affairs. Force was sometimes used for these appointments, and even simony and defiance of Church law and authority.

The popes, and especially Pope Gregory VII (1073–1085), fought this harmful influence of feudalism in the Church.

10. How did the popes acquire the Papal States and temporal power?

The Patrimony of St. Peter, as it was called, came from frequent donations of estates in and around Rome which started in the first centuries of Christianity and were made by devout and wealthy Christian families. By the seventh century, these possessions of the Holy See included a large portion of middle Italy.

After the seventh century, when the emperors had moved to Constantinople and abandoned their rights, leaving Rome and Italy exposed to the invasions of barbarian nations, the popes could look for no help from the East. The people turned to the Pope for protection from the destructive forces. The popes had to act as rulers, for such was the will of the people.

When the Lombards attempted the conquest of Rome and the emperor in the East did not answer requests for help, Pope Stephen II appealed to Pippin, king of the Franks. Thus were the Lombards defeated and Rome saved. Pippin gave the Patrimony of St. Peter back to the pope, laying the keys of the cities taken from the Lombards on the tomb of St. Peter to express possession of the papal lands by the Holy See.

The son of King Pippin was Charlemagne, who confirmed this decision of his father. This marked the beginning of temporal power for the popes.

The pope was now temporal ruler of Rome and the surrounding area. The city of Rome was divided into fourteen districts. Twenty-five cardinal-priests formed a senate to advise the Holy Father. The real administration was the work of seven cardinal-deacons, under the direction of an archdeacon. The government was supported mostly from the income of the land belonging to the Holy See. Peasants who worked these farms formed a rural militia to guard the domain of the pope.

Former government officials, who had belonged to the nobility, and former civil servants were never willing subjects of papal temporal power, and they formed political factions. This opposition of the lay nobility in Rome continued for 300 years. They did not want to accept clerical government.

11. How did papal temporal power affect the relationship of the Holy See to other nations?

In its time, it had advantages. The Holy See's temporal power enabled it to be independent in ruling the Church, free of interference by worldly, temporal powers. After Constantine, emperors had continuously claimed and practiced, as an imperial right, interference in church affairs. The Holy See was now on neutral ground in relationship to other nations and could deal without suspicion or partiality with the new Christian states which developed after the downfall of the Roman Empire of the West.

The property of the Church, which increased through gifts, enabled the Church to develop a grand system of charity which was administered chiefly by the religious orders and was permeated by the spirit of Christ in the gospels.

Hospitals for the sick and homes for orphans and the elderly were developed. The homeless, crippled, and mentally deficient were taken under the charitable care of the Church. When leprosy infected large numbers, the lepers were nursed. The poor became "guests of Christ" rather than mere beggars. The poor and sick received medicine, clothing, and daily food from parishes and convents which supported these charitable causes from their endowments.

The Church used its property to do the work of Jesus Christ, for the Church is the Mystical Body of Christ.

12. What was the principle of relationship of the Church to the state during the Middle Ages?

In general, the principle was that there should be a friendly union, while each would be independent. The Church should rule in the spiritual sphere and the state should control temporal affairs. They should help each other, and in this way the honor and glory of God would be promoted. Also, the temporal happiness of the people upon earth would thereby be protected, while they worked for eternal happiness in heaven.

13. How was this Christian view implemented?

The Christian nations protected the Church, as they were grateful for having been civilized and taught advantages in social living while receiving the true faith. The nations used their power to promote law and order, education at all levels and for all people, and public works of charity for the good of the people. In the holy Catholic faith and love, people formed one great Christian commonwealth of nations, while the pope as universal spiritual father tended to the salvation of souls and the Roman emperor of the German nation acted as the pope's anointed protector.

The popes often acted as peacemakers between the Christian nations. On local levels, bishops and abbots acted as peacemakers in their districts. The councils of the Church established what was known as the "truce of God." This forbade, under pain of excommunication, any feuds from Wednesday night until Monday morning and throughout Advent, Lent, and Eastertime.

Popes and councils worked to reduce slavery and to protect commerce by sea and land, so as to promote public safety and order. The popes promoted universities and lower institutions for education. Weak princes and unfortunate people often found protection from tyrannical rulers by turning to the pope.

14. What countries worked closely with the Church in this manner?

France, the "oldest daughter of the Church," became a great Christian nation with rulers like St. Louis IX. It was the cradle of the Crusades.

Hungary, the former home of the barbarian Huns, now a Christian land, was called the Kingdom of Mary. It embraced the faith as a nation when its king, St. Stephen (997–1038), was converted. St. Stephen saw that bishops were established and he drew up a Christian code of laws for his kingdom. He was given the title King by pope and emperor after he put down the insurrection of pagans.

Boleslaw I, king of Poland (known also as Chrobry), is considered the national hero of the Christian Poles. He reigned from 992 to 1025. King Boleslaw outlawed paganism and brought about the spread of Christianity. Poland became one of the greatest Christian nations during the Middle Ages, and a bulwark of Christian resistance in Europe against the invading Turks.

Aided by the Church, Spain and Portugal fought the Mohammedans for hundreds of years, shook off their power, and extended their Christian influence to Africa, Asia, and eventually America. Portugal is still known as the Land of Mary. It has long been devoted to our Lady's Immaculate Conception, with its national shrine at Brago, called the Rome of Portugal to this day.

The kings of England during the Middle Ages (with few exceptions) followed the example of King Alfred, who raised England from ruinous disorder with the help of the Church. England was called the Dowry of Our Blessed Lady.

The Frankish Empire under Charlemagne, the friend and anointed protector of the Church, became the greatest and most famous Christian nation.

King Malcolm and Queen St. Margaret led Scotland to temporal and religious prosperity by working with the Church.

Ireland became the Island of Saints and the cradle of Christian learning for northern Europe. St. Patrick's influence is well known, for it spread a Christian heritage to other nations.

The Scandinavian countries became civilized and Christian nations under men like St. Olaf in Norway, St. Erick and Magnus in Sweden, and Canute the Great and St. Canute in Denmark. St. Ansgar became the Apostle of the North; he preached the gospel to the Scandinavians.

Germany became a great Catholic empire. with its emperors anointed and crowned by the popes. Its national unity became strong under the one, holy, catholic, and apostolic faith.

Saints Cyril and Methodius became the Apostles of the Slavs, who in the ninth century occupied all of eastern Europe. Farthest east were the Russians. Ruric, the leader of a Swedish tribe, settled in the part of Russia known as the Ukraine, make Kiev the capital of his domain, and named the new country Russia. (It was from Constantinople that Christianity came to Russia.) St. Olga was the daughter-in-law of Ruric and was baptized a Christian in 957. Her grandson, Vladimir, married the sister of the Greek emperor and came to the faith. From this influence, all of his people were converted.

15. What dispute arose between Church and state over investiture?

It was a dispute whereby princes claimed the right to invest newly elected bishops and abbots with ring and crosier. The Church considered this meddling in the spiritual affairs of the Church, which alone had this authority. The princes claimed *they* had the authority because of the temporal power bishops and abbots received from them as vassals.

The Concordat of Worms was called in 1122 under Pope Calixtus II and King Henry V, emperor of Germany, to settle the matter. It was decided that the pope should invest prelates with ring and crosier as emblems of their spiritual power, while the emperor would confer the temporal power by his imperial scepter.

16. Did any emperors and kings abuse the Church–state relationship?

Yes, kings and emperors sometimes desired to increase their powers and over-stepped their authority in the Church. Emperor Henry IV of Germany tried to appoint bishops and sell Church offices. Henry had to do penance for this sacrilege at Canossa in 1076, when he was checked by Pope Gregory VII. He relapsed from his penitence and invaded Rome with an army, forcing Pope Gregory to flee to Salerno. The king's own son later revolted and robbed him of his crown and power, and the king died in exile, excommunicated from the Church.

Emperor Frederick Barbarossa of Germany even attempted to have an anti-pope crowned while deposing Pope Alexander III. A pestilence destroyed the emperor's army. Frederick Barbarossa saw the judgment of God in this and sought reconciliation with the Church.

In England, St. Thomas à Becket, archbishop of Canterbury, was killed when he opposed King Henry II of England, who in 1164 had laws passed giving the state the "right" to appoint bishops, while appeals to Rome were forbidden. The pope had the king excommunicated but the people compelled the king to seek peace with the Church.

Even Philip the Fair of France made similar claims, which hindered the freedom of the Church in her work of Christ. The king died despised by his own people and his three sons died in rapid succession, ending the family line of royalty.

17. Did God continue to manifest his power in miracles during the early Middle Ages?

Yes. Christ promised that he would continue the power of miracles in his Church. One of these was the eucharistic miracle of Lanciano, whereby the species of bread and wine, according to accounts of the time, were changed into actual flesh and blood which are manifest in our own day and stand up under modern scientific research.

Our Lord, in his human life upon earth, performed miracles as proof of his divinity. The miracles of Christ are divided into five classes: (1) nature miracles, e.g., water into wine (Jn 2); (2) healing miracles, e.g., the leper and the paralytic suddenly cured (Mt 8 and 9); (3) miracles of raising the dead, e.g., Lazarus (Jn 11) and the daughter of Jairus (Mt 9); (4) miracles of the possessed, e.g., the demoniac at Capharnaum (Mk 1), the woman with the spirit of infirmity (Lk 13); and (5) victories over hostile wills, e.g., in John 7:30, when no man dared lay a hand on Jesus, the casting out of sellers (Jn 2), and Jesus' escape from the hostile crowd at Nazareth (Lk 4).

18. Relate more details about the eucharistic miracle of Lanciano.

For twelve centuries the city of Lanciano, Italy, has been the scene of a eucharistic miracle that even the latest scientific investigations support as unexplainable by the laws of nature. Scientific and historical elements unite to testify for those who have made investigations of the authentic reality of the mircale of Lanciano, as it is called.

Informed Catholics know that it is a doctrine of faith that under the "species" of bread and wine in the Sacrament of the Altar (the holy Eucharist) are the body, blood, soul, and divinity of our Lord and Savior, Jesus Christ. The bread and wine are no longer present after the consecrating words of the priest, "This is my body; this is my blood." Pope Paul VI reaffirmed that a correct term to describe what takes place at the Consecration of the Mass is "transubstantiation." The Lanciano miracle appears to reaffirm what is already of Catholic faith (while it is not the source of our faith).

In ancient days Lanciano was called Ansiano and was famous for its fairs. About the year 750, in the Monastery of St. Legontian, lived the monks of St. Basil (today it is known as the Monastery of St. Francis). In this monastery, about the middle of the eighth century, lived a monk, educated in the sciences of his time but not strong in the faith. He had serious doubts whether the body of Jesus really exists in the consecrated altar bread and whether the wine is really changed into the blood of Jesus at the Consecration.

The same monk, in prayer, begged God to resolve the doubt in his heart. According to documents of that time, one morning when he was offering the sacrifice of the Mass, after pronouncing the words of consecration, the priest-monk was again overcome by his doubts. Then he *saw* the bread change into Flesh and the wine into Blood.

According to the documents handed down through the centuries, the monk became confused and frightened at the stupendous miracle of the Eucharist. He stood looking at the miracle as if in divine ecstasy. Finally, filled with joy and shedding tears, he spoke to the congregation: "O fortunate witnesses, to whom the Blessed God, to confound my unbelief, has wished to reveal Himself in this Most Blessed Sacrament and to render Himself visible to our eyes. Come,

Brethren, and marvel at our God, so close to us. Behold the Flesh and the Blood of our Most Beloved Christ."

The people rushed to the altar and beheld the miracle, and reports of the miracle spread throughout the city. The miracle had a profound effect on the city, and old and young alike. Some invoked the divine mercy of God while others beat their breast in sorrow, accusing themselves of sins. Still others acknowledged themselves unworthy to behold so precious a treasure. And others praised God in thanksgiving, that he had willed to have their mortal senses behold his immortal and incomprehensible majesty.

Authorities in the city had an exquisite tabernacle made of ivory to contain the priceless relic. Later they made a magnificent silver vase in the form of a chalice, and finally a crystal de Rocca, in which it was preserved.

Flesh appeared around the Host. Through the centuries the Host pulverized and disappeared while the Flesh remains intact after 1,200 years. Scientists have identified it as flesh of the heart muscle. On the outside rim it is thick, but almost paper thin on the inside, where it was in contact with the Host. Scientists have been unable to find any trace of chemical preservatives, as in mummies.

There are five parts to the Blood in the eucharistic miracle of Lanciano. Each part, though different in size, nonetheless weighs as much as all—two as much as three, and the smallest as much as the largest. The Blood has divided and dried into five pellets. Its entire weight is 15.85 grams or .56 ounce.

An account by Reverend Sebastiano de Dinaldis in 1631 tells how the Turks in 1566 were overruning the shores of the kingdom of Naples, burning and laying waste the cities. Friar Giovanni Antonio di Mastro Renzo of the Minor Conventuals on August 1 took flight with many youths, carrying this holy relic so that it would not fall into the hands of the infidels. They walked with speed all night and, having considered themselves to have made a very long journey, found themselves the next morning at the same gate of the city from which they had escaped.

The Monastery Church of St. Legontian, which was under the Basilian monks at the time of the miracle, was abandoned by these monks in the twelfth century, when they left the region, and it became the property of the Benedictines. Fifty years later it passed into the hands of the Friars Minor Conventual, who were in possession in 1252. In 1258 the Franciscans built a new monastery with a new church on the ruins of the ancient monastery and church. The present Church of St. Francis is therefore the guardian of this eucharistic miracle.

At present, the holy relics are contained in this manner. The Flesh is in a round, gold-plated silver lunette between two crystals. This lunette is in an ostensorium of silver, into which the holy relic was placed on April 16, 1713. The Blood is contained in a chalice of crystal with a cover of crystal and is part of the base of the ostensorium which contains the Flesh.

With the approval of Church authorities, on rare occasions the holy relics have been investigated. Monsignor Rodrigues made an authentication on February 17, 1574, in the presence of people who testified to the preternatural weight of the congealed Blood, viz., the total weight of the five pellets is equal to the weight of each pellet. This is attested on a marble tablet in the church. A second authentication was made in 1637, when the holy relics were transferred to the Valsecca Chapel. A third authentication was made on October 23, 1770, when it was desired that the reliquary be refurbished and the Host of Flesh was removed for a short time.

In 1886 the seals and silk cords were broken which sealed the chalice of Blood at its authentication in 1770. The archbishop of Lanciano, Monsignor Petrarca, and a commission of canons and ecclesiastics joined in breaking the seals and cords of the chalice, but the seal of the Host was not touched. It was certified that fragments of the species of bread were still clearly visible in the Flesh.

Through the centuries there have been historical and ecclesiastical notes concerning and restating testaments regarding the miracle of Lanciano which are documented to the present day.

Readers of this book on Church history will be interested in scientific investigations of our own times, when many advances have been made. Two hundred years had elapsed since the authentication of 1770, when, on July 1, a Saturday in 1972, before well-known witnesses, the holy relics were enclosed in a new lunette, sealed, and placed in a renovated ostensorium. This was after a scientific investigation, conducted from November 18, 1971, to March 4, 1972, by Professor Odoardo Linoli, an expert in histology and human anatomy. A summary of the results of modern scientific investigations lists the following points:

1. The Blood of the Eucharistic Miracle is real blood and the Flesh is real flesh.
2. The Flesh consists of the muscular tissue of the heart.
3. The Blood and the Flesh belong to the human species.
4. The blood type is identical in the Blood and in the Flesh and this stands to indicate that the donor is a single person, whilst there remains open the possibility of their origin from two different persons who, however, have the same blood type.
5. In the Blood there were found normally fractioned proteins with the percentual proportions that are found in the sero-protein scope of normal fresh blood.
6. In the Blood there were also discovered the minerals Chlorides, Phosphorus, Magnesium, Potassium, Sodium in a reduced quantity, whereas Calcium was found in an increased quantity.

Summary

We must beware of judging history in terms of our own times. The popes as temporal rulers may seem strange to the modern mentality, but we must remember how the Church was born into a world largely pagan and how it had to Christianize the nations and use the circumstances of the time to serve the cause of Christ.

The Church was reorganized among the Franks by St. Boniface and came into closer union with the pope at Rome. In this chapter we have seen how Charlemagne served the cause of culture and truth for the Church and helped spread the gospel. Missionaries went forth to the Saxons, Scandinavians, and Slavs (among others).

Christ protects and preserves his universal Church primarily through the presence and action of the Holy Spirit, whom Jesus called the Spirit of Truth.

The attributes of the Church are three: authority, infallibility, and indefectibility, which means that the Church in its faith and morals and infallible interpretation will continue unchangeable until the end of time, essentially the same as when it was established by Jesus Christ.

A study of Church history reveals that Jesus protects his Church, as this chapter indicates.

Jesus promised that miracles would be performed in his Church. Miracles point to the divine power in the Church of Jesus Christ. This chapter has detailed just one of the many miracles in the Church, extending from the Middle Ages into our present age.

Questions for Discussion

1. Explain the role of Charlemagne in his relationship to the Church.
2. What happened to Charlemagne's empire after his death?
3. What does this say about the Church, which survives even when man's kingdoms are destroyed?
4. What kind of system developed with the passing of Charlemagne's empire and why was this system necessary?
5. Explain some characteristics of feudalism—how it operated.
6. How did papal temporal power develop?
7. Explain the dispute concerning the right of investiture which arose between the Church and the state.
8. What delicate situation did Pope St. Gregory the Great find himself in with relation to the Lombards and the emperor of the East?
9. What was the Patrimony of St. Peter and how did it develop?
10. How did Pippin enter into the Patrimony of St. Peter and how did he react to the emperor of the East in this regard?
11. Does history verify the promise of Christ of miracles in his Church?
12. Describe what is known as the miracle of Lanciano.
13. What scientific evidence in our time substantiates that faith and science can support one another, considering only the aspect of the miracle of Lanciano?

Chapter 9
The Greek Schism and Apostolic Succession

1. What is the difference between heresy and schism?

Heresy involves rejecting a true doctrine of the Catholic Church. In *material* heresy, a Christian rejects some truth of Catholic faith but does not realize he is rejecting a religious truth. *Formal* heresy means that one knowingly rejects Catholic doctrine and willingly continues in that rejection, even after the error is pointed out. Sincere Christians who may be in material heresy are not guilty of sin since they do not knowingly and willingly reject what they believe to be true faith.

Schism involves separation from the unity of the Church, especially from the visible head of the Church, the Supreme Pontiff. It is a rebellion against the authority of the pope and differs from heresy in that it retains the doctrines of faith.

2. What two big schisms are known in history?

History speaks of the Schism of the East and the Schism of the West. The Eastern Schism was a series of disagreements and breaks which finally led to the separation of Catholics of the Eastern Church from the authority of the pope and from Catholics of the Western Church.

The Schism of the West, also called the Great Schism, was not a schism in the strict sense but was due to political influence, whereby the popes lived for a time in Avignon, France.

3. Why speak of the Eastern Church and the Western Church if formerly they were united; were they not *one* Church of Christ?

Yes. The distinction has more to do with differences in character and temperament between Catholics in the East and in the West. Their mental outlooks differed. The authority of the bishop of Rome, the pope, held them together, but cultural differences often caused difficulties since complete understanding and proper communications were lacking between the East and the West.

4. What were some differences between the East and the West?

Christians of the East were more "idealistic" or mystical in outlook and expressions of faith. There was more learning and greater devotion to philosophy and mystical theology. The East, being Greek, put much emphasis on individual freedom. There was often contempt of material things among Christians of the East.

Christians of the West were more practical in their thinking. The Roman mind placed great emphasis on authority and organization. The Western mind saw the need to live the faith in the practical, daily actions of the people. The Western mind did not always probe so deeply into the reasons of things, with their deep underlying mental challenges.

5. Which of these two mentalities is correct?

Both are correct but balance is needed. There is room for both views in true Christian faith in the Church. In the course of centuries, greater appreciation developed for the insights which the East and the West have to offer.

6. What was the Greek Schism?

This was the separation of the Eastern Church from the Western Church because of the power assumed by Photius about the middle of the ninth century, whereby he became patriarch of Constantinople and refused to accept the authority of the papacy in the West. He won the backing of the emperors of the East and drew the Church of the Greek Empire—of Asia Minor, Syria, Palestine, and Egypt—into schism.

In the eleventh century, Patriarch Michael Cerularius led another schism in the East which came to a head with the fall of Constantinople in 1453 to the Turks, making the Greek Church subservient to the Turkish sultan.

The Church in Russia separated from the patriarch of Constantinople in the sixteenth century, only to become a state church under the despotic czar Peter the Great, who became its head in 1721. After that the czars directed much of its affairs through synods, or councils of bishops and laymen, which the czars appointed.

7. Explain more about the schism of the Eastern Church under Photius.

Ignatius, a holy man and the patriarch of Constantinople, brought the emperor to task for his violence and unworthy life by publicly refusing him Communion. The emperors in the East had become accustomed to dictating to the patriarchs of Constantinople and controlling them; so the refusal of Communion angered the emperor, who had Patriarch Ignatius deposed, sent into exile, and replaced by a layman, Photius.

Photius, in one day's time, at the command of the emperor received minor orders and was ordained a priest, then consecrated a bishop. The year was 863, when Pope Nicholas called a synod in Rome to study the matter. The pope declared that Ignatius was the only lawful patriarch of Constantinople and that Photius was not to exercise any priestly powers that had been conferred upon him.

Three years later the emperor was assassinated and his assassin, Basil, seized the throne and immediately ordered that Photius be returned as patriarch of Constantinople. Photius, a learned man, was ambitious and made the most of the opportunity by convincing people that he had holy motives. Photius was willing to go even further than the emperor had envisioned. Playing on the vanity of the emperor, Photius stirred up resentment of the people against the pope, charging that the Church of Rome was spreading false doctrines among the Bulgarians, when in reality the issues did not involve doctrines but discipline applicable to Christians of the West. Photius tried to convince the emperor that the bishop of Constantinople should be the head of the Church.

Photius found what seemed like a doctrinal difference, expressed in the word *Filioque*. This expression meant that the Holy Spirit proceeds from God the Father and God the Son. Photius said that the belief of the Greek Church was that the Holy Spirit proceeds from the Father *only*, and not from the Son.

Photius finally lost favor with the emperor and was deposed and excommunicated by the pope, who repeated his recognition of Ignatius. But shortly thereafter, Ignatius died and the emperor again recognized Photius as patriarch of Constantinople. The pope insisted that Photius make certain promises, but these were broken and he was excommunicated again. When the emperor died, Photius was forced to retire to a monastery, where he died in 891.

The next 150 years gave evidence, at least externally, of harmony with Rome, but the Greek Church maintained an uneasy feeling toward the pope.

The Council of Constantinople (869–870) condemned the position of Photius and settled the Greek Schism, at least outwardly, for the time being.

8. Give a sketch of the second fall of the Greek church into schism.

Patriarch Michael Cerularius was excommunicated by Pope Leo IX through delegates. Cerularius, 1043, repeated Photius' old charges against the Church of

Rome. Emperor Constantine X ordered the patriarch to enter into dialogue with the Holy See to reconcile their differences. Pope Leo IX sent three delegates to Constantinople for this purpose.

The pope's delegates answered the charges made by Michael Cerularius. However, there was a language problem. The delegates knew no Greek and the Greeks could not speak Latin. It ended with the pope's delegates' excommunicating Patriarch Michael Cerularius and the patriarch, in turn, hurling excommunications at the Church of the West. This happened in 1054.

The separation has continued to the present day. In 1439, at the Council of Florence, the Greek bishops temporarily submitted and were received back into full union with the see of Peter. It lasted but a few years and the schism resumed.

9. Have the tensions created under Patriarch Michael Cerularius continued all these years?

The break hardened over the years, but Vatican Council II (1962–1965) was the beginning of relaxed tensions and hoped-for reunion. Some of the separated Eastern Christians over the centuries rejoined the Church of the West and accepted the authority of the pope. These are known as Eastern Rite Catholics today and they are in communion with the Holy See, although their form of worship is different.

The definitive Orthodox break with Rome dates from 1054, but there have been top-level negotiations in recent years through the efforts of the former ecumenical patriarch, Athenagoras I, and Pope John XXIII. Pope Paul VI and Patriarch Dimitrios I, their successors, continued the good relationships.

Most significant in improving relationships with the Orthodox churches (as the separated Eastern churches are now known) was the mutual nullification of the excommunications between the East and the West when Pope Paul VI and Patriarch Athenagoras met three times before Athenagoras died in 1972. Each lifted the excommunication imposed by the two Christian bodies upon each other in 1054. It was December 7, 1965, when the 1054 excommunications were mutually withdrawn.

10. Do the separated Orthodox churches today hold anything in common with their Eastern Catholic counterparts which are in union with Rome?

Yes. They have much in common regarding faith and morals, general Church discipline, valid holy orders and the other sacraments, and their divine liturgy or manner of worship. Both have a profound veneration of God's Mother and use beautiful icons. An important difference is that Eastern Rite Catholics accept the pope as the supreme authority and Christ's chief representative in the universal Church, while Orthodox Christians do not hold such communion with the pope. Many Orthodox would be willing to regard the pope as "the first among equals" but not as the Supreme Pontiff of the universal and apostolic Church.

11. Does the Catholic church recognize that Orthodox churches of today have a valid priesthood?

Yes. Orthodox churches are in the line of apostolic succession. When they separated from the authority of the pope as the successor of St. Peter, they retained valid bishops with the priestly powers of the hierarchy, so as to be able to ordain other priests and bishops. The powers of Christ's priesthood must be handed down in an unbroken line of apostolic succession through bishops who are full and true successors of the first apostles.

A Vatican International Theological Commission completed a historical and theological study in the 1970s, after Vatican Council II, reaffirming the valid apostolic succession of priestly powers for the Orthodox. While such Christian brethren in schism have a valid priesthood and a valid sacrifice of the Mass (divine liturgy) and all the sacraments, it is nonetheless the will of Jesus Christ that all his followers be perfectly one in authority as well as in doctrines of faith and morals. Catholics hold that all Christians—Orthodox and other communities which separated in later centuries—should be united with the see of Peter, the rock upon which Christ Jesus built his Church and against which, he promised, the gates of hell will never prevail.

12. Summarize the historical importance of Constantinople.

Today, Constantinople is known as Istanbul, Turkey. When the new city of Constantinople was founded it became the capital of the Roman Empire, which shifted its authority to the East and was at first called New Rome but later called Constantinople after its founder, the emperor Constantine.

Constantinople was built on a natural harbor called the Golden Horn and was protected by its location from attack. It was a crossroads for trade routes by land and sea, and a bridge between Europe and the East. It was completed in 330 and was considered for more than 1,100 years the most important city in the world, until it fell in 1453.

The Roman Empire became less Roman and more Greek in language and culture as the new capital was established and moved from West to East (Rome to Constantinople).

By the end of the fifth century, the old Roman Empire had disappeared, as the Western part was under attack by the barbarians and the Byzantine or Eastern Empire had little concern about the West. All this pushed the pope, in the West, into a more dominant role, politically as well as spiritually (as described earlier). In the East, the emperor exercised much authority over the Church, and even appointed the patriarchs of Constantinople and removed them when he was not pleased with them. This was known as cesaro-papism. Constantinople was the major see in the East, but Antioch and Alexandria were also important patriarchates of the East. They were much troubled with heresies.

To the present day, Orthodox churches are organized in jurisdictions under patriarchs, who are the heads of approximately fifteen jurisdictions organized along lines of nationality or language. While the ecumenical patriarch of Constantinople (Istanbul) still has primacy of honor among his equal patriarchs, his jurisdiction is limited to the title and he has power only over his own patriarchate. As spiritual head of worldwide Orthodox Christians, he keeps the Book of Holy Canons in which are recorded registrations of the recognized Orthodox churches. He has the right and privilege of calling a pan-Orthodox assembly.

13. Summarize the conclusions of the Vatican's International Theological Commission Study in the 1970s.

In the light of recent scholarship and good will, the study commission offered the following conclusions:

"*Institution by Christ:* Christ instituted a ministry for the establishment, animation and maintenance of this [common] priesthood of Christians. This ministry was to be a sign and the instrument by which he would communicate to his people in the course of history the fruits of his life, death and resurrection. The first foundations of this ministry were laid when he called the Twelve, who at the same time represent the New Israel as a whole and, after Easter, will be the privileged eye-witnesses sent out to proclaim the gospel of salvation and the leaders of the new people, 'fellow workers with God for the building of his temple' (see 1 Cor 3:9). This ministry has an essential function to fulfill toward each generation of Christians. It must therefore be transmitted from the apostles by an unbroken line of succession. If one can say that the church as a whole is established upon the foundation of the apostles (Eph 2:20, Rv 21:14), one has to add that this apostolicity which is common to the whole church is linked with the ministerial apostolic succession, and that this is an inalienable ecclesial structure at the service of all Christians. . . .

"*The Apostles and Apostolic Succession in History:* The documents of the New Testament show that in the early days of the church and in the lifetime of the apostles there was diversity in the way communities were organized, but also that there was, in the period immediately following, a tendency to assert and strengthen the ministry of teaching and leadership. . . .

"The church lived in the certain conviction that Jesus, before he left this world, sent the Twelve on a universal mission and promised that he would be with them at all times until the end of the world (Mt 28:18-20).

"*Ordination and Succession:* During the second century and after the letter of Clement, this institution is explicitly acknowledged to carry with it the apostolic succession. Ordination with the imposition of hands, already witnessed to in the pastoral epistles, appears in the process of clarification to be an important step in preserving the apostolic tradition and guaranteeing succession in the ministry. The documents of the third century (*Tradition of Hyppolytus*) show that this conviction was arrived at peacefully and was considered to be a necessary institution.

"Clement and Irenaeus developed a doctrine on pastoral government and on the word in which they derived the idea of apostolic succession from the unity of the word, the unity of the mission and the unity of the ministry of the church; thus apostolic succession became the permanent ground from which the Catholic Church understood its own nature.

"*Sacrament of the Effective Presence of Christ:* An apostolic succession is that aspect of the nature and life of the church which shows the dependence of our present-day community on Christ through those whom he has sent. The apostolic ministry is, therefore, the sacrament of the effective presence of Christ and of his Spirit in the midst of the people of God, and this view in no way underestimates the immediate influence of Christ and his Spirit on each believer.

"The charism of apostolic succession is received in the visible community of the church. It presupposes that someone who is to enter the ministry has the faith of the church. The gift of ministry is granted in an act which is the visible and efficacious symbol of the gift of the Spirit, and this act has as its instrument one or several of those ministers who have themselves entered the apostolic succession."

Thus the Vatican's International Theological Commission tells us that a validly ordained bishop, going back in an unbroken line to the first bishops, who were apostles, is needed validly to ordain a new priest or bishop with the indelible character (mark or charism) which bestows the priestly powers to consecrate bread and wine into the Lord's living Body and Blood, soul and divinity, and to forgive sin in Jesus' name, as well as all the powers Catholics believe are conferred through the sacrament of holy orders. In the ordination and consecration of a Catholic bishop, more than one ordaining bishop is employed to assure that the apostolic chain is not broken.

The study commission of the Vatican continues:

"*Transmission through Ordination:* Thus the transmission of the apostolic ministry is achieved through ordination, including a rite with a visible sign and the invocation of God (*epiklesis*) to grant to the ordinand the gift of his Holy Spirit and the powers that are needed for the accomplishment of his task. This visible sign, from the New Testament onward, is the imposition of hands. The rite of ordination expresses the truth that what happens to the ordinand does not come from human origin and that the church cannot do what it likes with the gift of the Spirit.

"The church is fully aware that its nature is bound up with apostolicity and that the ministry handed on by ordination establishes the one who has been ordained in the apostolic confession of the truth of the Father. The church, therefore, has judged that ordination, given and received in the understanding she herself has of it, is necessary to apostolic succession in the strict sense of the word.

"The apostolic succession of the ministry concerns the whole church, but is not something which derives from the church taken as a whole but rather from Christ to the apostles and from the apostles to all bishops to the end of time."

The study commission thus indicates that it is not the people of the Church as a whole who commission the ordained priest or bishop and that one does not thereby receive the powers of holy orders. Rather, only through ordaining a new candidate by a validly ordained bishop (or several bishops), in communion with valid orders, is apostolic succession of priestly powers maintained from the time of Jesus Christ and his apostles. The powers of the priesthood come from God and not from any authority of the people.

The Church reaffirmed its position, traditionally held since the Schism of the East and the Protestant break of the sixteenth century (which shall be studied later) when the Vatican's study commission noted:

"*Orthodox and Others with Succession:* In spite of a difference in their appreciation of the office of Peter, the Catholic Church, the Orthodox Church, and the other churches which have retained the reality of apostolic succession are at one in sharing a basic understanding of the sacramentality of the church which developed from the New Testament and through the Fathers, notably through Irenaeus. These churches hold that the sacramental entry into the ministry comes about through the imposition of hands with the invocation of the Holy Spirit, and that this is the indispensable form for the transmission of the apostolic succession which alone enables the church to remain constant in its doctrine and communion. It is this unanimity concerning the unbroken coherence of scripture, tradition and sacrament which explains why communion between these churches and the Catholic Church has never completely ceased and could today be revived."

14. What did this International theological commission say about apostolic succession in the Protestant Reformation churches?

"The communities which emerged from the sixteenth-century Reformation differ among themselves to such an extent that a description of their relationship to the Catholic Church has to take account of the many individual cases. However, some general lines are beginning to emerge. In general it was a feature of the Reformation to deny the link between scripture and tradition and to advocate the view that scripture alone was normative. Even if later on some sort of place for tradition is recognized, it is never given the same position and dignity as in the ancient church. But since the sacrament of orders is the indispensable sacramental expression of communion in the tradition, the proclamation of *sola scriptura* [scripture alone as the norm of faith] led inevitably to an obscurring of the older idea of the church and its priesthood.

"Thus through the centuries, the imposition of hands either by men already ordained or by others was often in practice abandoned. Where it did take place, it did not have the same meaning as in the church of tradition. This divergence in the mode of entry into the ministry and its interpretation is only the most noteworthy symptom of the different understanding of church and tradition. . . .

"In such circumstances, intercommunion remains impossible for the time being, because sacramental continuity in apostolic succession from the beginning is an indispensable element of ecclesial communion both for the Catholic Church and the Orthodox Churches."

15. What is the position of the Catholic Church today toward Eastern Rite Catholics in union with the pope?

Eastern Rite Catholics (many of whom are descendants of Orthodox Christians who came back into union with Rome) are in full communion with Western Rite Catholics. Vatican Council II spoke of them as follows:

"Such individual Churches, whether of the East or of the West, although they differ somewhat among themselves in what are called rites (that is, in liturgy, ecclesiastical discipline, and spiritual heritage), are, nevertheless, equally entrusted to the pastoral guidance of the Roman Pontiff, the divinely appointed successor of St. Peter in supreme government over the universal Church. They are consequently of equal dignity, so that none of them is superior to the others by reason of rite. . . .

"All Eastern Rite members should know and be convinced that they can and should always preserve their lawful liturgical rites and their established way of life, and that these should not be altered except by way of an appropriate and organic development. . . .

"This sacred Synod. . . decrees that their rights and privileges should be reestablished in accord with the ancient traditions of each Church and the decrees of the ecumenical Synods.

"The rights and privileges in question are those which flourished when East and West were in union, though they should be somewhat adapted to modern conditions."

16. What has been the condition of the Orthodox churches in modern times?

The Orthodox churches today are not under one head, as is the Catholic Church under the pope. The Orthodox live on both sides of the Communist Iron Curtain. Up to 85 percent of practicing Orthodox today live under Communist rule. There are seven Orthodox churches outside the Iron Curtain. Four of them are predominantly Greek and include Constantinople, Greece, Cyprus, and the Sinai; the other three are mainly Arab and include Alexandria, Antioch, and Jerusalem.

The Orthodox have often suffered greatly, especially the part administered from Constantinople. In the Turkish-Greek War (1920–1922) it was almost destroyed, along with other Christian churches in Turkey. Survivors formed a huge exodus, with more than a million Christians leaving Turkey. One night in September 1956, sixty of the eighty Orthodox churches in Istanbul were gutted or sacked.

The patriarch Athenagoras reacted with great dignity, and it was to this patriarch that Rome made the first moves toward unity when it invited observors from Constantinople to Vatican Council II (1962–1965). The letter of invitation (September 20, 1963) was the first letter sent by a pope to a patriarch of Constantinople since 1584. It was the beginning of an ever growing sense of unity between Orthodox and Catholics.

On July 25, 1967, Pope Paul VI visited Athenagoras in Istanbul. This historic visit did much more than many encyclicals or other messages might have accomplished, and is already noted in history as one of the greatest gestures in ecumenism. Their sole purpose in meeting was to seek the Lord's will for unity. This time both sides were free of *political* elements, which in the past have so often injured Christian unity.

Dimitrios I became the new patriarch in 1972 and Pope Paul VI sent word to him: "In the bishop of Rome you will always find a loving brother." Dimitrios pledged to seek unity, as had Athenagoras, his predecessor. He pointed out that the Catholic concept of the universal primacy of the pope is still a major difficulty, saying: "The highest authority in the Church is the Ecumenical Council."

In 1975 the tenth anniversary of the mutual lifting of the excommunications between East and West was celebrated in the Sistine Chapel in the Vatican, with Pope Paul VI meeting a delegation from the patriarchate of Constantinople. Pope Paul knelt before Metropolitan Meliton and kissed his feet on the occasion, which greatly shocked and edified all present and those who heard about it. The pope, in humility, gave an external sign that the pope of the Roman Catholic Church is and can be a unifying sign for Christians everywhere.

On the same day, Metropolitan Meliton, who had come as the envoy of Dimitrios I, placed a bouquet of white carnations at the tomb of Pope Leo IX, the pope who had signed the bull of excommunication against the Orthodox patriarch in 1054.

The two gestures, of the pope and the Orthodox envoy, were further signs of healing the schism that is over 900 years old.

Dimitrios sent a plaque to the Vatican to commemorate Pope Paul's historic meeting in Istanbul with Patriarch Athenagoras ten years earlier. It carries this inscription: "As a sign of the reciprocal love and profound esteem that exists between you and us, and grows ever stronger. July 25, 1977."

Summary

Catholic and Orthodox Christians have always held a common faith in the same God, in the same sacraments, and in their devotion to God's Mother. It was cultural differences, accompanied by tactless political mistakes, which estranged the Church in the East from the Church in the West.

When the Great Schism happened in 1054, most ordinary Christians were not aware of the mutual excommunications hurled between East and West. Christians on both sides hoped to clear up the misunderstandings.

The Crusaders and the sacking of Constantinople caused hatred and bitterness that brought the schism to the popular level, which has endured for over 900 years. It was not, essentially, theological differences that caused the separation. Prejudice, stemming from abuses, has scarred the memories of Eastern Christians.

It is significant that after more than 900 years of separation the Catholic Church and the Orthodox Church still remain so close in faith.

Growing independently and without communication with the West, the Eastern church developed a loose organizational structure. The West, with its different mentality, developed a highly centralized structure. The Catholic doctrine of the primacy of the pope is now a major theological stumbling block in the dialogue between Catholic and Orthodox Christians. The East has also permitted a married clergy and permission for divorce and remarriage under certain conditions.

Eventual reunion will be aided by Catholics' understanding the important position of Eastern Rite Catholics in union with the pope, the validity of holy orders in the Orthodox traditions, and how much of our faith is completely one.

The strong devotion of Orthodox to the Mother of God, whom Catholics consider the Mother of the Church, may well serve as a further bond of unity.

Questions for Discussion

1. When is heresy *material* and when is it formal?
2. Are sincere Protestant Christians in material or in formal heresy? Explain.
3. When historians speak of the Church of the East and the Church of the West, are they speaking of more than one church when they note their union in former centuries? Explain.
4. Explain how mental outlooks of the East and the West affected religious concepts.
5. What role did Photius have in the Greek Schism?
6. What date is given as the definitive date for the separation of Western and Eastern Christians, and what took place in leading up to it?
7. What good signs of developing union between East and West have occurred in recent times?
8. How can the Catholic Church recognize Orthodox priests as having the true powers of Catholic priests if the Orthodox do not recognize the pope as the true successor of Peter, in possession of the supreme authority in the universal Church?
9. What study commission in modern times reaffirmed the Catholic position regarding apostolic succession?

10. In summary, what did the study commission of the Church say about apostolic succession?
11. Explain the position of the Catholic Church, that the powers of the Catholic priest and bishop, received in the sacrament of holy orders, do not come from the people.

Chapter 10
The High Middle Ages, a Time of Faith and Achievement

1. What is meant by the high Middle Ages?

It is a term that covers the years from approximately 1050 to 1450. "Middle" is a term some historians have used to express the period between ancient and modern times. The age is often misrepresented, as if nothing good or important existed or happened until the height of the Renaissance in the sixteenth century.

2. Explain the life of Pope Hidebrand, who lived at the beginning of this period.

Hildebrand was born of poor parents in Tuscany about the year 1020. He grew up in a monastery in Rome that was under the jurisdiction of the abbot of Cluny in France. Cluny was founded in 910 and, from the very first, held to the strict observance of the ideals of St. Benedict; it never fell under control of temporal powers but was always under the supervision of the pope. Cluny had many holy abbots who advised kings and popes. Hildebrand grew up under such influence and received his education at the Lateran Palace.

From early boyhood Hildebrand loved Rome deeply, and the Church even more. After his studies were completed in Rome, he spent a number of years in prayer and study at Cluny in France under Abbot Odilo, who was later canonized St. Odilo.

One of Hildebrand's teachers at the Lateran Palace had been a man who later became Pope Gregory VI. Hildebrand eventually became secretary to this pope and learned the problems and difficulties of the Church. Whenever Hildebrand learned of abuses among Church members who were not living an authentic Christlike life, he worked zealously to correct such things.

When Pope Gregory VI died, Hildebrand retired to the Abbey of Cluny, but not for long. Pope Leo IX brought him back to Rome, ordained him a deacon, made him a cardinal, and thereafter he was made the administrator of the property of the Church in Rome and became an advisor to succeeding popes in the reform of the Church.

Under Pope Nicholas II (1059–1961), Hildebrand was named archdeacon of the Roman Church, and during this time a constitution was drawn up for the election of new popes. No longer could German emperors or Italian nobles have undue control or influence. Only cardinals could vote in a papal election. (The name "cardinal" originated as a title for priests who were attached to the cathedral churches of Rome and acted as intermediaries between the bishops and other priests. They were like hinges, connecting parish churches to the mother church, or cathedral [cardo is Latin for "hinge"].)

Since the death of Pope Leo IX, the people and their clergy had wanted and even demanded that Hildebrand become pope. Their desires were fulfilled in 1073, when he was elected pope and took the name Pope Gregory VII.

3. What reforms did Pope Gregory VII (Hildebrand) bring about in the church?

Pope Gregory VII sought to correct three major abuses immediately:
1. The sin of simony, or the buying of spiritual offices and favors.
2. The attempted marriage of the clergy. Certain unworthy members of the clergy had been ordained and placed in charge of souls through the influence of kings and princes. They did not have the real, Christlike spirit of the priesthood and insisted on marrying.
3. Lay investiture, by which princes bestowed the ring and crosier on bishops in return for their oath of fealty.

4. Did Pope Gregory VII find his reform of abuses in the Church an easy matter?

No. Correcting abuses is never easy when Christians become more worldly minded than spiritual minded. The emperor and princes, and the bishops and clergy who were their vassals, all fought Pope Gregory in a storm of opposition. The spiritual monks of Cluny and all the monasteries united to Cluny supported the pope, as did other clergy who were faithful to their duties. The common faithful also desired a return to proper Church discipline in all quarters.

5. Describe Pope Gregory's encounter with the emperor over the reforms.

Henry IV had become head of the Holy Roman Empire, as it was called. His career from the beginning had been dishonorable. In his court, spiritual offices were bought and sold. Henry IV defied the pope on lay investiture. When Pope

Gregory VII commanded Henry to come to Rome, the emperor ignored the summons. Instead, he called the bishops of his kingdom in council. He declared the pope deposed and sent a decree to Rome which was addressed "to Hildebrand, not pope, but false monk." Pope Gregory VII immediately excommunicated the emperor and declared that Henry's subjects no longer owed him obedience. This shocked Europe, and Henry found himself deserted by all.

6. How was the excommunication of the holy Roman emperor, Henry IV, resolved?

The princes of the empire held that Henry must stand trial before the pope, and they recognized that the pope had the right to depose unworthy rulers. They decreed that Henry must live in retirement until the trial, and since he was excommunicated, he had no right to his office.

In 1077 at Augsburg, on Candlemas Day, a council was called to try the emperor. Henry knew he stood no chance of winning. To prevent the trial, Henry went to the pope at Canossa in northern Italy, where the pope had stopped on the way to the council. It was winter time, and for three days Henry stood barefoot in the snow-covered courtyard of the palace at Canossa, wearing the gown of a penitent.

This put the pope in a difficult position. As a priest, he could hardly refuse absolution to one who acted so humble and repentant—even though the pope was suspicious of Henry's sincerity. It would be better to have the trial at Augsburg. But if he refused forgiveness to Henry, Henry could appear a martyr and the pope would lose support. He finally received the king and required that he promise to obey the laws of the Church. Thus absolution was granted.

7. Did the emperor persevere in his promises and penitence?

No. Henry had won a "diplomatic victory" at Canossa through his humble actions and the council was not held at Augsburg, but the princes met there and deposed Henry. They elected Rudolf of Swabia king of Germany. The pope remained neutral in the civil war which resulted. When Henry continued to disobey the laws of the Church, Pope Gregory excommunicated him again in 1080 and recognized Rudolf as king.

Henry IV marched on Rome with an army to depose Pope Gregory. He captured the city in 1084, while Pope Gregory fled to the Castle of St. Angelo and appealed to Robert Guiscard, a Norman who ruled an area in southern Italy. Robert Guiscard drove Henry out of Rome, but then his soldiers, many of whom were Saracens, sacked Rome and proved a worse scourge. The pope then fled to Monte Cassino and finally to Salerno, where he died May 25, 1085.

The dying Pope Gregory VII said: "I have loved justice and hated iniquity, therefore I die in exile."

8. Did Pope Gregory fail in his attempts at reforms against abuses within the Church?

No. The popes who succeeded Gregory VII continued his reforms. Pope Gregory VII brought to the attention of the Christian world the true meaning of spiritual authority in the Church. He made worldly rulers understand that they could not control the Church—that their power did not extend over that which Christ gave only to his Church.

Pope Gregory VII is credited with saving European society by his uncompromising and strong leadership. Had he not been a holy and strong pope, historians hold, general anarchy and disorder would have prevailed, with feudal kings and nobles becoming a law unto themselves. Europe would have fallen back into barbarism.

9. What great religious orders were founded during the high Middle Ages?

At the beginning of the thirteenth century the two great orders of the Franciscans and Dominicans were founded. St. Francis of Assisi, called the Saint of Seraphic Love, founded the Franciscan Order, stressing evangelical poverty and missionary zeal in building the Church of Christ Jesus. St. Francis, two years before he died, received the five bleeding wounds (stigmata) of our Lord. St. Anthony of Padua, who is also loved the world over, was one of his great disciples, as was Francis' spiritual daughter, St. Clare, who founded the Order of the Poor Clares and who was declared Patroness of Television by Pope Pius XII in modern times.

The Dominican Order was founded by St. Dominic and his rule was approved in 1216. Dominican friars later spread the devotion of the rosary. St. Dominic worked for the conversion of the Albigenses.

The Cistercian Order was founded by St. Robert in the monastery at Citeaux, near Dijon in France, when laxity crept into the early fervor of the monks of Cluny. The Cistercians wear a white habit and are dedicated to the Blessed Virgin Mary. They were so strict they almost died out, until in 1112, St. Bernard, with thirty relatives and friends, begged admission. St. Bernard was only 21 years of age, but his holiness and personality led so many to give up the world that soon it was necessary to build a new monastery, and eventually seventy more monasteries. St. Bernard restored the Cistercian Order to its original greatness.

St. Bernard, greatly devoted to the Blessed Virgin Mary, wrote the prayer The Memorare, which is still recited the world over. St. Bernard became an advisor to popes and settled disputes between bishops and clergy, and also between warring cities.

The Premonstratensians were founded by St. Norbert. In 1120 in the hills of France, in an area known as Premontre, the holy man Norbert retired to a life of prayer and fasting so as to found a new religious order. The new community was approved by the pope in 1126 and within a few years had 100 abbeys. They are also known as Norbertines.

The Carthusians were founded in 1084 by a holy priest named Bruno. Bruno remained only six years in a life of solitary prayer, in huts and a chapel to imitate the early monks in the desert, before the pope called him to Rome. Before he died in 1101, St. Bruno established several monasteries of this same kind in southern Italy.

Each monk lived in a little hut, but they came together for the divine office and holy Mass. They ate no meat, and only one meal a day. Although very severe, in the thirteenth century the order grew to fifty monasteries.

The Trinitarians were founded by St. John of Matha and worked to deliver Christians from Mohammedan slavery.

10. What were some of the great achievements of this time?

Great cities developed. Magnificent cathedrals were built, which still stand as monuments of faith. There developed convents, universities, art, libraries. In 1340 there were 30,000 students at the university in Oxford, England, and 36,000 at Prague in 1403. Medical science was an important branch of university studies.

Serfs were freed and new inventions made it possible to cultivate more land, producing a greater supply of food. Farmers were given more free time. The Church protected the serfs from bad treatment by their nobles. Education developed, and parishes developed their own schools.

In the high Middle Ages, St. Albert the Great and Roger Bacon were responsible for the initiation of modern science. Bacon, an English monk, wrote *The Secrets of Art and Nature* after he had observed and experimented with nature. God's knowledge and power are hidden in nature, and Bacon did much to discern them. His book predicted steamboats, balloons, submarines, microscopes, telescopes, and even gunpowder. He explained the laws for reflection of light.

More important than natural science (which the Church sees as God's blessing) was the birth of the philosophy and theology known as Scholasticism. Great literature also appeared during this time, such as the *Divina Commedia* by Dante Alighieri (1265–1321). He developed, in poetry, teachings on the doctrines of hell, purgatory, and heaven.

Many beautiful hymns, still in use in the modern Church, were written: "Veni Sancte Spiritus" (Come, Holy Spirit), "Jesu Dulcis Memoria," "Alma Redemptoris Mater" (Loving Mother of the Redeemer), and the famous "Salve Regina" (Hail, Holy Queen). Others are "Stabat Mater" (Stood the Sorrowful Mother), composed by Franciscan friars and still famous for Lenten use, and beautiful hymns to Jesus in the Blessed Sacrament by St. Thomas Aquinas, "Pange Lingua," (Sing, My Tongue) and "Adoro Te" (Humbly We Adore Thee).

"Mystery plays" were introduced, as the Church used drama as a means of preaching to the people. The great liturgical seasons were dramatized. "Morality plays" were develoepd to teach true morals as well as faith. Plays dealing with our Lord's life and death were called "passion plays," and this type continues unto the present day.

Music, literature, and drama were great means of popular education in the high Middle Ages, under the influence of the Church, and had a deep effect on the culture of the people. While some, looking back in retrospect, may criticize these educational means, they were more effective and noble than many of today's newspapers, books, movies, and radio and television programs.

During this epoch of the Middle Ages, people developed a keen sense of the relationship of their life on earth to God and eternity. They found spiritual joy in living in preparation for eternal life. It produced such great mystics as St. Francis of Assisi, who still inspires men of all religions today. Monuments to their faith still stand, e.g., the Cathedral of Chartes (in France) of the twelfth century, with its flying buttresses and magnificent windows dedicated to different religious themes, as well as the magnificent Gothic cathedrals at Rheims, France, at Cologne, Germany, and many others.

11. Were achievements made in understanding and teaching our holy faith?

Yes. Great doctors (teachers) of the Church flourished during this age. Theology during the Middle Ages became distinguished according to a method of study known as Scholasticism.

Until the twelfth century, scholars were mostly concerned with discovering and publishing anew the writings of the early fathers of the Church and wrote little of their own. Now there developed an interest in studying things for themselves, so as to understand the faith better. For tools they turned to ancient Greek philosophers, and especially to the writings of Aristotle.

Scholasticism, a science of study of philosophy (the "handmaid of theology"), demonstrates that there is no quarrel between faith and reason, and reason can aid a deeper understanding of true faith. Gratian, a professor of law at Bologna, did the same thing for the laws of the Church by collecting the decrees of the councils and the edicts of the popes.

12. Who were some of the most important theologians and spiritual writers of this epoch?

St. Anselm, archbishop of Canterbury, was one of the most important of the early theologians of the Scholastic system and is considered the founder of Scholastic theology. Peter Lombard taught at the cathedral school at Paris, and became bishop of Paris in 1160. Lombard was the author of *Four Books of Sentences,* a collection and explanation of the opinions of the fathers of the

Church on every doctrine of faith. It became the theology textbook throughout Europe.

St. Albert the Great, St. Thomas Aquinas (the Angelic Doctor), and St. Bonaventure (the Seraphic Doctor) became teachers and promoters of Scholasticism at its best.

During this epoch there also developed mystical theology, which follows methods of contemplation. While Scholastics sought for fuller understanding of the faith through reason and philosophy, other scholars preferred a method of uniting themselves to God by means of prayer and profound meditation. They were called "mystics" and they worked harmoniously with Scholasticism. The great theologians of the thirteenth century were both Scholastics and mystics.

Thomas à Kempis, author of the *Imitation of Christ*, still widely read, lived in this period.

13. Who was the greatest scholar the Middle Ages produced?

St. Thomas Aquinas. He was born near Naples in 1224 of a noble famliy and went to school at the Benedictine abbey at Monte Cassino. After his father died he determined to become a Dominican. He went to Paris, where he studied under St. Albert the Great, one of the greatest scholars of his time.

St. Thomas Aquinas joined the Dominicans in 1223. He taught in different universities after he obtained his doctor's degree. His fame as a theologian became widespread. Ordained a priest, he taught at Paris, Rome, and Naples. He was called to Rome in 1261 by Pope Urban IV and for three years served as an advisor to the pope. It was during this time that he composed the Mass and office for the Feast of Corpus Christi, and the hymns "Pange Lingua" and "Adoro Te."

St. Thomas wrote many books, but his principal books were the *Summa Contra Gentiles*, a defense of Catholic truth against the Arabian philosophers, and (in three parts) the *Summa Theologica*, which covers the entire teachings of the Church in matters of faith and morals. His other principal works consist of short writings in philosophy and theology and various hymns.

St. Thomas combined his scholarship with the prayer of the mystics. He said that he learned more from meditating on the "book of the crucifix" than from all other books he studied.

St. Thomas died in 1274. In 1923 Pope Pius XI declared him *Doctor Communis*, the teacher who belongs to all of us. He is the Angelic Doctor and Angel of the Schools. He was canonized a saint of the Church in 1323 and proclaimed a doctor of the Church in 1567.

Even in modern times, the philosophy and theology of St. Thomas Aquinas have been the guide in training of priests in seminaries. The Council of Trent recognized his *Summa Theologica* as next to the Bible in authoritative presentation of the faith. Vatican Council II again recommended St. Thomas Aquinas' teachings for the training of future priests.

14. Did the Church provide for the education of common people during this epoch?

Yes. Besides cathedral and monastic schools and universities dedicated to higher learning, other schools were encouraged by the Church for the elementary education of boys and girls. Some of these were parish schools and others were under the charge of towns. In guild schools an apprentice received not only a general elementary education but vocational training, to develop a skilled craft or trade.

There was also chantry schools, in charge of a priest, who in addition to offering the sacrifice of the Mass for the repose of souls in the chapel (connected to a cathedral or parish church) conducted the school for "teaching gratis the poor who asked it humbly for the love of God."

By the end of the Middle Ages almost the entire population of towns was able to read and write. This is why the art of printing, once discovered, spread so rapidly, since there was a great demand for books.

The Third Council of the Lateran in 1179 decreed: "The Church of God, being like a good and tender mother obliged to provide for the spiritual and corporal wants of the poor, is desirous of procuring for children, destitute of pecuniary resources, the means of learning to read and of advancing in the study of letters, and ordains that every cathedral church shall have a master who will instruct gratis the ecclesiastical students of that church and the poor scholars, and that a grant be assigned him which, by sufficing for his maintenance, will thus open the door of the school to studious youths."

The Fourth Council of the Lateran (1215) renewed this decree, and historical evidence indicates the decree was obeyed.

15. Did the Church have to struggle against any heresy within its ranks during the golden thirteenth century?

Yes. The Church must always beware of wolves in sheep's clothing, as Christ predicted. There are always those who become unbalanced in the Christian faith and attempt to bend it too far one way or the other, right or left.

The heresy of the Albigenses arose in the twelfth century and continued into the thirteenth. It was so called from the city of Albi in southern France. During a decline in the twelfth century, various sects of heretics arose. The most dangerous was the Albigenses, who denied the sacraments and the right of the ecclesiastical hierarchy or the power of the state to punish crimes. Their errors were related to the old Manichean assumption that two supreme principles of good and evil are operative in creation and life, and the supreme objective of all human endeavor is to be delivered from evil matter. This heresy denied the humanity of Jesus Christ and the authority of the Church, while endorsing a moral code which threatened the fabric of social life in southern France and northern Italy in the twelfth and thirteenth centuries.

There were two classes among the Albigenses. The "perfect" were forbidden to marry, to eat meat or any animal products, and had to observe rigorous fasts. The "believers" had two duties: to join the "perfect" before they died and to perform certain acts of reverence when meeting one of the "perfect." Whatever vices they were guilty of would be forgiven upon entering the ranks of the "perfect." The transition consisted of a ceremony called *consolamentum*, which they thought gave them absolute certainty of eternal salvation.

There could be no "second change" once one entered the ranks of the "perfect." Should one commit a serious sin, he or she would be irretrievably lost because there could be no repetition of *consolamentum*. To prevent relapse, friends sometimes resorted to murder. Sometimes the "perfect" starved themselves to death.

Another small, heretical sect was the Waldenses. Founded by Peter Waldo, a merchant of Lyons, it claimed to be a return to pure Christianity. This heresy rejected the hierarchical structure of the Church, as well as its sacramental system and other doctrines. Its followers were excommunicated in 1184 and its beliefs were condemned by the Church several times after that.

Somewhat earlier, the Church had to deal with the Berengarian heresy, the first clear-cut eucharistic heresy. It denied the real presence of Jesus Christ under the appearances of bread and wine in the Blessed Sacrament. Various synods of the Church condemned this denial, and a council, held in Rome in 1079, also condemned it.

16. Explain what is meant by the Inquisition.

Courts of inquisition were set up to deal with heresies of the time, and the pope appointed inquisitors for the various countries of Europe. Dominicans and Franciscan friars were usually appointed to this office. The inquisitors went from town to town, and those accused of heresy were brought to trial, after a month's time to renounce their errors and receive a *secret* penance. A *public* trial was held when they refused correction. If they remained obstinate, heretics were turned over to the *civil* authorities. This often meant death at the stake.

The Christian states of the Middle Ages often punished heresies severely because they threatened the social order established by law. Many of the great Church leaders were opposed to the harsh penalties inflicted by the state in the Inquisition. St. Bernard was against the death penalty. While prejudiced historians will criticize the Catholic Church for the Inquisition, we should remember that the death penalty is not mentioned in any of the councils of the eleventh or twelfth centuries as a punishment for heresy, and was not, when inflicted, a work of the Church.

The nations of the West were only a few generations from the times of barbarianism, and now that unity had been found through the Christian faith, people loved the Church and the state hated anything that threatened her new order. (It is always a mistake to judge history entirely in terms of one's own time; rather, one should judge present times in terms of all the history that has gone before us.) The custom of the time was to punish all crimes severely. One convicted of theft would have his hand cut off or be hung. Counterfeiters, murderers, and those guilty of arson would be burned at the stake or buried alive. Sometimes they were tied to horses and drawn and quartered.

Not all was glorious about the Inquisition, and many will come to the conclusion that the mercy of Christ could have been better shown. History reveals that people who call themselves Christian (Catholic or non-Catholic) have been known to inflict cruelty on each other when they got the upper hand or wanted to suppress the other.

17. How did the Church prevent the spread of the dangerous Albigensian heresy?

It was condemned by the councils of Lateran III and IV in 1179 and 1215. The Fourth General Council of the Lateran, held by Pope Innocent III in 1215, established the Inquisition, which was an ecclesiastical tribunal which tried persons accused of this heresy. If they were guilty but penitent, they were reconciled to the Church. If they remained obstinate, they were handed over to the secular power, for their teachings contained the seeds of treason to society as well, it was believed.

18. What did the Fourth General Council of the Lateran decree regarding the Eucharist?

This council ordered annual confession and Communion as a minimum and defined and made official the term "transubstantiation" to explain the faith and teaching of the Catholic Church on the Eucharist. This word expresses the Catholic faith that the substances of bread and wine, at the time of consecration during the Mass, with the words spoken by an ordained Catholic priest, are changed into the Body and Blood of Jesus Christ. A real and true presence of Jesus Christ occurs at Mass when the priest speaks the words of consecration.

The "accidents" of bread and wine—touch, taste, appearances—remain the same, but the words "This is my Body . . . this if my Blood," effect transubstantiation, or conversion, of the entire substance of bread and wine into the Body and Blood of Jesus Christ, our Lord God and Savior.

The Catholic Church in 1215, in response to the heresy of the Albigensians, thus clearly defined what had always been the Catholic faith concerning the Eucharist.

19. What mysterious and precious relic, documented from the high Middle Ages, has gained great interest among scientists in the twentieth century?

The Shroud of Turin, which many believe is the most precious relic in the world, because there is evidence that the crucified body of our Lord and Savior Jesus Christ was wrapped in it and left the details of his crucified body upon it. It is in the Chapel of the Holy Shroud in the Cathedral of St. John the Baptist in Turin, Italy. Its documented history goes back to 1354.

20. Explain the Shroud of Turin more fully.

In September 1978 the Shroud of Turin, believed by many to be the winding sheet which enfolded the dead body of our Savior, Jesus Christ, was again displayed for inspection. Scientists continue to study their 1978 testings which seem to verify the Shroud's authenticity.

It is a 14-foot piece of linen cloth with the front and back impressions of a crucified man who was whipped, stabbed in the side, and crowned with thorns—which meets the exact details of the crucified Jesus as given in the Bible. It is in the possession of the exiled monarchy of Italy, the house of Savoy.

While documented history goes back only to 1354, there is strong circumstantial evidence that it existed as far back as the first century A.D. While an unbroken line of documents is lacking, there is evidence that it was treasured at Constantinople from the fifth century on. In 1204 Constantinople was looted by renegade Crusaders and it was carried away to France and given to the cathedral at Besancon. In 1349, according to some accounts, it was stolen from the cathedral and later passed into the hands of the de Charny family at Lirey. In 1452 it was given by the de Charnys to the Italian family of Savoy and kept at Chambery. In 1578 it was sent by the Savoys to the Cathedral of Turin, Italy, where it has been kept to the present day.

Scientific testing of the priceless relic has continued to the present day, but scientific interest in the shroud began in 1898, when the first photographs were made by S. Pia. It was discovered that the light and dark areas of the body are reversed and the images on the shroud's surface are like photographic negatives. Pia discovered a positive image of the crucified man when he developed his picture, and thus one sees a much clearer image, which on the shroud is like a negative.

This discovery caused much excitement, which has continued to the present and convinces some scientists that it is the authentic linen cloth that was given by Joseph of Arimathea and thickly sprinkled with myrrh and powdered aloes brought by Nicodemus. (The Bible gives an account of this.) Since Egypt exported much fine linen in ancient times, this cloth may well be Egyptian, imported into Palestine and bought by the wealthy Joseph of Arimathea as his own burial shroud (see below).

That the image is in the negative on the shroud is of great interest to scientists, since the very concept of a negative would hardly enter into the mind of a forger as photography would not be invented for 500 years after the documented records.

Scientists conclude that the images were not painted. There is no sign of brush strokes and the images follow no known style. Furthermore, with modern knowledge of photography, efforts of renowned artists to paint negatives which, when photographed, would turn into recognizable positives were miserable failures.

Scientists are convinced the images are of a corpse in rigor mortis. There is evidence of the separation of serum and cellular mass, characteristic of dried blood. Anatomical realism is precise. Pathologists concluded that there is evidence of swelling around the cuts and bruises.

The following conclusions were reluctantly made by Ives Delage, a member of the prestigious French Academy: "The shroud had not wrapped a random crucifixion victim. The man in the shroud is severely lacerated about the head, suggesting the crown of thorns. He exhibits a gaping wound in the chest, such as a Roman lance might make. A swollen face and lash marks all over the body show that he was beaten and flogged as the New Testament says Jesus was. There is a large lacerated area on one side of the shoulders, indicating he had carried a heavy, rough beam."

There is no contradiction between the gospels and the images on the shroud, and Delage could not conclude that the images are a clever fake, the product of a body mutilated to look like the Jesus of the gospels, for any forger would have followed the Christian depiction of Christ in making the fake. The shroud differs from the traditional way Christians thought in that the nail holes are in the wrists, not the palms, and the lacerations on the man's head show he wore a *cap* of thorns, rather than the traditional wreath. The man whose blood-stained image is on the shroud is nude, and nowhere in traditional Christian art is Jesus naked as an adult.

The public was able to see the shroud on May 4, 1613, but not until 1931 and 1933 would this great relic again be fully displayed. Following the first exhibitions of the shroud in this century, Pierre Barbet, a Parisian anatomist, published a book, *Doctor at Calvary*. The book points out that the nails pierced the crucified man's wrists and not the palms of his hands, and the palms are not strong enough to support the weight of the body, as Doctors Barbet and Parigi proved. But the statements in scripture concerning the piercing of our Lord's hands are not contradicted, for among the Jews the word for hand included "wrist" as well.

New theories in the latter part of the twentieth century have developed, suggesting that some burst of heat or light "scorched" or "photographed" the negative images onto the linen fibers. This theory is supported by those who have seen the shroud. It lends itself to the supernatural and suggests the Resurrection. Christians have commonly held that Christ's risen body passed through substantial things, such as closed doors when he appeared to the apostles. Likewise, supernatural powers rolled the stone back from the tomb, not so Christ would emerge but so it could be seen "He is risen!"

There is no other known case of a shroud with such images. Other shrouds have blood-stained masses of splotches and swirls, due to body decomposition. According to the latest theory, the "picture" on the shroud does not seem to have resulted from normal chemical interaction.

By this theory, the absence of such splotches on the holy shroud means that, somehow, the body was free of the shroud *before* decomposition. This agrees with the New Testament and the Christian faith. The evidence of the Turin relic indicates that the body of the crucified existed in some mysterious manner. The natural way would have been for someone to have unwrapped the shroud and removed the body, but the natural way by which the crucified body might have been removed from the shroud is precluded.

There are hundreds of bloodstains on the body. If they were wet, removal of the body would have left smudges on the shroud. But scientists say the borders on many stains are so perfect that they appear more like pictures of blood clots than absorbed stains. If the bloodstains had dried and thus been enmeshed in the linen fibers, removal of the body would have torn the cloth and the clots. Christ, rising from the dead, could have come *through* the cloth, as he came through the closed doors.

Dr. Max Frei, an internationally known criminologist, was given permission in 1973 to examine the shroud. He found traces of 2,000-year-old pollen on the cloth, and the pollen is the same as pollen that was produced in Palestine about 2,000 years ago.

It will doubtlessly prove interesting to all who study the high Middle Ages as a time of faith and achievement to learn that our modern, scientific age, so often lacking in faith, is taking intense interest in a relic whose documentation extends back to and perhaps before the period we have studied in this chapter.

Summary

Much can be learned from the high Middle Ages and we can profit by the lessons. The strength of leadership by Pope Hildebrand (Pope Gregory VII) shows not only how the Church was saved and prospered, but society as well. Without strong authority, crisis and chaos result. But authority must always blend justice and mercy; there are always grave temptations when anyone obtains too much worldly power.

Christ said, "Give to Caesar the things that are Caesar's and to God the things that are God's." In our country, church and state are separate, as in many other countries. Unfortunately, however, there is an exaggerated sense of separation of church and state in modern times, and the state, intentionally or not, sometimes fosters the "religion" of atheism or secularism when it upholds such things as the abortive murder of unborn infants or forbids prayer in schools, even when no particular form of religion is preferred to another.

The high Middle Ages saw much success, and the development of science and art. But all worldly knowledge is as nothing compared to the knowledge of God.

Worldly knowledge and power rank infinitely below spiritual knowledge and blessings, which, when received and used well, give glory to God and lead men to eternal happiness. That, after all, is what religion is all about. There was much in the high Middle Ages that speaks well for the Church and its members.

Even though heresies arose during the high Middle Ages, such as the Albigensian heresy (which, among other things, denied the sacraments), yet God, in his Church, continued to draw good even from the failings of men by reemphasizing in the official doctrines of the Church the faith of the Church in the real presence of Jesus Christ in the Eucharist. Lateran Council IV used the term "transubstantiation," as did the Council of Trent (1545–1563), which also spoke of the *sacrificial* nature of the Mass.

When the Fourth Lateran Council used the word "transubstantiation," it was not defining a new doctrine for the Church but stating precisely what has always been the faith of the Church. To the present day, the Catholic Church officially uses "transubstantiation" in counterdistinction to the term "transignification."

The glory of the Church shines forth in the thirteenth century. The daily lives of the people were enhanced by their holy Catholic faith, and society was Christianized. More people began to live in towns, and mendicant orders enriched the spiritual lives of people.

When conflicts broke out among townspeople in the Middle Ages because it seemed the clergy and rulers of the Church possessed too much worldly power, God raised up great spiritual leaders among the people themselves, as, ultimately, priests and bishops are always the product of the faith of the families of the people.

Mendicant orders developed, with their apostles serving the towns. ("Mendicant" means the members of such an order took the vow of poverty and supported themselves by begging.) Examples of the mendicant orders are those founded by St. Francis of Assisi and by St. Dominic, who was born in Calaroga, Spain, in 1170. His followers became the Order of Preachers, approved by Pope Honorius in 1216. St. Dominic held that a successful preacher must have a solid foundation in philosophy and theology, and in imitation of Jesus Christ he sent his followers, two by two, into all the towns and cities of Eruope, preaching the faith. Their preaching had great success, and by learning and eloquence (as well as holiness) they stemmed the tide of heresy in the high Middle Ages.

One of the most celebrated members of the Dominican Order is St. Thomas Aquinas, whose writings in philosophy and theology influence Catholic thought to the present day.

Questions for Discussion

1. What do some historians mean by "middle" in speaking of the Middle Ages?
2. Who was the pope who led reforms against abuses among Christians in the high Middle Ages? Give some of his history that prepared him for his great role.

3. What three abuses especially needed correcting at this time?
4. What experiences did Pope Gregory VII have with the "holy Roman emperor" that subsequently proved the emperor was insincere?
5. What contribution did Pope Gregory VII make to secular rulers' understanding of their limitations vis-à-vis Church authority?
6. Give a summary of at least one great religious order that was established during this period.
7. What were some of the great achievements in society at this time?
8. Did Christians during this period grow in appreciation of the next life? Explain.
9. What is meant by Scholasticism, which developed during the high Middle Ages?
10. Explain the importance of St. Thomas Aquinas' contribution to the Church and why he is still important today.
11. What was the heresy of the Albigenses?
12. What is meant by "mendicant orders"?
13. What was the Inquisition?
14. What happened during the high Middle Ages which demonstrates that the Church is not the enemy of science?
15. How did a heresy of this period lead the Church to define its faith in the real presence of Jesus in the Eucharist? (In answering, explain the word that Lateran Council IV used to express our faith in the Eucharist.)
16. Give a brief account of the treasured Christian relic whose existence is documented from 1354 and stimulates the interest of scientists and Christians in modern times.

Chapter 11
Perils of the Church and Decline of the Middle Ages

1. What perils seemed to threaten the Church in the last part of the Middle Ages?

Trials afflicted the Church when the papacy fell under the control of the king of France, as Rome was left without the papal court for seventy years in what is known as the Babylonian Captivity of the Church. The pope went to Avignon, France, to live. Christians were torn by devisions in what is known as the Great Schism of the West. Three men, at the same time, claimed to be pope, so that the Church was involved with "anti-popes." The heresies of Wycliff and Hus spread. The Renaissance developed, which created problems for faith and morals in the unhealthy study of pagan literature and law.

Great harm was done to the faith of Christians by the popes' living at Avignon, and the Great Schism and clouds of darkness seemed to overshadow the Church. The bark of St. Peter was tossed on stormy waves. Christ was still with and in his Church but he seemed to be asleep as he was in biblical days, when the apostles awoke the Lord in the midst of the wind and waves, saying, "Save us, Lord, we perish." Just as the Lord rebuked the apostles for not having greater faith, so in subsequent history, down to the present day, man must always trust in the word of God that his Church will never be destroyed.

2. What is meant by the "Babylonian Captivity" of the Church?

Since the days of the first pope, St. Peter, the popes had lived at Rome, which became the center for governing the spiritual lives of Christians all over the world. The popes had to rely heavily on the kings of France during their troubles with the German emperors. As history advanced, this reliance proved harmful to the Church.

Pope Boniface VIII quarreled with Philip the Fair, king of France, when Philip placed a tax on the clergy and on the income of the Church. Pope Boniface excommunicated Philip, but the king then sent armed forces into Italy. They captured the pope and held him prisoner. Their abuse hastened the death of Pope Boniface VIII.

Within two years another man, who was not a Roman cardinal and was not at the conclave for the papal election, was elected pope. He became Pope Clement V, who never went to Rome and was deeply influenced by the king of France. He was crowned in France and took up residence at Avignon. Pope Clement V became the first of the Avignon popes.

Pope Clement and the other popes for the next seventy years lived in France. Saints and scholars begged the popes to return to Rome. St. Bridget of Sweden wrote letters to the pope to return to Rome. Finally, St. Catherine of Siena fearlessly persuaded Pope Gregory XI in 1377 to return to Rome.

3. How did the popes' residing at Avignon do great harm to the Church?

The nations of Europe were not happy that the pope resided in France, which, they were convinced, was to the political advantage of France. The Christian world felt the pope was too much under the control of France, and it did not have confidence that he could effectively govern the entire Christian world.

When taxes were laid upon priests, bishops, religious orders, and kingdoms to provide the money to build palaces and buildings for the administration of the Church in France, this caused ill feelings, whereas good Christians should have strong devotion and loyalty toward the papacy. The cardinals who were appointed were largely Frenchmen. The clergy of Rome and the Papal States lost all influence in administering the Church. This enabled the nobles to come into power in Rome, throwing the traditional Holy City into chaos.

4. Who was St. Catherine of Siena and what influence did she have on the Church?

St. Catherine was born in Siena, Italy, in 1347. From the age of 7 she led a strict religious life, joining the Third Order of St. Dominic. She had such charisms as reading hearts and was instrumental in the conversion of hardened sinners.

St. Catherine was also devoted to helping the poor and the sick. She showed great heroism in the plague which broke out in Siena in 1374, by administering to the afflicted.

Catherine was instrumental in bringing peace when war broke out in 1375 between the republic of Florence and the Papal States.

Catherine made the long trip to Avignon to visit Pope Gregory XI, to persuade him of the necessity of returning to Rome for the good of the universal Church. Pope Gregory XI (1370–1378) had made a secret vow, at the time he was elected pope, to bring the papal residence back to Rome. He had not fulfilled the vow, as he lacked courage in face of the strong opposition he met from the French king and the many French cardinals.

Pope Gregory was overwhelmed when Catherine of Siena told him she knew he had made a vow to return to Rome and was not keeping it. Pope Gregory had told no one about that vow, so he knew Catherine must be a spokeswoman for God.

It was with great difficulty that Pope Gregory secretly escaped from France. He became discouraged along the way, but at each stop on the journey he met Catherine. Catherine was at Marseilles when he boarded the ship for Genoa. She met the pope again in Genoa when he landed, and went with him into Rome.

Pope Gregory was not in Rome long when he died (March 26, 1378). His successor was Pope Urban VI, as the citizens of Rome wanted an Italian who would stay in Rome. The reign of Pope Urban VI (1378–1389), the true pope, was to see much trouble as other men claimed to be pope. Catherine of Siena stood by the true pope, Urban, encouraging and advising him.

St. Catherine worked tirelessly to bring order back to the city of Rome and peace to Christians throughout the world. She wrote letters to influential people throughout the world, asking them to support the true pope.

St. Catherine lived to be only 33 years old, because of the strenuous role she played for the good of the universal Church. Almost 400 letters are still on record which this great saint wrote to important men in her time. The magnificent style and spirituality of this saint are found in her many letters, as in her book *Divine Doctrine*.

5. Were the popes who lived at Avignon unworthy of the papacy?

In reality, no man is worthy of the papacy or the priesthood of Jesus Christ. The Avignon popes were not only holy men, they were scholars, even if at times lacking in courage, but we must remember the extreme pressures brought upon them by the French kings. Popes Clement V (1305–1314) and John XXII (1316–1334) completed the Code of Canon Law at that time.

Blessed Pope Urban (1362–1370), when he was dying, stretched himself on the bare floor, covered with ashes. He held a crucifix in his hands. He was declared blessed March 10, 1870.

6. What is the Great Western Schism and how did it come about?

In brief, the Western Schism was the division among Christians caused by more than one man's claiming to be pope. This lowered the trust of Christians in the papacy and encouraged civil rulers to infringe on the affairs of the Church. It gave encouragement to the false opinion that general councils of the Church have greater authority than the pope.

We must remember that never in the history of the Catholic Church has there been more than one pope at a time. There is always only one successor to St. Peter. The problem was not more than one pope at a time but more than one man *claiming* to be pope.

It came about this way. Pope Gregory XI died in 1378, not long after returning to Rome from Avignon. The Roman people had gathered during the election, shouting "Elect an Italian or you die!" The great number of French cardinals elected the Italian Urban VI, thinking he would come to Avignon. He did not do so. The cardinals then claimed that his election was not lawful because they had been forced by the Roman people to vote for him. Pope Urban was not the most tactful man, and that did not add to his popularity, but he was the true pope.

Dissatisfied with Pope Urban VI, some of the cardinals held a conclave of their own to elect another "pope," who called himself Pope Clement VII. This anti-pope went to live at Avignon and won recognition from France and other Western countries. The majority of Christians, however, stood by the true pope, Urban VI. This was the beginning of the Great Schism of the West.

After thirty years of two men claiming to be pope, several cardinals thought they would put an end to the confusion. They called a council at Pisa, which was not legal by Church law. This council nevertheless deposed both the pope at Rome and the anti-pope at Avignon and elected a new pope who took the name Alexander V. But now matters were worse than ever. Now three men were claiming to be pope.

7. How did the Schism of the West end, with only one man claiming to be Pope?

The schism was ended by the Council of Constance (1414–1418). The German emperor, Sigismund, persuaded the "pope" at Pisa and the true pope at Rome to agree on a council at Constance. At this council the lawful pope, Gregory XII, agreed to resign (a pope has the right to resign, but he will always be a priest and bishop). The council set aside the other two anti-popes and agreed to elect Pope Martin V (1417–1431). This was a true election because it was authorized by Pope Gregory XII.

Once again, after forty years, the Church was united, with Christians throughout the world recognizing but one man as pope. Pope Martin V was a good and holy man who won the love and respect of the Christian world.

8. Who were Wycliff and Hus and what teachings did they spread which caused harm to the Church?

John Wycliff about the year 1360 was a professor at the University of Oxford, England. John Hus was a professor at the University of Prague and took up the errors of Wycliff. Though Wycliff was from England, his false doctrines took hold in Bohemia. Hus, of Prague, had great preaching ability and his false teachings proved popular with the people.

These men taught that every Christian can interpret and explain the Bible for himself, without need of the Church as the guide of official interpretation. Although Christ founded a Church which at once has visible *and* invisible qualities, these men taught that the Church is *invisible* and exists only in the hearts of the "predestined."

As a consequence, Wycliff and Hus rejected that Jesus Christ, the God-Man, had instituted the hierarchy of pope and bishops and the priesthood itself. They said that wrong done by temporal and spiritual rulers deprives them of the right to govern or own property. This, they said, also gives their subjects the right to judge them and rebel against them.

9. What would be the consequences of the false doctrines of Wycliff and Hus?

Their false teachings struck at the very roots of the Church, which Jesus established. It lay the groundwork of false doctrines which would later be adopted by Martin Luther and other Protestant revolters in the early part of the sixteenth century. The doctrines of Wycliff and Hus, proclaiming principles of revolution and revolt, have not only disturbed the Church since then, but society in general. Their false principles of revolution and liberation from all authority arose strongly again after Vatican Council II in our own era. As many Catholics were greatly disturbed over four centuries ago and confused at the time of the Protestant Revolt, the same would happen in recent decades.

The Council of Constance (1414–1418), which ended the Western Schism, rejected the teachings of Wycliff and condemned Hus as a heretic.

10. During this decline of the Middle Ages was the Church without holiness in its members?

An essential mark of the true Church is holiness, and during this time (as always) the Church was blessed by holiness in its Founder, who still lived in and guided the Church, and in many of its members. Holiness was still present in many Church members. Outstanding were St. Catherine of Siena and St. Vincent Ferrer, a Dominican who preached penance much like St. John the Baptist. There was the Franciscan St. Bernardine of Siena, who, after a youth of angelic purity, was a mystic and spread devotion to the holy name of Jesus. Other mystics of the time were St. Bridget of Sweden and St. John Nepomucene, who died a martyr in Prague (he died rather than break the seal of the confessional).

Prayer and penance, with various forms of mortification and self-denial, were practiced by many Christians of this period (as many do today), while others ignored the teachings of Jesus Christ.

A book that was written in this period is a spiritual classic and is still recommended by Church authorities: *The Imitation of Christ* by Thomas à Kempis.

Other saints of this period who manifested sanctity and heroic virtues were St. Francis of Paola, who founded the Hermits of St. Francis and is known for his ascetic life. There was St. John Capistran, who preached a crusade against the Turks and led an army of Christian men to victory when their enemies outnumbered them ten to one. St. Nicholas of Flue was a hermit in Switzerland and, like Theresa Neumann in our own century, took no food for twenty years except Communion. St. Frances of Rome was given the privilege of having the visible presence of her guardian angel always with her. There were many other saints whose lives testify to the mark of holiness in the Church.

11. What happened to the great achievements of Scholasticism and how were the minds of many Christians turned to pagan values?

Unfortunately, after the death of scholars like St. Thomas Aquinas, St. Albert the Great, St. Bonaventure, and others, no scholars replaced them. Professors in universities frequently lost the spirit of searching for a deeper penetration into the truth and instead spent their time arguing foolish matters. They did not develop the art of good literary style. Their books were dull.

Without good writings dedicated to intellectual pursuits on behalf of true religion, men in search of good and beautiful literature at that period turned to ancient Greek and Roman writings. At first, such poets were studied only for their literary style. Everything we are exposed to affects us for good or bad, and pagan ideas gradually affected their mentalities and their manner of living.

12. What is meant by the Renaissance?

The Renaissance refers to a period in Italy beginning in the fourteenth century and reaching its height in the early sixteenth century. It designates the movement in Western Europe that had many unfortunate effects on moral, spiritual, and artistic life. The turning to pagan Greek culture and scholarship in the midst of profound social changes that were then taking place (such as the printing press, the compass, gunpowder, and geographical discoveries in Africa and America) caused profound changes in the thinking of people. There were also the astronomical theories of Copernicus, which disturbed people. It was a time, in some respects like the present, when technological progress was not matched by intellectual adaptation in spirituality. A humanistic approach to the arts developed.

Some outstanding men of the period were Machiavelli, Donatello, Michaelangelo, Raphael, da Vinci, Fra Angelico, Titian, and Correggio. England had St. Thomas More and others. They began a renaissance known as the Elizabethan Era. A rationalistic approach to the Bible was initiated in the Low Countries by Erasmus, Melanchthon, and others.

A reaction to Scholasticism set in in France, where scholars of the University of Paris led the movement.

During this period a style of architecture and decoration known as Classical developed, which was borrowed from the ancient Greeks and Romans. It deter-mined the style of St. Peter's Basilica.

Not all was bad in the Renaissance, but there were many dangers which would affect the spiritual lives of Christians.

13. What were some of the achievements of the Renaissance period?

Good uses were made of modern inventions. Printing's first use was directed toward the Bible, which was printed in all the languages of Europe. Commen-taries on the gospels and the lives of the saints were printed in books for the laity. The Church was in favor of using this invention to help men spiritually.

Popes during this period became leaders in the arts and sciences. Pope Nicholas V (1447-1455) was a scholar of Latin and Greek authors. He was also a scholar in theology and philosophy, as well as law and medicine. He desired to make Rome the world center for art and science, and he founded the Vatican Library.

Pope Pius II (1458-1464) composed beautiful hymns to the Blessed Virgin. A history book he wrote is recognized even today for its value. Pope Sixtus IV (1471-1484) built the Sistine Chapel. He wanted to make Rome the world's most beautiful city. Pope Julius II (1503-1513) commissioned Michaelangelo to do the paintings in the Sistine Chapel, which are world famous. Frescoes on the ceiling relate the biblical accounts of the creation of the world, as well as the Last Judgment. Pope Julius obtained the artist Raphael to decorate the rooms of the Vatican Palace.

Constantine had built the church over St. Peter's tomb at this world center of Christianity, and now, after more than a thousand years, it needed to be re-placed. Pope Julius II had Bramante, an architect, make plans. Michaelangelo was commissioned to carry out the plans and complete them. Pope Leo X (1513-1521) saw the church to its completion.

Popes of this period are known as the "popes of the Renaissance." While they were scholars and great politicians, their role of leadership in the spiritual realm often suffered. Added to this was the evil of nepotism, which consisted of placing their relatives and illegitimate sons in key positions in the Church. Popes at times made their nephews cardinals. Relatives were given governing positions over the Papal States, to the enrichment of their families. The popes needed much money to support the artists and literary men around the papal court. Not all was bad, amid the abuses, as great contributions (often of spiritual value noted yet today) were made at that time.

14. Explain the evils the Church experienced under nepotism.

The spirit of nepotism saw ten out of thirteen popes related by blood between 1431 and 1534. Some of the popes lived sinful lives, and brought disgrace upon the Church. Demands were made upon Catholics the world over to support the beautiful buildings and art, and much scandal resulted.

The papacy, however, even in its saddest hours, did not teach false doctrine. The Holy Spirit, the soul of the Church, with Christ Jesus as head, was still there, protecting the Church from heresy. Even schismatic councils did not destroy the Church, which Christ has promised will continue until the very end of the world. While most of the 264 popes of the Catholic church have been good men, and even holy (often to a profound degree), the fact that a few of them left much to be desired in their private lives—but never led the Church into false teachings—has led various non-Catholic historians to conclude that this Church is divine, the true Church of God. Even when it has had weak and sinful men as its visible head, it has never contradicted its teachings. Only God could preserve the Church in such a manner.

We must remember that Jesus Christ never promised the first pope, St. Peter, or his successors that they would never sin. He promised only that the Church, in its official teachings under the guidance of the Holy Spirit, would never teach error. "Upon this rock I will build my Church and the gates of hell shall never prevail against it" (Mt 16:18).

By faith, the Catholic Church is always certain that Jesus, its divine founder, will never leave it. The Holy Spirit will always keep the bark of Peter, tossed at times by mighty storms and winds, in the truth. It is sad when heresies attack the Church from without. It is sadder still when men *within* the Church are not loyal.

Summary

Even during the decline of the Middle Ages, there were great and holy men and women. Holiness is forever a mark of the true Church. It is always there in its Founder and in the power of the Church's sacraments, for they are the acts of Christ extended in time and space. But the devil will always use men to sow tares of evil among the good wheat and attempt to choke holiness in the Church. Ultimately, the devil can never succeed.

The papacy, as we have seen, fell under too much control of the king of France. The Church suffered during the removal of the papal court from Rome. Added to this was the Schism of the West, when three men claimed at the same time to be pope.

St. Catherine of Siena's great spirituality and strength of character brought the pope back from "exile." She bears testimony to the great influence women can have and have had in the life of the Church. Nevertheless the pope, returned to Rome, did not immediately undo the harm that had been done and the storms were not immediately quieted. More trouble lay ahead for the Church. The removal of the papal court from Rome is often called the Babylonian Captivity of the Popes.

In earlier days, when men had to spend all their time and energy just to keep body and soul together, they did not have time to become intensely interested in themselves as human beings but rather, in the difficulties of life, looked to things spiritual and the eternal happiness of heaven in the next life.

The Church saved civilization after the fall of the Roman Empire. The barbarians had been civilized and Christianized and there developed the greatness and beauty of the Middle Ages. With much success, unfortunately, men began to look for an easier life on this earth. Nothing is wrong with that in itself, if one does not forget eternal life, for the best and most beautiful of this world is but a faint image of eternal bliss with God, which eye has not seen, nor ear heard, nor has it even entered into the mind of man what God has prepared for those who love him.

Questions for Discussion

1. Explain how the popes, residing at Avignon for about seventy years, weakened the influence of the Church.
2. What great role did St. Catherine of Siena play in regard to the papacy?
3. Were there *actually* three popes at one time? Explain.
4. Explain how the false teachings of Wycliff and Hus would cause the Church much trouble in the years ahead by their type of thinking.
5. Name some saints who are known for great holiness during the decline of the Middle Ages.
6. In brief, explain what is meant by the Renaissance.
7. Explain how an individual pope could be a weak spiritual leader, even a sinner, and this would not disprove the Catholic claim of being the true Church founded by Jesus Christ, which will last until the end of the world.
8. What circumstances led men away from spiritual principles and to turn in on themselves, in what is known as humanism?
9. Explain how study of the weaknesses of the leadership of popes during the decline of the Middle Ages can actually help one with an honest and open mind to realize that the Catholic Church is indeed of God.

Chapter 12
The Disunion of Christians: The Protestant Revolt

1. Where did the Protestant Revolt, also called the "Reform," begin?

The Protestant Reform, really a religious revolt, began in Germany. Until the close of the fifteenth century, there were almost ideal social and religious conditions in Germany. Family and parish life were ideal, with people regularly at Sunday Mass, and even daily Mass. There were splendid forms of religious education and works of charity. With the invention of the printing press, the Bible and other religious books became popular in the reading habits of the people.

2. What, then, made it possible for serious religious disruption in Germany?

There were many causes in Europe in general. In particular, changes were taking place in Germany, with growing emphasis on the wealth of certain individuals. Cities grew and trade and commerce developed, and emphasis was placed on the money a man owned, rather than on land devoted to agriculture (which often assures a stable family life). Certain men got control of capital, whereby, with much money, a few men could determine what many others would do. Their lending and spending brought many of the common people under their control. The Church resisted this, but, unfortunately, the Church herself had acquired wealth that was not well used.

A division developed among the "higher" and "lower" clergy. Archbishops and bishops were often chosen from among the nobility and wealthy families. This meant that such churchmen were often more interested in the things of the world than in the souls of men and the next life. Pastors and priests, tending to the spiritual needs of souls, were often financially poor and had to find other work to make a living, in addition to their priestly ministrations.

People who lived on the land, or "peasants," became dissatisfied with the abuses of the wealthy. People in cities, who were often wealthy, looked down upon the peasants, who had little voice in political matters but were heavily taxed.

At the beginning of the sixteenth century, the peasants in Germany (as well as Austria) began to rise against such abuses.

3. How did indulgences become involved in the Protestant controversy?

Pope Julius II (1503–1513), in the attempt to rebuild St. Peter's Basilica, offered a plenary indulgence to those who, in addition to the sacraments they received worthily, would contribute, according to their means, toward the rebuilding of St. Peter's. There was nothing wrong in this as such, for the Bible itself favors almsgiving as a form of penance. When Pope Julius died, Pope Leo X (1513–1521) continued to proclaim the same indulgence. The archbishop of Mainz sent the Dominican priest, John Tetzel, to preach it in Germany.

Tetzel was imprudent in his manner of preaching as he went everywhere in Germany with this assignment. Historians conclude that he misrepresented the Church's position, at least in his manner of preaching, on the indulgence and the spiritual conditions required. An Augustinian monk, Martin Luther, was angered at the preaching of this Dominican priest and challenged him to a public debate on indulgences.

On November 1, 1517, Martin Luther nailed his ninety-five theses to a door of the church at Wittenberg, proclaiming his position (such was the manner of scholars of that day). By December, Luther's ninety-five theses, originally written in Latin, had been translated into German and were widely read by the people. He became popular with the laboring people who were suffering economic abuses.

The ruler of Saxony, Frederick the Wise, gave support to Luther. Frederick had never permitted the indulgence for St. Peter's to be preached in his district. A year after posting his ninety-five theses, Luther insulted Cardinal Cajetan, the Dominican papal legate, sent by Rome to deal with the problem.

The ninety-five theses of Luther were translated into French and became known all over Europe. By 1519 Martin Luther had gone so far as to deny the authority of the pope and a general council of the Church. He said that the Bible is the sole source of faith and is to be privately interpreted by each individual.

4. Who was Martin Luther?

Martin Luther was born at Eisleben, Saxony, on November 10, 1483. His parents were Catholic. His father was a miner and Martin Luther was brought up in poor conditions, but his father worked his way up to run several mines and became middle class. Martin left home at the age of 14 and received his education free by singing as a chorister in a church. He later went to the University of Erfurt. His father wanted him to study law; instead, Luther studied philosophy and proved a good student. Against advice from his father and others, Luther joined the Augustinians and was ordained a priest in 1507. (There are accounts that he had made a vow to become a priest while in danger of death.)

Martin Luther continued his theological studies at Erfurt, taught at the University of Wittenberg, and led an extremely busy life. But he became scrupulous, developing concepts of God that were most demanding and rigorous.

Luther's scrupulosity caused him many personal problems and only gradually did he discover God's mercy, which should have been "automatic" for a Christian. His "discovery" about good works was nothing new (even if unbalanced in presentation) and should have offset his scrupulous fears.

Scholars hold that Martin Luther developed a neurosis of scrupulosity which affected his theology. It appeared to him, due to his temperament and the type of philosophy and theology he studied, that nothing was good enough for God; man could not be good, but only evil. Luther claimed to discover God's mercy in 1519, realizing that man is saved by faith and confidence in God the Father, and not by his own good works. He absorbed the Bible, which he considered the "story of hope." While men are basically evil, according to Luther, God sent his Son, Jesus Christ, the God-Man, to die for mankind and to rise from the dead, thus meriting eternal life for humanity.

Luther's theology is commonly spoken of this way: *Man is saved by faith, not by good works.* "Faith alone" became the emphasis of his theology. Man had to believe in Jesus as the Lord and Savior. Man's good actions would follow, not by compulsion but freely, and God would save him. (All this, properly interpreted, is not new teaching. It is God who saves through his Son made Man. We are saved through the merits of Jesus Christ and, strictly speaking, do not merit salvation ourselves.)

Luther's ninety-five theses developed into a jealous dispute between the Dominicans and the Augustinian Luther. The Dominicans (John Tetzel was one of them) had powerful influence in Rome. They wanted Martin Luther's position condemned. Luther's weakening and unsure position is portrayed by his words: "For I myself did not know what the indulgences were, and the song threatened to become too high for my voice." As sound theologians of our day see it, there was at the beginning no deep theological difficulty, but misunderstandings, imprudence, stubbornness, and pride on all sides. That makes sense, for it is never sound theology, and certainly never true faith, which divides men from one another, but rather their sins.

5. Did Luther go astray in his theology on the priesthood?

Yes. In 1520 he wrote *An Appeal to the Ruling Class of German Nationality as to the Amelioration of the State of Christendom.* In this writing Luther denies that

Catholic priests have any special religious powers of Christ. He became confused on the Church's teaching on the "priesthood of the baptized," also called today the "priesthood of the faithful" or "priesthood of the laity."

The Catholic Church teaches that all men participate in the priesthood of Christ if they are baptized. At the same time, the Church teaches that certain men, who have received the sacrament of holy orders, participate in the priesthood of Christ in a special manner with special powers, especially the powers of consecrating the bread and wine into the Body and Blood of Jesus and of forgiving sins in Jesus' name. The priesthood of the ordained (holy orders) differs not only in degree but in *essence* from the priesthood of the laity.

Martin Luther by 1520 was writing that men ordained, whether by bishops or the pope himself, are only baptized Christians. It is the community which designates certain men for particular functions. The priesthood, then, is purely functional. This means that one is not a priest for all eternity. Some men are shoemakers, carpenters, farmers, or merchants; so, in religion, certain men specialize in religious functions but have no more powers of God than the Christian farmer or carpenter or cook. Priests, then, should be subject to the state.

Luther called for the nobility in Germany to break with Rome. There should be local elections for bishops. Papal legates should be ignored. No German money should flow into Rome for support of the universal Church or the see of Rome. Celibacy should be the business of each priest, just as other men decide for themselves whether they want to marry. Luther claimed that no cases should be appealed to Rome, for it had no authority over the local church. Feast days should be abolished.

The list of reforms which Luther called for in the Church in Germany was long. Luther's denial of the priestly order had the effect of denying the power of the Mass and sacraments, and even losing its power for Protestants who broke with the ancient Church and lost the powers of the priesthood handed down in an unbroken line of the apostolic chain.

The extent to which Luther went left little room for Pope Leo X to do much else, in 1520, except excommunicate him.

6. How did Luther respond to his excommunication?

Martin Luther was hardened in his position, which removed him and his followers even further from the Church which Jesus Christ had founded almost 1,500 years before.

Luther wrote *The Babylonian Captivity of the Church,* in which he speaks of the "papal captivity" of the Church. There is a priestly caste which keep members of the Church in slavery to the sacraments. He again denies the priesthood of the ordained and the power of the sacraments. To Luther, they are nothing more than signs, without special powers of Christ.

Luther came out with yet another treatise, *The Freedom of a Christian.* In this work Luther says that the Catholic Church is wrong in saying that salvation comes from fasts, penances, devotions, ceremonies. He accuses the Roman Church of not teaching that salvation comes from faith and hope in God the Father and Jesus. Luther says that it is man's faith and confidence in God the Father, not his good works, which save him. He does not deny that there should be good works; they are free responses as the fruit of man's faith.

Much of what Luther was saying was true in some respects, but it was unbalanced in emphasis and not the complete truth of the teaching of the Catholic Church. What was seriously wrong was Luther's denying the authority of the pope and the powers of Christ in sharing his priesthood with certain men and Christ's acting in and through the sacraments. This would finally result in millions of separated Christians being deprived of authentic and full means of worship and sources of grace that Jesus intended in founding his Church.

7. What did Luther substitute for the authority of the papacy?

Even in his own time, Luther was accused of making a "paper papacy" of the Bible, in that everybody "became pope" who interpreted the Bible for himself. Such was the accusation of Sebastian Franck (1499–1542), who as an Anabaptist favored religious toleration.

Revolts against authority began to break out on behalf of the theories promoted by Luther. Two of his disciples, Andreas Carlstadt and Thomas Muntzer, became fanatical. They accepted Luther's doctrine that all Christians are priests (an exaggerated doctrine concerning the "priesthood of the baptized"); they held that since all Christians possess the Holy Spirit, God's people should be free of all Church organization. They abolished the Mass, getting ahead of Luther's movement and intention. The faithful were invited to eat a communal meal, but they went further than Luther and denied any real presence of Jesus Christ in the Eucharist. Communion was only in memory of Jesus, a reminder—nothing more.

Without the central authority of the papacy and bishops who worked in harmony with the chief bishop of the universal Church, Luther was unable to form and hold unity among his disciples. He lost the friendship of Carlstadt. Thomas Muntzer became Luther's enemy, who spoke of Luther as "leader of the synagogue of Satan... the pope of Wittenberg... Doctor Liar."

8. Who were the Anabaptists?

Anabaptists taught that baptism received in infancy must be repeated, as baptism received as a child was of no value. Thomas Muntzer taught that infants would not make a conscious, free decision to accept Jesus as Lord and Savior. Without such a commitment, all must be baptized again. The rebel followers of Muntzer and his like became known as Anabaptists, promoting teachings that were not acceptable to Lutherans or Catholics. According to

Anabaptists, all worldly things are evil, and they did not stop short at what they considered worldly, including even worship ceremonies.

In Munster (northern Germany) they announced another kingdom of Christ on earth, an Anabaptist kingdom of a communistic character. John of Leyden, who had been a Dutch tailor, was chosen as their king and prophet. John took seventeen wives. He ruled in an eccentric, crude manner. He defended his crimes by quoting the Bible. Finally, the government had to step in to restore order.

9. What is Calvinism?

It is a form of Protestantism named after John Calvin (1509–1564), a French-man who was a lawyer with anticlerical tendencies. He had a passion for theology and reform of the Church. As a student at the University of Paris, Calvin became affected by Lutheran teachings. He became established in Geneva, Switzerland, in 1541, and Protestantism discovered in him a genius at organization who could make up for Lutheranism's weaknesses in discipline.

Calvin taught salvation by faith alone, because, he believed, human nature is totally evil through original sin. He taught predestination—that God has pre-destined part of mankind for heaven and the other part for hell. The Holy Spirit brings an individual to Christ and "elects" him for salvation.

Calvin's theology is found in his *Institutes of the Christian Religion*. He did not believe in having the state replace Church authority. With his great ability at law, he organized his church with pastors, elders, doctors, and deacons, who controlled law in the church and order in the Christian community.

Geneva became the stronghold of Calvinism and he ruled it with intolerant power. While claiming private interpretation of the Bible for himself, he was not consistent. For example, he had Servetus burned at the stake for denying the Trinity.

The new religion was carried into France. Calvin in 1541 translated his *Institutes* into the French language. Calvin himself trained ministers at his Academy of Geneva.

John Knox (1513–1572), founder of Presbyterianism in Scotland, became his disciple and Scotland was won for Calvinism.

10. Give a Summary of the Spread of the Revolt to the Various Countries.

GERMANY. It was here that the first big upheaval centered. Martin Luther is often made to appear (by Protestant historians) as the great liberator who broke the Church's hold on the common people, thus giving them religious liberty. The Church is made to appear as a society which not only issues excommunica-tions but, at the slightest provocation, puts to death those who do not agree with her. Great fear and mistrust are instilled in some non-Catholics by this type of lopsided historical reporting. (There are, of course, objective non-Catholic historians.)

ENGLAND. King Henry VIII wanted a divorce from his wife, Catherine of Aragon, so as to marry Anne Boleyn, a young, beautiful lady of his court. Pope Clement refused. Henry VIII then declared himself head of the Church in England and forced the entire country into apostasy. Bishops and priests had to take an oath to recognize the king's spiritual supremacy. There were 72,000 Catholics who refused and were thus put to death, including Cardinal Fisher and St. Thomas More.

Henry VIII, as he grew tired of his wives, married another (six in all, after beheading two of them).

Pressures against Catholics grew even stronger under the successors to Henry, his son Edward and Elizabeth, his daughter by Anne Boleyn. Priests were hanged and quartered. Catholics who refused to assist at Protestant services were fined and put in prison.

Pressures were still greater under King James I, Cromwell, and William of Orange. No Catholic could hold public office. A Catholic child who turned Protestant would inherit the parents' entire estate, excluding Catholic brothers and sisters—even when the parents were living.

SWEDEN. Gustav Wasa, who became king of Sweden in 1523, saw that by seizing Church property and abolishing the hierarchy he would obtain absolute power. He therefore introduced Lutheranism by force and deceit. For fifty years the Swedish people were deceived into believing that they still belonged to the ancient Catholic Church. Preachers feigned saying Mass while wearing traditional Catholic vestments. Finally, Catholics were excluded from office and their worship was forbidden by law.

DENMARK, NORWAY, ICELAND. Protestantism was introduced in these countries by Christian II and Frederic I, contrary to the will of the people. All Church property was confiscated and bishops were beheaded.

FRANCE. In this country there were undesirable actions by both Catholics and Protestants. Catholics were provoked by the Protestant Huguenots. In Orthey, 3,000 Catholic men and women were massacred. At Nimes, hundreds of Catholics were killed with daggers in one night. In return, in 1572 King Charles of France was informed by Catholics that the Huguenots had conspired against his life, and he commanded that during the night (St. Bartholomew's Night) his soldiers should fall on the Huguenots and kill them. The pope, when he learned of this, after it happened, condemned the actions of these Catholics.

The Calvinist heresy seduced many Huguenots. Conspiring against the king in order to bring one of their party upon the throne, they waged bloody wars against their lawful sovereign.

HOLLAND. Calvinism was adopted as the state religion and the Catholic religion was forbidden when William of Orange led the people to rebel against their king, Philip II of Spain, and became head of the Dutch republic in 1578.

An army was sent out by the government to enforce Calvinism, and bishops were imprisoned. Catholic priests of Amsterdam were put on a ship and sent out to sea, never to be heard of again. At Gorkum, nineteen priests became martyrs. Churches were desecrated and the sacred images were burned. In spite of this, Belgium and several provinces of Holland remained true to the Catholic faith.

PRUSSIA. This country had been civilized and Christianized by German knights. Albrecht of Bradenburg in 1522, then superior of the order, became a Lutheran. He broke his religious vows and married, and made himself prince of the country. Lutheranism became the religion of the country.

SCOTLAND. In a sense, Catholic Queen Mary Stuart became a martyr to the true faith as the nobility rebelled against her. This was due to John Knox's preaching of Calvinism and urging rebellion against the lawful government. Queen Mary fled to England, where her cousin, Queen Elizabeth, had her imprisoned and beheaded, as Mary Stuart was the lawful heir to the English throne and would not renounce her Catholic faith.

IRELAND. Cromwell invaded Ireland with an English army. About 10 million acres of land were confiscated and 29,000 people sold as slaves to America. Still, Ireland refused to accept Protestantism. Catholics in the northeast (Ulster) were driven into the poverty-stricken province of Connaught. Five pounds was offered for the head of every priest. This persecution continued to 1800 in various ways. In 1829 Daniel O'Connell obtained religious liberty from England for his country.

11. Protestantism, since it has no unifying structure, split into many denominations. What are some of the later sects?

At present, there are over 400 different Protestant denominations in the world. (Some counts have that many in the United States alone.) In general, there are two main branches of Protestantism: (1) classical or traditional Protestantism, which includes original groups which broke from the ancient Catholic Church, such as Lutherans, Calvinists, and Anglicans, and (2) radical Protestantism, such as Baptists, Congregationalists, Methodists, evangelical sects, and fundamentalists.

The Methodists were founded by John Wesley, an Episcopalian preacher, at Oxford, England, in 1738. He was assisted by his brother, the great hymn writer Charles Wesley.

The Baptists were founded by Roger Williams at Providence, Rhode Island, in 1639.

Congregationalists (sometimes called Puritans) were founded by Robert Browne in England in 1600. Many of them came on the *Mayflower* to America, landing at Plymouth Rock in 1620.

The Quakers were founded by George Fox in England in 1647.

Hundreds of contending sects eventually sprang from the Protestant Revolt, with its doctrine of private judgment and interpretation of the word of God. However, there have been ecumenical tendencies toward unity among many Protestants in recent decades.

12. Was a reformation needed in the early sixteenth century?

Yes. Catholic historians generally agree that a reformation was needed during those troubled times. Catholic historians, however, whose understanding of their Church as the divine institution founded by Jesus Christ, the Son of God, and which was promised by its divine Founder that it would never be destroyed ("Upon this rock I will build my Church, and the gates of hell shall not prevail against it"), do *not* admit that the Church, in itself, in its divine teachings and powers, needed to be reformed.

13. What, then, needed to be reformed?

The *moral lives* of many Christians needed to be reformed or spiritually renewed. Even some leaders in the Church—some priests and bishops, and even a few popes preceding the sixteenth-century Protestant Revolt—were not living lives according to the desires of Christ and the teachings of his Church. During the 2,000-year history of the Catholic Church, most of her 264 popes have been good and even saintly men, but a few have not brought honor to the papacy. This should not surprise us. Rather, it serves to prove the divine institution of the Catholic Church, which survives even when unworthy men occupy her highest post.

Too many members of the Church were spiritually sick and needed moral reform of their personal lives. The Christian principles and truths for reforming their lives existed, as always, within the ancient Catholic Church, which should ever renew itself spiritually in its members. Many sad events prepared the way for moral laxities.

14. Why then, does the Catholic Church object to the Protestant Reformation, which took thousands of her members away, resulting in the protestant sects of today?

Men must be changed by religion, not religion by men. While a reformation was needed, the Catholic Church objected to the *kind* of reformation. Christ had given his Church its teachings, its sacraments, its authority, and all that was necessary for man's salvation and to lead a good moral life while giving glory to God. It was by living according to this Church that a true reformation would result. It should have been toward such an end that the revolters worked, rather than attempting to change the Church of Jesus Christ by multiple interpretations.

15. Did such a reformation take place within the Catholic Church, which remained true to the word of God and as Jesus established it?

Yes. The Counter Reformation, as history calls it, took place within the Catholic Church after the revolt. Rather than trying to change the nature of the Church itself, in the sense of changing doctrines or denying rightful authority set up by Jesus Christ, it worked at correcting abuses of certain churchmen and strengthening the faith and morals of all Church members. Sadly, the Counter Reformation came too late to prevent the Christian breakup.

The Council of Trent was called by Pope Paul III to begin the reform within the Church by condemning false doctrines. The Council of Trent established practical rules for the promotion of faith and morals. It opened at Trent on December 13, 1545, and remained in session until December 4, 1563, being often interrupted by plague, war, and other causes. The council strove to lay down standards of doctrine which a Catholic must believe to consider himself a sincere Catholic.

16. What, in summary, did the Council of Trent decide?

There were long debates. The council nonetheless officially taught that both the Bible and tradition are common sources of faith, with God as the single supreme source. Man is not completely evil. Man has free will to accept God's saving grace, which God freely gives man. The sacraments communicate to men the saving graces of Jesus Christ. The Mass is truly the sacrifice of the cross perpetuated. Holy Communion is truly the living substance of the Body and Blood of Jesus Christ, together with his soul and divinity, and only the appearances of bread and wine remain after the consecrating words of a validly ordained priest. This change is best described by the word "transubstantiation." (Martin Luther held that Jesus Christ is present *together with* the bread and wine, while the Catholic Church held, and still holds, that no substance of bread and wine remains after the consecration.)

While Luther pushed for the vernacular or the language of the people in church services, the Council of Trent said that the language of worship was to remain Latin. This language, a source of unity, would also distinguish those who remained loyal to the true Church of Christ. The council, however, did *not* condemn use of the vernacular as contrary to faith. It was rather a discipline judged necessary for the times.

Penance (confession) and extreme unction (annointing of the sick) are truly sacraments. The council also determined what is necessary for Catholics to enter a true sacramental marriage.

The Council of Trent defended the special spiritual powers of ordained priests and bishops. Holy orders confers a special character or indelible mark upon the ordained priest that will remain for all eternity.

To correct abuses, the Council of Trent required that bishops must live in their sees for the greater portion of each year. No longer could a bishop head more than one see at a time, as had been done previously. Seminaries were to be set up for both the intellectual and the spiritual formation of future priests. Trent forbade the marriage of ordained priests.

17. Were the deliberations of the Council alone sufficient to bring about the needed reforms?

No. Decisions on paper remain just that, until they are implemented into the lives of the Church's members.

The Society of Jesus, founded by St. Ignatius of Loyola in 1540, was approved by Pope Paul III in 1544. Ignatius was formerly a Spanish knight. Proclaiming undivided loyalty and obedience to the popes, the Jesuits (as they became known) were effective in implementing the reforms of Trent throughout the world. This did much to stop the spread of Protestantism. The Jesuits developed a great system of higher education. Jesuit missionaries were sent to pagan countries.

The Society of Jesus developed great theologians, such as St. Robert Bellarmine and St. Peter Canisius, the Apostle of Germany, as well as Petavius and Suarez.

Great religious orders founded to assist the Church at this time included the Order of Capuchins (1528), which practiced strict penance and poverty and performed missionary labors. The Oratorians were established by St. Philip Neri, the Apostle of Rome, who founded the Oratory to educate priests in the greatness and holiness of their vocation. The Discalced (bare-foot) Carmelites were established by St. Teresa of Avila and St. John of the Cross in Spain. The Passionists were founded by St. Paul of the Cross to practice penance and do missionary work.

St. Vincent de Paul founded the Priests of the Mission and the Sisters of Charity for corporal and spiritual works of mercy. St. Alphonsus Liguori founded the Redemptorists; St. John Baptiste de La Salle founded the Christian Brothers, with its Christian schools. St. Francis de Sales founded the Sisters of the Visitation; St. Angela de Merici founded the Ursuline Sisters.

Many other religious orders and leaders arose at this time to defend and to promote the Catholic faith. The Church was also blessed during these times with a long list of saints.

18. Did the Catholic Church experience gains in converts to make up for those who broke from full unity with the ancient Church of Christ?

Yes. Missionaries who went to non-Christian lands brought millions into the true Church. St. Francis Xavier went to India and Japan. Other Jesuits continued his work. Countless conversions were experienced. The Church spread to China. In Mexico, where formerly 20,000 human victims were sacrificed each year to false gods, converts were made by the millions, helped by the reported miracle of Our Lady of Guadalupe as God's Mother in 1531, who left her miraculous image on the *tilma* of Juan Diego.

Franciscan fathers from Spain went not only to Mexico but into New Mexico and California, as is attested in the life of Fr. Junipero Serva. Breboeuf, Jogues, and Marquette labored in North America among the Indians, and many suffered martyrdom.

The newly discovered continent of the Americas offered rich fields for the harvest. In South America and Central America, as well as in the newly discovered regions of Africa, missionaries from among the Franciscans, Dominicans, and Jesuits evangelized the heathens.

Summary

Terrible failure, neglect, and the laxity of some Church leaders paved the way for the men who in the sixteenth century divided Christendom into hundreds of bickering churches. However, the Church as such was still a holy organism. There were even great saints at that time, but general purification in many quarters was seriously needed.

Martin Luther frequently doubted the wisdom and rightness of his position. Having replaced papal authority with private interpretation of the Bible, Luther's middle-class church became undermined. Wycliff and Hus (before him) had set the stage, and now men found opportunity to strike out against all authority, political and spiritual, while helping themselves to the property of their betters. Luther himself approved of violence. The Peasant's Revolt in Germany ended with the loss of much blood. Luther, in the pamphlet *Against the Murderous and Thieving Hordes of Peasants*, said: "Let everyone who can, slay, smite and stab."

The term "Protestantism" is general and describes Christian denominations that are not Catholic or Eastern Orthodox. The word came from those who *protested*. The term came into use in 1529 in Germany when the Diet of Speyer decreed that the Mass should be restored in those German states where it had been discontinued. No new doctrines were to be preached before a general council could be held. Six powerful princes and rulers of fourteen rich cities *protested* the action of the Catholic emperor, Charles V, who tried to limit Lutheranism. At the Diet of Augsburg in 1555, Charles had to accept Lutheranism as a fact. This diet said that the ruler of each imperial territory would decide the religion of his state. It kept the peace until 1618, when the Thirty Years' War started the controversy anew.

Today, almost 500 years since the Protestant Revolution started, men are still religiously divided, and this has also affected social and legislative relationships among citizens. Mistakes were made on all sides in handling the problems. Too late, Luther came to recognize that his revolt had not improved things, but conditions among Christians were far worse. If Luther was destined to be a prophet, he bungled his vocation.

Christians can still heed the words of Christ: "Sanctify them in the truth. Thy word is truth. Even as thou hast sent me into the world, so I also have sent them into the world. And for them I sanctify myself, that they also may be sanctified in truth. Yet not for these only do I pray, but for those also who through their word are to believe in me, that all may be one, even as thou, Father, in me and I in thee; that they also may be one in us, that the world may believe that thou hast sent me" (Jn 17:17–22).

Questions for Discussion

1. Can the Protestant Revolt of the sixteenth century in the true sense of the word be called a "reform"?
2. What conditions in Germany prepared it for spiritual unrest and revolt?
3. What was the controversy about indulgences?
4. In brief, describe the type of man that Martin Luther was.
5. Summarize the high points of his teachings.
6. Was Luther incorrect in saying that all baptized Christians are priests? Explain your answer as it applies to holy orders.
7. Explain the difficulties in the substitution Luther made for the authority of the papacy.
8. Explain the chief position of the Anabaptists, which gave them their name.
9. Did the followers of Luther remain united?
10. What kind of religion did John Calvin promote?
11. Henry VIII at first seemed to remain loyal to authentic Catholic doctrine. Describe what led him to spiritual difficulties and how he responded.
12. Describe the kind of reformation that was really needed in the early sixteenth century.
13. Explain the statement "Men must be changed by religion, not religion by men."
14. What was the Counter Reformation?
15. What, in brief, were the conclusions of the Council of Trent, as opposed to false doctrines promoted by Protestants?
16. How were the conclusions of the Council of Trent implemented after they were put on paper?
17. What kind of special vow of obedience does the Society of Jesus (Jesuits) make?
18. How did God provide for increase in the Church to offset those who broke away?
19. Name various causes that led to the breakup of Christendom.

Chapter 13
Catholicism Advances in the New and Old Worlds: The Catholic Offensive

1. What country sent missionaries to bring the true faith into the newly discovered Americas?

Spain was the instrument God used to bring the true faith to the lands newly discovered to the west. Spain won prominence under Ferdinand and Isabella, who drove the Moors out of their country in 1492. That year Christopher Columbus reached America. The Spanish kingdom was under the rule of the Catholic emperor, Charles V. Under Charles and Philip II, his son, Spain reached its height of power and influence.

Ferdinand and Isabella saw to it that Protestantism made no serious advances in Spain. With the help of Franciscan Cardinal Ximenes, they tended to needed reforms in Spain. Modern historians question some of the methods they used, such as the Spanish Inquisition, which was directed principally against the Jews and the Mohammedans. It was also used to stamp out heresy, and at times was guilty of cruelty.

2. How did the Catholic faith come to the New World?

Queen Isabella helped the Genoese sailor, Christopher Columbus, who was seeking a new route to India. She gave him three ships, one of them named *Santa Maria* (Holy Mary). Columbus did not find his new route but he discovered America, which he took possession of in the name of the king and queen of Spain. Other Spaniards came to explore the new land and were accompanied by Spanish missionaries, Franciscans, Dominicans, and Augustinians. They preached the gospel to the natives of the new lands.

Cardinal Ximenes saw to it that Spain passed laws to protect the liberties of the Indians. Schools were to be opened in each mission. Besides the Spanish language, students were to be taught music and the arts of industry, agriculture, and homemaking.

In Peru, the first university in the New World was founded in Lima in 1551, although Mexico City had a university, established in 1533 by Franciscan Peter of Ghent. The Jesuit fathers came to Lima in 1568 and set up the first printing press in the New World. St. Rose was born in Lima in 1586. She joined the Third Order of St. Dominic and became the first canonized native saint of the New World.

The Jesuits settled in Paraguay in 1586 and set up magnificent Christian communities among the Indians, known as "reductions." Unfortunately, they were done away with by the Portuguese in 1750, and the Jesuits were driven out in 1767.

After Cortes conquered Mexico for Spain in 1521, Franciscans came. (Mexico already had a high culture among its Indians.) The Franciscans founded missions and were later aided in this by Dominicans and Augustinians. Colleges were established from which native priests later went northward to spread the faith. For centuries the Church worked hard in Mexico, until almost the entire country was Catholic.

3. Give a summary of the tradition which relates the part heaven played through Our Lady of Guadalupe in the conversion of Mexico.

Hernando Cortes, the conqueror of Mexico, established Christianity after conquering the land. He ordered the destruction of pagan temples, which were replaced by Christian churches. (The Mexican Empire fell to Cortes in 1521.) The first Christian church was that of Santiago, and one year later Juan Diego and his wife were baptized there. The baptismal font where Juan Diego was baptized still stands.

Juan Diego was one of the first to be converted to Christianity after the Spanish conquered the Mexican Empire. By 1531, ten years after the conquest, the Mexican people were on the verge of revolting against the Spanish because of conflicts and tensions. It was through our Blessed Mother that the revolt was prevented by the great miracle of December 1531.

Juan Diego became the human instrument, together with the miraculous portrait the Mother of God left imprinted on his *tilma*, in establishing Christianity in a pagan society and thus starting a great growth of the true religion in the Western Hemisphere. The Mother of God transformed part of the clothing Juan was wearing into a continuous miracle that still thrills the world as it learns about it for the first time and discovers deeper and deeper messages. In recent years, images of men reflected in the eyes of the Lady of Guadalupe painting have been discovered.

It is said that God gives special revelations to persons whom he has fitted to receive them. This would be especially true when the revelations are not just for oneself but for others and for hundreds of years to come. The true God prepared the people of Mexico, somewhat like the people of the Old Testament, for revelations of the one true God. In 1464 God sent his angel to Nezahualcoyotl, the king of Texcoco, who then gave up the pagan religion and built temples to the true God. He prayed before altars containing offerings of flowers and incense. Nezahualcoyotl, shortly before his death, made a great speech and said: "How deeply I regret that I am not able to understand the will of the great God, but I believe the time will come when he will be known and adored by all the inhabitants of this land."

Nezahualpili, the son of this king of Texcoco, was just like his father. He continued the great devotion to the true God and became known as the wisest man of his time. He died in 1515, but before he died he told the emperor, Montezuma, that he had had a dream a few days before. The dream said that Montezuma was soon to lose his throne to invaders from across the sea, who would bring the true religion.

This explains why Montezuma surrendered so easily to Cortes in 1521. It has often confused worldly historians, why Montezuma surrendered his great Aztec Empire without much resistance. Prophecies had also been made to his sister, Princess Papantzin, in 1509.

Princess Papantzin was with Juan Diego, his wife, and uncle in the first group baptized into the true religion when the Franciscan missionaries came. Juan and his wife walked 14 miles to Tlatelolco for Mass, until she died in 1529, after which his devotion to the Blessed Virgin became even stronger.

It was on the Feast of the Immaculate Conception, 1531, that the Virgin of Guadalupe first appeared to him. He was 57. The Mexicans, who at this time were treated badly, had conspired and were planning to attack and destroy the Spaniards. Bishop Zumarraga realized that things had become so serious that only a miracle could forestall the uprising and prevent destruction. The bishop, who was devoted to the Blessed Virgin and had begged her for help, had secretly asked Mary for Castilian roses as a sign that she would help. That in itself would be a miracle, for Castilian roses did not grow in Mexico but in Spain.

The bishop had asked Juan for a sign from the Lady to verify the truth of his words about a chapel to be built on Tepeyac Hill at the request of God's Mother. Coming into the bishop's house, Juan fell to his knees, carrying the Castilian roses which the Mother of God had helped him arrange in his *tilma*, after he had picked them on the hill. As he told the bishop about the roses, he opened his white *tilma* to permit them to fall to the floor and said: "Behold! Receive them!"

Suddenly there appeared on the *tilma* the image of the Virgin, holy Mary, Mother of God, just as it can be seen now in her temple at Tepeyac in Mexico City. The bishop and all who were with him lifted their eyes from the roses to the tilma; then fell to their knees in awe, admiring the image of the Mother of God.

The bishop, in tears, prayed and begged forgiveness for not having been more prompt in answering the will of the Mother of God. He rose to his feet and took the cloth from Juan's neck which the Mother of God had tied to him and placed it in his chapel. The next day the bishop said to Juan: "Come show us the place where the Queen of Heaven wants her temple built."

The image of God's Mother meant much to the millions of Indian people. To them it was picture-writing, telling them of the falsehood of their past gods and to turn in prayer to the Son of this Queen. The brooch with a black cross at the neck of the Lady's tunic reminded the Mexicans of the cross, which was a sign of the religion of the Spaniards. When the Mexicans asked Juan Diego for a meaning for the cross, he told them that the true God, who is invisible, had become a Man. His name is Jesus, and he died on a cross and rose to life again. The Son of God made Man had offered his life to God the Father for the salvation of the entire world.

There was no longer need for the 20,000 bloody human sacrifices which the pagan Mexicans had been offering to a false god each year. Almost at once the natives wanted to embrace the true Christian faith. In great numbers they went to the Catholic missionaries to be baptized.

In 1548 Bishop Zumarraga was appointed the first archbishop of the New World and that same year made a trip to the town of Tepetlaztoc. In four days he baptized, confirmed, and married about 14,000 natives. Millions of native Mexicans were baptized into the Catholic faith in the years immediately following the gift from heaven of the miraculous portrait of God's holy Mother.

The above account helps explain how Hernando Cortes, an explorer with a military force between 700 and 1,300 men, conquered a great empire that stretched for about 2,000 miles and comprised about 9 million people, highly civilized and with a fully developed society. In reality, our Lady "conquered" this people for her Son.

The Guadalupe shrine has become a center for eucharistic devotion which draws millions to the present day. Popes have repeatedly recognized the miraculous image of Guadalupe. Even in the sixteenth and seventeenth centuries, approval of the Holy See was given in the form of popes' granting indulgences to encourage devotion to Our Lady of Guadalupe. To the present day, artists and scientists remain perplexed at how this image could have been painted on rough cactus fiber, which should have turned to dust hundreds of years ago.

At the very time when the Catholic Church was in crisis in Europe with the Protestant Revolt and millions were separating from the fullness of the true faith and union with the pope, heaven was using our Lady's image and the lay apostle, Juan Diego, to bring an even greater number into the true Church on the new continent. Five million separated from the Catholic Church due to the Protestant Revolt; eight million were added in Mexico in a short time, to grow into millions more.

The New World was one vast continent at that time, and our Lady appeared at its center. Pope Pius XII placed the integrity of the faith in *all the American continent* under the patronage of Our Lady of Guadalupe. Pope Pius X spoke of her as belonging to the whole world: "Among the most celebrated sanctuaries of all the Christian world one must count [especially], with all right and justice— the one in Mexico in honor of the Virgin Mary of Guadalupe."

Only in recent decades, especially since Mary was crowned by Pope Pius XII as Queen of All the Americas, has understanding and devotion to Our Lady of Guadalupe made great inroads throughout the United States.

In January, 1979 Pope John Paul II, in his first trip outside Italy after his election, visited the Shrine of Our Lady of Guadalupe in Mexico City.

4. Summarize the beginnings of the Catholic Church in the United States of America.

The Franciscans began active work among native Indians near the present city of Santa Fe in 1544. The Jesuits moved along the northern coast of Mexico to the present state of Arizona. Fr. Junipero Serra first came to the harbor of Veracruz, Mexico, on December 6, 1749. Fr. Serra was a man of great ability in oratory and a scholar of philosophy; his desire, nonetheless, was to go to the missions to carry the gospel to those who had never heard of God. From 1750 until his death in 1784 he led a historic "conquest" of America.

Leading a group of Franciscans, his only weapon the crucifix and his watchword "Love God," Fr. Serra converted California into a paradise of faith, according to historical writers. He founded nine major missions in California and his successors founded twelve more. Around these missions the great cities of California grew (the first mission was San Diego in 1770).*

Missionaries accompanied Spanish explorers into Texas. As late as 1785 the government of Spain supported the missions. Only when Protestant settlers came from the United States in 1821 were the inhabitants of Texas other than Spanish and Catholic.

St. Augustine was founded in Florida on September 8, 1565 (so named because the peninsula had been found on the saint's feast day). It was the work of a leading naval figure of the Spanish Empire, Admiral Pedro Menendez de Aviles, who had been ordered by Philip II to found a colony in Florida. From this center missionaries spread out, as the admiral had taken with him twelve Franciscans and four Jesuits to work for the conversion of the Indians. Many priests were martyred but always more priests came, and gradually, with much bloodshed, this area of the New World became civilized and Christian. Missions and monasteries were founded throughout Florida and almost all the Indians north of the Gulf of Mexico and east of the Mississippi River became Catholic.*

---

*The above is a summary account of the life of Juan Diego (1476–1548) from the book, *Saints and Heroes Speak,* by Fr. R. J. Fox, O.S.V. Press. The account is based on historical accounts preserved from the times of Juan Diego and the conversion of Mexico.

*More detailed accounts will be related in chapter 16 regarding missionary efforts in the United States.

5. Give a brief account of missionaries in North America.

In the northern part of the New World, the French were the first settlers. Henry IV of France invited the Jesuits to come to Canada in 1608, and they established a college at Quebec. Indian tribes—the Hurons, Algonquins, Montagnais—were converted and organized into villages. The Iroquois, who were enemies of the Hurons, could not be converted. Missionaries came into the United States from Canada, and the Mass was said in 1604 in Maine. In 1633 the Capuchins founded a mission on the Penobscot River and the Jesuits settled on the Kennebec.

Fr. Isaac Jogues visited Manhattan Island and went 1,000 miles into the interior, reaching the region of the Great Lakes. Captured by the Iroquois, he was tortured, and two fingers were burned off. Rescued by the Dutch, he returned to Europe but later returned to Canada, burning with great love to convert the Indians. He visited the Iroquois near the present city of Albany, trying to bring peace between them and the Hurons. He discovered the beautiful lake in New York State which he named Lake of the Blessed Sacrament (later the English changed it to Lake George). There the Iroquois put him to death in 1642. In 1930 Pope Pius XI canonized Fr. Isaac Jogues and his five Jesuit companions, who also were put to death by the Iroquois.

Fr. Jacques Marquette explored the Mississippi River with Louis Jolliet in 1673 and called it the River of the Immaculate Conception. Fr. Marquette preached the gospel to the Indians who lived along its shores.

Fr. Louis Hennepin, a Belgian Franciscan, worked among the Mohawks. He joined La Salle in 1679 in his second expedition to the west. While on his way back to Quebec he discovered Niagara Falls.

The Venerable Kateri Tekakwitha belonged to the Mohawk Indians, who were hostile to Catholic missionaries. Despite opposition from her own tribe and family, she became a devout Catholic, devoted to our Blessed Mother and the Blessed Sacrament and practicing great penances.†

6. Did the Virgin Mary occupy a place in early American history?

Yes, right from the early explorations through the colonial period to the founding of the Republic. Coumbus' flagship was the *Santa Maria*. After their love for God's Mother, pioneers gave many cities in the South and West her name. Los Angeles is an "abbreviation" of *St. Mary, Queen of the Angels of the Portiuncola*. In 1565, when Menendez landed in Florida and founded the city of St. Augustine, the oldest U.S. city, one of his first acts was to have the Mass

---

†A detailed account of the life of Kateri Tekakwitha, whose cause has been introduced for canonization may be found in *Saints & Heroes Speak*, OSV Book Dept. The book is authored by the same priest who wrote the *Catechism of the Catholic Church*.

offered in honor of the nativity of Mary. Our Lady of La Leche is still venerated there.

French missionaries traveled south from Canada (up the St. Lawrence), naming establishments after our Lady. St. Isaac Jogues and his companions, who were martyred, spread devotion to our Lady, and today at Auriesville one finds Our Lady of the Martyrs Shrine.

The first bishop of the United States was Bishop John Carroll, who was consecrated in 1790 on the Feast of the Assumption. He declared our Lady, Mary, patroness of the diocese of Baltimore, Maryland. The Cathedral of Baltimore, which he began, was dedicated on completion to our Lady's assumption.

On May 13, 1846, at the sixth provincial Council of Baltimore, the country's bishops requested of the Holy See that our Lady be named the patroness of the United States under her title the Immaculate Conception. This was granted by Pope Pius XI in 1847.

On November 20, 1959, the National Shrine of the Immaculate Conception was solemnly dedicated at Washington, D.C., which had been under construction for many years in the foundations were built, 1931). This magnificent church was built by Catholics throughout the United States to honor God's Mother, their patroness.

7. How did the popes strengthen the unity of Catholics throughout the world with the Holy See after the Council of Trent?

Pope Gregory XIII (1572–1585) established national colleges in Rome. Priests were to be educated in the Holy See to learn how *to think with the Church* and thus return to their countries filled with knowledge of the government of the Church and loyalty to the pope. Pope Sixtus V (1585–1590) organized cardinals in more than fifteen "congregations" to look after the different aspects of the Church's work throughout the world.

8. How did Catholics fare in countries where Protestantism was strong?

In countries where Protestantism had become predominant, Catholics were forced to give up many public ceremonies they had been accustomed to enjoying. Riots sometimes resulted when Catholics had public processions. Those who participated in Mass in England and Ireland were considered enemies of the state. Priests had to offer Mass in secret. The doctrine of the Catholic Church which was most attacked was the Real Presence of our Lord Jesus Christ in the Blessed Sacrament.

Devotions multiplied to "compensate" for the lack of the Mass and sacraments when, because of persecutions, the people were deprived. The Catholic devotions were directed primarily to our Lord in the Blessed Sacrament, but also to our Blessed Lady and the saints. Many litanies were developed, and became so popular that the pope by 1601 had limited their public use to the Litany of Loretto (in honor of God's Mother) and the Litany of the Saints. The Litany of Loretto had just become popular because it was used at the shrine in Loretto, Italy to which—according to Pious tradition—the House of Nazareth had been miraculously transported by angels. (To the present day, this shrine is considered one of the world's most famous religious shrines—the small house in which Jesus, Mary, and Joseph lived. It is enclosed inside a large and magnificent church.)

The Dominicans spread the rosary devotion widely, and it became very popular in the sixteenth century. Societies were established to promote the rosary. Popes generously granted indulgences for its recitation and for carrying the beads on one's person. About the same time (fifteenth and sixteenth centuries), shrines begin to appear in the open air in honor of the various scenes of our Lord's passion and carrying his cross to Calvary. These became known as Stations of the Cross. Gradually, the Church officially recognized this practice by granting the same indulgences to one meditating on the sufferings of Jesus (when they were erected inside parish churches) as when one journeyed to Palestine to pray at the actual sites of our Lord's passion and death.

9. What happened to education after the religious revolt of the sixteenth century?

Education in general was greatly hindered. It has sometimes been falsely claimed that Protestantism was the first to establish public schools, but historical records inform us that there were more free schools and opportunities for elementary education *before* the Protestant Revolt than for the next 100 years.

The Catholic Church's efforts were greatly hindered in education after the unhappy breakup of Christian unity. The Church no longer was recognized by many as a source of authority and she had lost means of support. The universities and cathedral schools, which had been so closely identified with the Church, now found they had little to depend upon without Church support. The great scholar Erasmus, who was a contemporary of Luther, wrote: "Wherever Luther prevails, the cause of literature and learning is lost." It was the result of chaos, disunity, and the breakdown of authority.

The Jesuits did much to remedy the plight of education. They developed a system of studies known as *ratio studiorum*. They taught the Catholic faith to youth in schools and colleges and lectured in universities. They also attempted to prepare youth for higher education. The schools were free, and no poor student was turned away. All that was necessary was ability and willingness to study.

10. Did Catholicism spread to other parts of the world besides the New World after the Protestant Revolt?

Yes. While the Church lost about one-third of its territory in the Protestant Revolt, it more than made up for it, not only in the New World but throughout the world. St. Francis Xavier, one of the first group of seven Jesuits under St. Ignatius, went to India. In the Portuguese colonies, he converted more Indians in thirty days than the Portuguese had in fifty years. In Malaysia, St. Francis met a Japanese who encouraged him to bring the faith to Japan, where St. Francis met terrible obstacles. Still, fifteen years after he left Japan, there were 150,000 Catholics, who grew to 300,000 by 1592.

How well St. Francis sowed the seeds of faith in Japan is testified to by the persecution of Christians in 1623 under a new ruler. Thinking he had completely destroyed the Church, the Catholics went underground. They had no priests. Yet they baptized, prayed the rosary, and passed on the true Christian doctrines, so that when missionaries were permitted back in the country in the nineteenth century, they found communities of 20 to 50,000 Catholics that had survived and were ready to receive the priest-missionaries.

While St. Francis Xavier did not get into China, other Jesuits continued the efforts. A young, talented Italian by the name of Matteo Ricci went to China, finding an introduction through his talent in science and mathematics. He had much difficulty and some success. By 1650 there were 150,000 Catholics in China, a small number indeed, but an opening had been made by the West to a mysterious and difficult land.

While Catholicism was spreading to new parts of the world, a reformation was taking place within the Catholic Church.

11. Explain some aspects of the Catholic reformation within the church.

The period of the Catholic reformation produced some of the greatest saints in Church history (some of whom were mentioned in the last chapter). St. Charles Borromeo became one of the greatest bishops in the period of the Catholic reformation. One would never have expected it when Pope Paul III (1534–1549), who first called the Council of Trent, made him a cardinal at the age of 22. Because he was the pope's nephew, it looked like another case of nepotism.

This was the situation St. Charles Borromeo found in Milan. No bishop had lived there for sixty years. The priests were without knowledge of Latin, in which they were to offer Mass and administer the sacraments. The churches were empty, were even used as barns. Monasteries were not fostering religion but were gathering places for worldly recreations, such as dances and parties.

St. Charles avoided the worldly spirit which had characterized the Renaissance. He led a life of prayer, penance, and poverty, and led his priests to do the same by establishing seminaries with strict discipline. He also established hospitals and schools for teaching the fullness of Catholic doctrine. St. Charles was not immediately popular or accepted by all. His life was even attempted. But the saint continued his heroic efforts and saintly life, and by the time of his death Milan had developed into a model diocese.

St. Teresa of Avila (1515-1582), declared the first woman doctor of the Church by Pope Paul VI on September 27, 1970, with much difficulty established many Carmelite houses throughout Spain. She reformed the lenient Carmelite life she met when she joined the Incarnation Convent in Avila, into which the sisters had fallen, without realizing how far they had fallen from the ideals of the Carmelite Order. From her convents, thus reformed, some of her nuns carried the reform throughout Europe, which eventually came to the United States via Belgium.

In Rome itself, as a result of the spirit of the Renaissance, much corruption had seeped into the lives of the people, causing them to forget true Christian values, which are eternal, and the infinite power of Christ in the Mass and the sacraments. St. Philip Neri (1515-1595) took to preaching, even as a young layman on the streets of the city, and won many followers with his happy disposition. He established oratories and converted priests and lay people to the authentic Catholic life.

One of the outstanding apologists who explained and defended the Catholic faith—so as to spread it—was St. Peter Canisius. His efforts were directed to converting Protestants back to Catholicism, the ancient and original Church of Christ Jesus. This saint was received into the Jesuit Order in 1543, and by 1549 he had gone to Germany, where the Protestant Revolt had got its start. St. Peter Canisius labored in Germany most of his life, until he died in 1597.

St. Peter Canisius got Protestants into dialogue and pointed out the reasonable truths of Catholicism, once one accepted Jesus Christ as Lord and Savior. He pointed out the weaknesses of the Protestant positions. He wrote three catechisms, according to a concentric method, for the different age levels of children. These were translated into other languages for other countries.

Proving by teaching the fullness of Catholic faith and by apologetics that truth wins out once it is known and explained, Peter converted southern and central Germany back to the Catholic Church. He also brought Protestants back to the Catholic Church in Hungary, Bohemia, Poland, and Austria. So successful was he in Poland that this country, which had turned largely Protestant, came back almost entirely to the Catholic faith.

St. Francis de Sales (born in 1592) as an ordained priest went as a missionary among the Calvinists of southern France. He brought more than 70,000 back to the Catholic Church. At the age of 25 he became bishop of Geneva. St. Francis directed his efforts to holiness among lay people, as well as among priests and religious. To the present day his book, *An Introduction to the Devout Life*, is considered a masterpiece of spiritual writing, as is his *Treatise on the Love of God*.

It was during this period that St. Vincent de Paul (1581-1660), founder of the Vincentian or Lazarist Order, appeared. When he was ordained a priest, St. Vincent was no more zealous than the average priest of his time. Five years after ordination, while on a voyage, he was taken to Tunis as a slave, having been captured by Mohammedan pirates. For three years he was held captive but finally converted his master, an apostate Christian. Then the two escaped to France.

The charitable works which began to develop in the life of St. Vincent de Paul inspire people to the present day. He had special compassion for the poor and developed a system for distributing aid to the poor and unfortunate. He founded the Association of Charity among women for this purpose. He himself lived a life of poverty, even going without fuel so that the poor would not be cold.

The charity of St. Vincent extended to helping those in prison, providing free schools for poor children, visiting the sick, and founding orphanages and homes for the aged, where he insisted husbands and wives should not be separated. Countries ravaged by war found his followers assisting the unfortunate ones. He was assisted by the Sisters of Charity. Large groups of laymen and laywomen followed his example.

It was shortly after the time of Martin Luther that God raised up an order of nuns in Italy known as the Ursulines. Their founder was St. Angela Merici (1474–1540) and they worked especially to teach children. She founded the first teaching order of nuns in the Church. St. Angela was inspired by God to direct her efforts in this direction, as well as caring for the sick. They came to Canada in 1636 and by 1727 had opened a convent at New Orleans and established the first school taught by nuns in the United States of America.

What happened after the Protestant Revolt, when one-third of the Christians lost their loyalty to the true Church which Christ established under St. Peter and his successors, is answered by God, who raised up great saints and heroes, guiding his Church with the constant presence of the Holy Spirit. While Protestantism lacked the missionary spirit, the Catholic Church spread throughout the world. The Catholic Church is the Church of God, and men weak in faith in every century have predicted its destruction, which Christ promised will never happen. The aftermath of the Protestant Revolt is sufficient proof of Christ's promise.

Summary

The Catholic Church did not remain simply on the defensive but, in the spirit of the gospels, went on the offensive. The missionary spirit, in which Jesus expects his Church to live, seeks constantly to evangelize more and more souls, until every last soul in the world is brought to Jesus Christ. Thus the period immediately following the Protestant Revolt could not be spent simply fighting enemies and misunderstandings, but included a positive approach to reforming weaknesses within its own ranks, among the Church's own members.

The aftermath of the split among Christians meant that the spirit of the times was a setting aside of the authority of God's Church, with each individual interpreting of the Bible for himself, with private interpretation much in vogue.

What this principle means in reality is that each man becomes his own church, the framer of his own religion, if private interpretation is taken seriously. The denial of doctrines led to the denial of all revealed religion, and thus a new paganism began to take hold in countries once Christian. Against that spirit of infidelity the Church has struggled ever since.

The reforms of the Council of Trent began to be put into effect with the election of Pope Pius V in 1566. This pope lived in poverty—contrary to the spirit of the Renaissance. Devoted to the passion of Jesus, he declined the wearing of rich robes. He had great devotion to Mary and her rosary. As a result of the reforms led by Pope Pius V, respect for the authority of the papacy began to return to the hearts of people. The sacraments were frequented and Catholics became better informed on Catholic doctrines. One cannot live and love what one does not know.

Sometimes it is called the Catholic Counter Reformation, but a better name would be the "Catholic Reformation," for it represented what should have been the spirit of all Christians: remaining united while reforming their individual and inner lives in Christ, rather than splitting off and forming new churches.

Protestants during this period did not want anything to resemble Catholicism. Their churches were lacking in artistic beauty, and often very bare. The Catholic Reformation, on the contrary, produced great achievements in art and architecture. A new style developed, known as Baroque. Churches became very beautiful, with stress on color, paintings, statues, and much decoration. St. Peter's Basilica (at the Vatican) was designed by Bernini (among others), with twisted, gilded columns around the high altar.

Questions for Discussion

1. In exploring the New World, did the Church bring Christianity to the native peoples? Explain.
2. Who was one of the first converts to Christianity after the Mexican Empire fell to Cortes in 1521? Summarize the events of his life.
3. Explain from the account of Our Lady of Guadalupe, why Montezuma surrendered so easily to Cortes?
4. What was the first name given to the Mississippi River?
5. What was the name of the beautiful lake in New York State before the English changed it to Lake George?
6. What do the original names given the Mississippi River and Lake George indicate about early settlers?
7. What evidence is there that the Virgin Mary occupied an important place in the lives of Catholics early in the history of our country?
8. What was the trend in relationship toward Catholics after the Protestant Revolt, when Protestantism had become predominant in certain countries?
9. What contributed to the spread of Catholic devotions?
10. How did the devotion known as the Stations of the Cross develop?

11. Did the Protestant Revolt help or hinder education generally? Explain.
12. Give at least one example of how Catholicism spread to other parts of the world (besides the New World) after the Protestant Revolt.
13. Sometimes it is said that for more than 400 years after the Protestant Revolt the Catholic Church remained simply on the defensive. Would you agree? Explain.
14. Give examples of the Catholic Reformation.
15. What did St. Charles Borromeo do to reform the Church in Milan?
16. Who won many Protestants back to the fullness of true Catholic faith? Tell something of his efforts.
17. How did God bless the Church in a singular way after the Protestant Revolt, to compensate for the heavy losses as people became confused in the true faith or were forced out of it by deceit or compulsion?

Chapter 14
The Aftermath of the Religious Revolt and the Birth of the French Revolution

1. What was the spirit of the times after the Protestant Revolt?

With Luther, Calvin, and other Protestant leaders proclaiming the doctrine of private interpretation and setting aside the authority of God in his Church—as Jesus had established it upon the rock of the papacy and the bishops in union with the pope—chaos soon began to reign. Without authority, disunity and chaos are always the outcome. Having each man the interpreter of the Bible amounts to each man developing his own religion. In religious matters, every man becomes a law unto himself rather than God as the supreme Law Giver and the one Church, headed by Peter's successor, as the chief interpreter of the word of God with the power to make laws: "to bind and to loose" in the name of Jesus Christ.

The final outcome is not only the denial of certain doctrines of the Church but the denial of all divinely revealed religion, and a gradual return to paganism and atheism.

2. How did this affect political leaders?

Such false doctrines affected every level of society. Leaders announced that faith would not govern them but only reason. The movement, wrongly called the Enlightenment, arose, which was a turning to darkness as man turned in on himself and away from God and Jesus Christ, the true Light of the World. The Enlightenment was opposed to all religions, and especially the Catholic Church.

Kings and princes arose without respect for the Church, and attempts were made by kings to remove the Church from unity and loyalty to Rome.

3. What was the Thirty Years' War?

It was the result of a religious crisis in the Holy Roman Empire in the early years of the seventeenth century. The 1555 peace between the Protestant and Catholic princes in Germany was not successful. This "Augsburg agreement" held that the religion of the ruler should be the religion of the people. (Hardly any concept of religious freedom was present in that principle.) A rebellion against the empire broke out in Bohemia on May 23, 1618, started by Protestant princes who formed the Evangelical Union. They deposed Ferdinand as king of Bohemia and put a Protestant, Frederick of the Palatinate, in his place. A war broke out in 1620 which lasted thirty years.

Electors had elected Ferdinand and declared him Holy Roman emperor. Protestant leaders throughout the empire encouraged a revolt against the Catholic Ferdinand. The kings of Denmark, Sweden, and France became involved in the war. Cardinal Richelieu (1585-1642), the minister to the king, was really ruling France at the time. Tilly and Wallenstein were Catholic generals. The war amounted to serious plundering of the German countryside by both the Lutherans and the Catholics. A leading Protestant general was Gustavus Adolphus, king of Sweden. Cardinal Richelieu, fearing that Austria would become too powerful in Europe, threw support to the Protestant side, while Pope Urban VIII (1623-1644) remained neutral.

When both sides were exhausted with thirty years of war, the Treaty of Wesphalia was signed in 1648, which officially accepted the permanent split among Christians. The Catholic Hapsburgs had Austria, Hungary, and Czechoslovakia. Germany was disunited and kept from becoming a great power. Whoever owned Church property in 1624 would still own it. Calvinists, Catholics, and Lutherans were given freedom of worship.

4. What were the results of the Thirty Years' War and the Treaty of Westphalia?

Religion was no longer an aid to unite men in faith and society. This led to other wars as a spirit of nationalism developed. The Hapsburgs were removed as Holy Roman emperors. Germany was divided into 343 weak states. Catholics lost more than they gained. Germany had no supreme authority. France obtained the most powerful position.

Henceforth the prince or king of Protestant countries was considered the head of the church. If subjects did not join the Protestant faith of the ruler, they were imprisoned or even put to death.

Gallicanism, as it is called, developed. Catholic rulers, seeing how strong this made the Protestant princes, wanted to imitate them and destroy the influence of the pope in their countries. In France, Louis XIV claimed he was absolute ruler, subject to no one, and he set out to control the Church, even appointing bishops. He left the pope only the right to confirm the king's choice. The hierarchy (bishops) became little more than tools of the government. Clergy depended upon the favor of the king for promotion, rather than holiness of life and zeal for the cause of souls. When the people later resisted tyranny, seeing the Church and state as one, the Church was to suffer greatly. Louis XIV concocted a "modern" error which said the pope is not infallible, even in matters of faith, unless he speaks with the universal consent of the Church. He set forth the proposition that a general council has greater authority than the pope.

5. How did the Pope react to Louis XIV's infringement on Church Authority?

Pope Innocent XI (1676–1687) condemned the positions of Louis XIV. He would not confirm the appointment of any French bishop put forth by Louis. The papal nuncio in France was then thrown into prison and an army was sent to attack Rome. Louis XIV made peace with the Church only when his foreign enemies threatened France.

6. What were the Freethinkers, who arose at this time?

"Freethinkers" were Rationalists who refused to accept any authority in intellectual matters. They recognized no divine authority in religious matters. They formed their ideas only from weak human reason and nature. They would not accept the doctrine of original sin. Human beings, they claimed, could find goodness and happiness on their own by following their own inclinations.

7. Which country was the home of this new movement?

"Free thought" began in Protestant England, where deism was taught, which was a new idea of the relation between God and the world. Deists taught that while there is a God, he has nothing to do with the world he created. God, having created the world, leaves it on its own—sort of a God-is-dead mentality in relationship to man, who is removed from divine providence. The movement spread to Holland, France, Germany, and the United States.

8. Who was the great apostle of the Enlightenment or free thought?

In France, Voltaire (1694–1778) was its great prophet. He had led a life of immorality and blasphemy and had as his goal the destruction of the Church. He eventually died in despair.

Jean Jacques Rousseau, born in Geneva, Switzerland, in 1712, became a hero to the Enlightenment cause. He taught that the world could be saved by education, if education were based on the desires of human nature and not controlled by authority or any ideas that have come down from the past. Rousseau ignored God and taught that what is right and lawful comes only from the people's will. This ignored God as the ultimate truth and supreme law giver.

Rousseau wrote a book on education in which he has a beggar ask for alms "for the sake of God." Rousseau answers: "No, not for the sake of God, but for the sake of man." He developed a secular humanism to replace Christian charity.

9. What was the Order of Freemasons?

It was founded by Freethinkers who banded together into a brotherhood. They desired to build an international organization not connected with any church. Freemasony was founded in London on July 24, 1717, and adopted "free thought" as its fundamental doctrine. Members were bound by oaths of secrecy. It spread swiftly through the world and was opposed to the Church.

The Freemasons gained political power, especially in France. They were opposed to the Catholic Church because of her doctrines and international character. They advocated "separation of Church and state." Pope Clement XII excommunicated Catholics who joined Freemasonry, and succeeding popes continued this censure.

Rulers and governments of Christian countries began to uphold the ideals of Freemasonry and foster them among the people.

10. What happened to the Jesuits in their fight against such errors?

In France, the Jesuits fought against the Rationalists. Voltaire recognized that the Jesuits were a great strength in the preservation of Christianity. Lies were started against the Jesuits, and in 1762 the Parliament of Paris suppressed the Jesuits in France.

They had been ordered out of South America in 1759 because the Portuguese prime minister, Pombal, could not make political tools of them. In Portugal itself, Jesuits were arrested and sent to the Papal States. This also occurred in Naples, and France, Spain, Portugal, and Naples appealed to the pope to suppress the Jesuits throughout the world.

Pope Clement XIV compromised and, hoping to obtain peace for the Church, suppressed the Jesuit Order in 1773.

11. How did the Jesuits survive the suppression?

The Jesuits had been one of the strongest bulwarks of the Church and the greatest defenders of the papacy, and it was strange to have them suppressed, as Pope Clement XIV (1769–1774) was forced to do. Just as strange, non-Catholic princes came to the support of the Jesuits. In Prussia, Frederick II asked them to continue their work in education. Catherine II of Russia would not permit the papal document of suppression to be published. When Clement XIV died, Pope Pius VI (1775–1799) permitted the Jesuits to form a novitiate in Lithuania. Pope Pius VII permitted the order to exist in Russia. He reestablished the order for the entire world in 1814.

12. Was any American affected by the document of suppression?

Yes, a very special American in Church history. He was just finishing his term as a Jesuit novice in Austria at the time of the suppression. He had hoped to work for the Church in Maryland. He and several companions returned home and continued to live in community, but not as Jesuits. That novice became the first bishop of Baltimore, Bishop John Carroll.

13. What false doctrines during this period caused added problems for the Church?

Gallicanism and *Josephinism* gave the princes power in ecclesiastical affairs and the Church was reduced to a servant of the state. Joseph II, emperor of Austria, put these false doctrines into execution, as did other German princes (Josephinism). The government of Portugal and the king of the Bourbon family (ruling France, Spain, and several Italian states) joined for this purpose (Gallicanism).

14. Summarize the consequences of these false principles for religious and political liberty.

Princes, assuming absolute power, restricted the rights of the people. Rebellion and anarchy resulted from "free thought" that recognized no principles. The Church became the victim of unjust state laws and was not able to protect the people from their oppressors, as she had during the Middle Ages.

King Louis XIV of France declared himself the absolute power. He sent the representatives of the people home with these words: "I am the state."

The consequence of this was the French Revolution, which broke out in 1789, filling not only France with horror but Europe in general.

15. What condition caused the uprising in France?

For too long the kings of France had dominated the people, enriching themselves and supporting the nobles by oppressing the poor. The common people fell into a desperate condition. Leaders of the Enlightenment incited the people to revolt. The agitators had to work in secret because the kings held strictest censorship over all that was written. Freedom of speech did not exist. Agitators took for their watchwords "liberty, fraternity, equality." This became the battle cry of the poor, common people, until they revolted to overthrow the monarchy.

16. What effect did this have on the Church?

The Church had become so closely identified with the state in the minds of the people that they looked at the higher clergy with the same kind of hatred they had for kings and nobles. The "lower" clergy, who shared poverty in common with the people, held the confidence of the people. In the beginning, the lower clergy supported the revolution.

17. What was the "Civil Constitution of the Clergy" and the National Assembly?

The people forced the king to grant the right to send representatives to a National Assembly. This assembly, to handle the national debt and heavy taxes, decreed that all Church lands would become the property of the state. The state would take care of the support of the clergy (November 1789). In 1790, all monasteries, convents, and religious houses were suppressed.

Next, the National Assembly framed a "Civil Constitution of the Clergy," which was contrary to the canon law of the Church (July 1790). According to this constitution, bishops and pastors were to be elected by the people, with Protestants and Jews having a vote. No one could hold any office in the Church that was not connected with parish work. Bishops and priests who would not take an oath to this constitution could no longer serve in their priestly office.

Only a handful of bishops took the oath and hardly half of the priests. Pope Pius VI declared that the constitution for the election of bishops and pastors was not valid. The pope suspended all who took the oath. By this time Louis XVI was king, he refused to receive Communion from a priest who had taken the oath, and people in Paris became enraged.

Priests who refused the oath were banished to penal colonies in South America, while others went to England, Germany, and America.

18. Summarize the position and fate of King Louis XVI and the queen, Marie Antoinette.

Both have been seriously maligned by false accounts in history. The king has often been portrayed as stupid and dictatorial. The queen is seen as extravagant, immoral, irresponsible, and light headed. These two monarchs were victims of evil conditions which they inherited. After the death of Louis XV in 1775, Louis XVI found himself with a country deep in dept, unjust taxes, and an extravagant court at Versailles, accustomed to living in luxury and immorality and unwilling to permit Louis XVI and Antoinette to deprive them of their style of life. Under the preceding two kings (Louis XIV and XV), their life of careless gaiety had been accepted and they were opposed to any change. The court circulated pamphlets accusing the king and queen of the very evils of which they themselves were guilty.

"Liberals" among the people who hated all authority, and therefore the king and the queen, joined forces with the nobles in spreading falsehoods. The ordinary people heard so much of this that they began to believe it, whereas previously they had great respect for the king and queen. The king was deeply concerned about his people, and at first his reign went well. Louis and Antoinette had enjoyed great popularity, but this changed.

Louis saw much injustice in the tax structure, which favored the rich and burdened the poor. The king would have reduced taxes from 10 to 2½–5 percent, according to one's ability to pay. This would have favored poor people, but that is not the way Louis' enemies "advertised" it in the newspapers. They simply said that the government was going to raise more money through taxes. Rebellions were stirred up throughout the country.

Louis XVI was a good man but he was not a strong leader in resisting the forces of the deceivers. Louis was put under pressure to permit an "Estates General" to meet on May 4, 1789. The "Third Estate" delegates plotted to have their own way, broke away from the other delegates, and set themselves up as a National Assembly.

From this date on, revolution moved rapidly in France. Disorder broke out, with mobs running wild in Paris, and Louis was unable to keep order; his every effort to help the people and the country was turned against him by lies. By August, peasants were revolting throughout France. Monasteries were robbed; property was destroyed.

A group known as the Jacobins gained power and taught that everyone should have the freedom to do whatever he wanted. Total disorder and chaos began to reign, and the royal family feared for their lives, even attempting escape from Paris, but without success.

On September 14, 1791, a new constitution was adopted, leaving the king only the power to veto laws. Louis was convinced that in reality France had no king. When he vetoed a decree which ordered the arrest of priests who had not taken the oath to the Civil Constitution of the Clergy, he knew that behind the revolution was hatred of God and the Catholic Church. His enemies intensified their lies against him.

The leaders of the Jacobins were Robespierre, Danton, and Marat, who gained complete control by September 1792. Hundreds of people were massacred in a few days' time. When the king was told he must die, he pleaded for three days to prepare his soul, but was denied. On January 21, 1793, mounting the scaffold, King Louis XVI proclaimed his innocence of the charges and prayed to God for forgiveness of his enemies and for the good of France.

Antoinette was treated no better. She was separated from her young son Louis, the rightful new king of France. Her son was forced to sign documents accusing his mother of immorality, and eventually this young king died from mistreatment in prison. The queen kept her dignity, but on October 16, 1793, she was guillotined.

19. What happened after the death of Louis and Antoinette?

On November 10, 1793, less than a month after the queen's death, the worship of God was forbidden. A new calendar was adopted which abolished Sundays and holy days, and the months were given new names. An evil woman was placed on the altar of the Cathedral of Notre Dame and worshiped by the mob as the "Goddess of Reason." Robespierre in 1794 began executing his supporters, who in turn executed Robespierre.

A new government was established in 1795, known as the Directory. It had five directors who operated dishonestly. Only a wealthy minority was permitted to vote.

20. How did Napoleon Bonaparte rise to power?

The kings of other countries in Europe began to worry about their safety when they saw what happened in France. They declared war on the French government, and Pope Pius VI sympathized with them. The French Republic sent an army into the Papal States under the command of Napoleon Bonaparte, a young general. One of Napoleon's generals, Berthier, gained possession of Rome and declared the temporal power of the pope to have ended. Napoleon took the aged pope back to France with him as a prisoner, and the pope died August 29, 1799. When this pope (Pius VI) died, many said he would be the last pope.

The cardinals, however, under the protection of the German emperor, met on an island near Venice for a conclave to elect a new pope, who took the name of Pope Pius VII (1800–1823).

Napoleon Bonaparte continued to rise to power in France, replacing the leaders of the revolution. Napoleon, proclaimed First Consul in 1799, submitted a constitution to the vote of the people which won almost unanimous consent because the people were anxious for a leader who could keep order. It had the effect of making Napoleon dictator in France. The revolution was over and France had moved to absolute monarchy.

In spite of all that had happened, Napoleon saw that the people were still Catholic at heart. He recognized that the people still practiced their religion in secret. Therefore, in 1801 Napoleon made peace with the pope, and shortly after that became emperor of France.

21. What happened to the internal life of the Church during this period? Did sanctity still exist?

Holiness, one of the essential marks of the true Church, will always be present in the Church. The years 1647–1690 marked the life of St. Margaret Mary Alacoque, and according to accounts of her life, our Savior appeared to this humble and saintly Visitation sister in central France, showed her his Sacred Heart, and requested that devotion to it be spread throughout the world. On December 27, 1673, while she was kneeling before the divine presence in the Blessed Sacrament, Jesus appeared to St. Margaret Mary and spoke these words:

"My Divine Heart is so full of love for men and for you in particular that, no longer able to contain within itself the flames of its burning charity, it must spread these flames by means of you, and it must manifest itself to men in order to enrich them with its precious treasures. I have chosen you to achieve this grand crusade of love." Taking her heart, Jesus showed it to her within his own, as a tiny atom consumed in a burning furnace.

From that time onward the Sacred Heart was often revealed to her, especially on first Fridays. The Sacred Heart of Jesus asked that men make reparation and receive Communion in reparation, especially on first Fridays, and honor the image of his Sacred Heart.

The most famous apparition was in June 1675, during the octave of Corpus Christi. While praying before the Blessed Sacrament, our Lord revealed his Sacred Heart, saying: "Here is the Heart that has so loved men as to spare nothing for them, exhausting and consuming itself in order to prove its love for them. And in return I receive from most of them only ingratitude." Jesus asked her to have a special feast established in the Church in honor of his Sacred Heart.

In 1689 St. Margaret Mary was entrusted with a message for the king of France, and tried to carry out the message. When a nobleman, Armand Jean de Rance, left the court of Louis XIV and entered the Cistercian abbey of La Trappe, he discovered that its monks had departed from the strict observance of the rule of St. Bernard. He brought about a reform that resulted in the Trappist Order of monks.

During the troublesome years of this period, diocese after diocese began to observe the Feast of the Sacred Heart. Petitions poured into Rome and Pope Clement XIII accorded the feast to Poland in 1765. The devotion to the Sacred Heart kept spreading. By a decree of August 23, 1856, Pope Pius IX extended the feast to the universal Church, and in 1875 he encouraged all the faithful to consecrate themselves to the Sacred Heart of Jesus. Pope Leo XIII consecrated the whole human race to the Sacred Heart in 1899. St. Margaret Mary was canonized on May 13, 1920.*

The spirituality of the Sacred Heart devotion that grew and spread during this period of history remains strong to the present day, and has been encouraged by all recent popes of the Church.

New religious orders developed during this period too, such as the Congregation of the Most Holy Redeemer, founded by St. Alphonsus Liguori. He was devoted to the Mother of God and to giving missions and administering the sacrament of penance. When his body was exhumed, the brown scapular of Our Lady of Mt. Carmel, which was upon him at burial, was found incorrupt.

St. John Baptiste de La Salle (1651-1719) devoted much time to a free school in Rheims for poor children. He helped many teachers and eventually founded the Brothers of the Christian Schools.

St. Louis Marie Grignon de Montfort (1673-1716) lived during this period and developed outstanding devotion to the Virgin Mary. His writings have been considered an authority and guide to true devotion to the Virgin Mary to the present time. Indeed, God used this saint to usher in the Age of Mary, in which we live. Pope Pius IX declared that devotion to Mary, according to St. Louis de Montfort, is the best and most acceptable form of devotion to our Lady.

---

*A detailed life of St. Margaret Mary Alacoque of Paray le Monial can be found in the book *Saints & Heroes Speak* (OSV Press) by the author of this catechism.

The Montfort fathers are followers of this saint's manner of life in Christ. His book, *True Devotion*, remained hidden for over 125 years. The saint had predicted such a fate for it, because the forces of evil did not want it publicized. Louis de Montfort* was beatified by Pope Leo XIII on January 22, 1888. He was canonized by Pope Pius XII on July 20, 1947.

Summary

The spirit of liberalism (a vague term with different meanings from century to century and area to area) continues to the present day. It respects no authority and holds that man has no responsibility except to satisfy every human desire. Man's mind is greater than any other power, and God himself is ignored. These false doctrines arose from the Renaissance and the Protestant Revolt, were developed in the seventeenth century, and matured in a "reign of terror" in the eighteenth century. They not only crippled the Church for a time, but country after country found itself plunged in disorder and without effective government.

The deism of old, which held that God made the world and then left it to itself, returned in modern times under a theory known as "God is dead." Then too, "process theologians" have held to "ongoing revelation," without regard to the unchangeable truth which is God. In our own times, the same false thinking attempts to implant itself in the souls of man and in the minds of youth, claiming there is no such thing as objective truth or absolutes in morality. "Pluralisms" in theology are promoted which reject the authority of the pope, the magisterium (teaching Church), and the constant, irreformable doctrines of the Catholic Church. Thus we see that dangerous modern tendencies have their roots in errors centuries old.

The French Revolution shows the total confusion, chaos, and disbelief that can result when men seek unbridled freedom. They end by destroying all freedom if they succeed in implementing their false doctrines, such as those represented by the Enlightenment, Rationalism, private interpretation, and Josephinism and Gallicanism.

At the time of the Protestant Revolt, arguments were made that the clergy be free to marry. Four hundred and fifty years later, after Vatican II, identical arguments were brought up by some Catholics.

The period we have just studied attempted to make the will of the people superior in authority to that of Christ and his Church. The study of history can serve us in handling modern problems, lest we make the same mistakes.

Questions for Discussion

1. Explain how the principle of private interpretation, if taken seriously, leads to each man becoming his own church or developing his own religion.

---

*A detailed life of St. Louis de Montfort is part of the book *Saints & Heroes Speak* by the author of this catechism (OSV Press).

2. What was the movement known as the Enlightenment? Was it a just name?
3. What was the reason for the Thirty Years' War?
4. What was the Treaty of Wesphalia and what were its consequences?
5. What effect did the spirit of the Enlightenment and Rationalism have on Catholic rulers?
6. Explain, in brief, what Freemasons stand for.
7. What led to the temporary suppression of the Jesuits?
8. What did Gallicanism and Josephinism represent?
9. Why was France a choice battleground for a revolt of the people?
10. How did the Church suffer from too close an identification with the state in the minds of people?
11. What was the "Civil Constitution of the Clergy" and how did the pope respond?
12. Explain the position of King Louis XVI and his queen and how they were mistreated.
13. Explain what was attempted in the French Revolution, with the death of Louis and Antoinette.
14. How did the French Revolution affect the rulers of other countries in Europe?
15. How did Napoleon Bonaparte become the new ruler in France?
16. How did Napoleon react to the Catholic faith of his people?
17. In brief, explain how, during these years of turmoil and its effects on the Church, Catholic love and devotion spread from France throughout the world to the present day.
18. Name some of the false doctrines which developed during this period which contradicted the true teachings of the Church.

Chapter 15
The Catholic Church in the Nineteenth and Twentieth Centuries

1. How did Pope Pius VII and Napoleon get along together?

Pope Pius VII (1800–1823) was invited to come to Paris to crown Napoleon emperor of France in 1804. While advised not to go, the pope felt it could help the Church. The pope was well received as he traveled through France. Napoleon, however, received him coolly, and placed the crown on his own head after the pope had blessed it, after taking the crown out of the pope's hands. During his entire stay in France, Napoleon was discourteous to this chief Vicar of Christ on earth.

Napoleon, during his entire reign, attempted to force Pope Pius VII to obey his will. In 1809 Napoleon took possession of the Papal States and the pope was brought to France as a prisoner. The pope was kept from all communications from the outside world. He was not even permitted his breviary for the official daily prayers of the Church.

Napoleon had ambitions to rule the world. In the spring of 1805, Austria, Russia, and Sweden joined England against France. By 1808, Napoleon's Grand Army was the most powerful in Europe. It had annihilated the armies of Austria and Prussia, defeated the Russians, and forced the Hapsburg Holy Roman emperor, Francis II, to give up his title, held by the Hapsburg family since the fifteenth century. Napoleon's armies, having imprisoned the pope, occupied Portugal and brought all of Europe east of Spain under control.

Spain offered resistance but was weak. The city of Zaragoza put up a heroic fight against the French, as its leader dedicated his cause to the Mother of God in the chapel of the Pillar Virgin. This one city, alone, weakened French troops and morale, even though the Zaragozans finally lost the battle.

In 1808 the British landed in Portugal and, due to the weakened conditions of the French, caused by the Spaniards, succeeded in driving the French out of Portugal. Although the Spaniards had been despised throughout Europe for being weak, yet, due to them, Napoleon's power in Europe began to weaken. Still, Napoleon looked to Russia. His troops marched toward Russia thinking they would have an easy victory. On the snowy fields of Russia, Napoleon's immense army, estimated to be as many as 1 million, was reduced to hardly 50,000 men. Without success, Napoleon tried to build up his Grand Army again.

The Battle of Nations took place at Leipzig in October 1813. The armies of Austria, Russia, and Prussia defeated the French troops, and on March 31, 1814, the Allies captured Paris. Napoleon was sent into exile on the island of Elba.

Napoleon escaped from Elba and came back to France to rally an army around him, as men forgot the defeats and remembered only the glory. A great battle was fought at Waterloo in Belgium and the power of Napoleon was broken forever. He was taken prisoner and sent to the island of St. Helena in the South Atlantic, where he died.

In 1814 Pope Pius VII returned to Rome.

2. Relate the Pope's return to the Eternal City and the tradition of the confidence of Popes in Mary as Help of Christians in the Church's battles with worldly powers.

The treaty of peace, signed at Vienna in 1815, ended the War of Nations in Europe with Napoleon. The Papal States were given back to the pope.

While God respects man's free will, however badly he uses it, yet a close study of history reveals that Jesus Christ is Lord and King, and God is ultimately the author of all history. We recall how in 1571 a huge Turkish armada had set sail to capture the Eternal City and that Pope St. Pius V called upon every Catholic to invoke the aid of the Mother of God under her title Help of Christians. An insignificant Christian fleet was victorious, saving Christendom on that day of October 7, 1571, and the pope proclaimed a new feast in honor of Our Lady of the Most Holy Rosary, as he asked Catholics to storm heaven unceasingly with rosaries.

In 1683 the Arabs tried again with an army of 200,000 Turks, facing an army of 30,000 Christians whom they besieged in Vienna. Pope Innocent XI called upon Catholics to take the cause to our Lady Help of Christians, reciting her rosary. The Battle of Vienna began on the birthday of our Lady, September 8, and the Turkish army was crushed by the small Christian fleet on the Feast of the Holy Name of Mary. The Turkish fleet never again was a threat to Christendom.

Over a century later, in 1800, the French, under Napoleon, succeeded in doing what the Turks had failed to accomplish. Rome, the Eternal City, fell. Fifty venerated churches in Rome were burned and Pope Pius VI was imprisoned in France, where he died (as already noted). The pope died from ill treatment. The forces of atheism seemed to be triumphant. It was thought, "God is dead . . .

the Pope is dead." When the new pope, Pius VII, was elected, anti-Catholic newspapers said: "Not Pius VII but Pius the last!"

As noted, in 1809 Bonaparte again seized the Pope, dragged him to a prison in France, and made most of Europe his subjects. Faced with this, Pope Pius VII, according to tradition, made a vow to our Lady. If she would restore freedom to the Church, he would honor her with a new feast. The Pope succeeded in smuggling a message to the world's bishops to ask Catholics to pray to Our Lady Help of Christians for deliverance.

We have seen how Napoleon, at the head of an army of 1 million men, set out to conquer the world's largest country. By spring, most of his men were dead and Napoleon was no longer emperor. On the same day that Napoleon signed his abdication, Pope Pius VII, who had no armies, made his triumphal reentry into the Eternal City, Rome. He had spent five terrible years in prison. On that very day, May 24, 1814, remaining true to his vow to God's Mother, the pope proclaimed the Feast of Mary Help of Christians as his first official act.

3. Did the Church continue to work to show men how to preserve true liberty?

Yes. In the first part of the nineteenth century the Church worked hard to defend her rights against the new governments in Europe. The Church is a true friend of democracy because she has always preached that before God there is neither bond men nor free, rich nor poor. God respects all persons, and we cannot love God unless we love our neighbors as ourselves. We cannot recognize God as Father if we do not recognize one another as brothers.

Still, in the minds of people, the Church had become closely associated with the kings of the past. Therefore many looked upon the Church as the enemy of liberty. Many preached a "separation of Church and state," but meant that the state should be supreme over the Church. These men, called Liberalists, were suspicious of the Church, which was international, and held that man is a law unto himself and there is no divine authority.

When Pope Gregory XVI (1831–1846) became the Vicar of Christ in 1831, he worked hard to educate men on the true position of the Church. He opposed rebellion as a means of settling political questions. He encouraged the study of philosophy and theology to develop Catholic scholars throughout the world to bring to the attention of the world the true Catholic position on social questions.

4. How did the Church revive in France?

Some Catholic laymen came to the support of the Church, to defend her against the government. One of these was a brilliant newspaperman, who, though he made some mistakes, was humble and corrected his position when they were pointed out by the Pope. He then became a Dominican priest—Père Lacordaire, who became a great preacher. All Paris longed to crowd the great Cathedral of Notre Dame to listen to his sermons.

There was also Frederick Ozanam. Formerly interested in law, and besieged with doubts, he came, when only 20 years of age, with seven other young men to found the Society of St. Vincent de Paul. Interested in Catholic education, he worked to develop Catholic teachers so that children and youth would not lose the faith.

5. Tell about the Catholic revival in Germany.

The Romantic movement in literature, which turned to the study of the history of Germany during the Middle Ages, helped the Catholic cause in Germany. It was learned how the Church had helped the lives of people during the ages of faith.

There were also men like Clement Hofbauer, who became the great Apostle of Vienna; he died in 1820 and was canonized in 1909 by Pope Pius X. The government gave the Church much trouble regarding mixed marriages, until Joseph von Görres, a professor in the University of Munich, wrote a book called *Athanasius*. It became a best seller and the government was obliged to give victory to the Church. A prominent lawyer, Wilhelm Emmanuel von Ketteler, read the book and gave up his office to study for the priesthood. Eventually he became the bishop of Mainz and a great preacher and defender of the Church in Germany.

6. How were Catholics in Ireland given freedom?

A law that was passed in 1801 united Ireland closely to England and made it possible for the Irish people to be in Parliament, but not if they remained sincere Catholics. Members of Parliament had to take an oath which denied the doctrine on the Eucharist, viz., transubstantiation of bread and wine into the Lord's Body and Blood at the Consecration of the Mass—as well as the sacrifice of the Mass itself and the intercessory prayers of the saints.

Daniel O'Connell was the outstanding leader for the cause of Catholic emancipation. The French Revolution had closed the college at Douai, where Daniel was a student, and as a result he made a vow to become a champion for law and order. In 1827 O'Connell was elected a member of Parliament for County Clare, after he had been active in an origanization called the Catholic Association, which existed to win equal rights for Catholics in Ireland and England. The British government knew that the popular O'Connell would not take the oath against his faith, and they feared a rebellion among Catholics would break out in the two countries.

The king signed the Act of Catholic Emancipation on April 13, 1829, which permitted Catholics to sit in Parliament without taking the oath that was contrary to Catholic faith. O'Connell became one of the most popular orators of his time, entering the House of Commons in 1830. He fought for freedom for Ireland until his death.

7. Relate the Catholic Revival in England.

Since the Protestant Revolt, the freedom of Catholics in England had been restricted. The Act of Catholic Emancipation permitted Catholics in England to worship publicly. In 1835 Fr. Gentili (from Italy), a member of the Fathers of the Institute of Charity, arrived in England. This group introduced the Forty Hours' Devotion to Our Lord in the Most Blessed Sacrament, devotions to God's Mother through the month of May, and other Catholic devotions once popular among Catholics in England. Passionists and Redemptorists came from Ireland, France, and Belgium. The 1846 the Irish famine brought many Irish Catholics to England. Non-Catholics were edified at their piety. Interest in the Catholic faith began to develop in England, which had been forced out of the Church under Henry VIII.

The Church of England (Anglicanism) had been losing its hold on the people. Converts began to come into the Catholic Church from the Church of England. Dr. Wiseman, president of the English College at Rome, and who later became Cardinal Wiseman, preached in London and won many converts. Cardinal Henry Edward Manning was a convert in England. As archbishop of Westminster, he wrote the book *The Eternal Priesthood*, still considered a classic.

The Oxford Movement (1833–1845) represented growing interest in the Catholic Church in the Protestant University of Oxford. The most famous convert in the Oxford Movement was John Henry Newman, who had been considered the most famous preacher among the Protestants in England. He entered the Catholic Church in 1845, then studied for the priesthood in Rome, and returned to England to establish the English Congregation of the Oratory of St. Philip Neri. In 1879 Pope Leo XIII made this world-famous convert a cardinal of the Church. The writings of John Henry Cardinal Newman are considered some of the best explanations of the Catholic faith, and most valuable in answering problems and questions of faith in the latter part of this twentieth century.*

8. What happened during the early nineteenth century that greatly changed the manner of people's lives?

The Industrial Revolution caused people to leave the farms and villages and to move near the factories in the big cities. This brought many changes in family life, as its members were not so closely united, no longer living and working together on the farms. Members of all ages went off to the factories to work, and even children worked long hours away from home.

The Industrial Revolution began around 1769, when James Watt (in England) invented the steam engine. This aided rapid transportation, and large quantities of factory-made goods became available. While this had benefits, it

---

*The "life" of John Henry Cardinal Newman (as well as St. Philip Neri) can be found in *Saints & Heroes Speak* (OSV Press), by the author of this Church history.

also created social problems: individual, hand-made items became less important while men became almost parts of machines, working in drab factories for long hours.

It was mostly in England and America that the inventions that spurred the Industrial Revolution occurred. Inventions like the spinning jenny, steamboat, railroad engine, electric motors and generators, telegraph, reaper—all had a profound effect on the lives of people. "Capitalism" developed, by which a few with money could control the work and lives of many. Unequal distribution of wealth and property became more and more evident.

The theory of "laissez-faire" (leave alone) developed, which caused governments not to interfere in the management of capitalists. This led to many abuses: long working hours for children and teenagers, poor pay, inadequate working conditions, etc. Something began to be done about the abuses with the Factory Act, passed in England in 1833, which forbade the hiring of children under 9 years of age. Those from 9 to 13 could work no more than 48 hours a week, while teenagers could not work more than 69 hours a week.

In Ireland, the people suffered terribly as their grain was shipped to England under a landlord system, with the English government doing nothing to relieve the extreme hardship of the people whose stable crop, the potato, had repeatedly rotted in the fields.

9. What other developments began during the nineteenth century?

The spirit of laissez-faire capitalism led to much dissatisfaction among working people. They had little money to live on; wealth fell into the hands of a few rich capitalists; "liberal" ideas were espoused with little respect for authority. All this laid the groundwork for an economic theory of socialism which would have the government take over factories and businesses. Utopian ideals developed whereby life on this earth would be glorious if all men owned everything in common and no one had property of his own. Socialists set up communal farms, but most of them soon failed.

Later, socialists proposed that force be used to effect the goals of the peaceful communes. This was the beginning of communism, which we shall learn more about in a later chapter.

10. What was the Communist Manifesto?

The Communist Manifesto was published in 1848 by Karl Marx and Friedrich Engels, containing some of the most dangerous doctrines to freedom and belief in God in the history of the world. It played into the minds and hearts of working people who were dissatisfied with abuses of the day. It stated: "The history of all human societies up to the present time has been the history of the class struggle." It urged class struggle, and the overthrow of all in power by force. Religion is the "opium of the people," used by the powerful to keep others weak and ignorant. All law and religion would be done away with in the forceful overthrow by the "proletariat" (workers).

The false doctrines that had developed from the spirit of the Enlightenment, Rationalism, and revolutionary Liberalism, rejecting all authority and faith, and giving birth to the French Revolution, were to be born again in atheistic communism, with its bible the Communist Manifesto.

The Manifesto concludes: "The communists openly proclaim that the only way they can achieve their aims is by the violent destruction of the old order of society. The ruling classes may well tremble at the thought of a communist revolution! The proletarians have nothing to lose in the struggle apart from their chains. They have a whole new world to conquer. Workers of the world unite!"

11. What other abuse developed during the nineteenth century?

Imperialism. This involved European nations' getting economic and political control over non-Western nations. Such nations as Great Britain, France, Germany, and Italy spread their spirit of imperialism, with Liberal ideas, to Asia, Africa, and the Middle East. Instead of spreading Christianity, the spirit of nationalism fostered the desire for cheap raw materials.

12. Which saint flowered in France in the nineteenth century and is still considered the greatest modern saint?

St. Thérèse of Lisieux, also called the Little Flower, developed a spiritual, childlike form of spirituality, and her autobiography, which she wrote "under obedience," has offered inspiration to millions the world over, until and including the present day. She was born January 2, 1873, at Alencon in France and entered the Carmelite Order of nuns when very young. She made a special trip to Rome with her saintly father, Louis Martin, and sought special permission from Pope Leo XIII to enter Carmel at the age of 15, although her superiors wanted her to wait until she was 21.

She was miraculously cured, according to accounts of her life, through the intercession of our Lady. As a Carmelite nun, the Little Flower practiced great penance and mortification. She had a keen interest in the spirituality and work of priests and the missions.

Allowed to enter Carmel at 15, she died only nine years later, of tuberculosis. Her "little way" of spiritual childhood, described in her autobiography, is still a best international seller. She died September 30, 1897, promising to shower roses upon the earth.

Thérèse of the Child Jesus was canonized in 1925 and has been declared patron of the foreign missions.*

---

*A detailed life of St. Therese will be found in Saints & Heroes Speak (OSV Press) by the author of this book.

13. Who was a great priest-saint in France in the nineteenth century?

St. John Vianney, the universal patron of parish priests, was born in Dardilly in 1786. During the Reign of Terror of the French Revolution, priests were forbidden to practice their priesthood. To observe Sunday services was against the law and all religious feast days had been abolished. John Vianney's earliest recollection of participation in the sacrifice of the Mass consisted of his family and neighbors' gathering in secret in a barn outside the village for this holiest of mysteries.

After the revolution, Napoleon permitted greater religious freedom and the Mass could be offered publicly. The father of the future patron of parish priests Matthew Vianney, was a farmer and taught young John to love our Lord in the Sacrament of the Tabernacle. It was Matthew's practice, while on his way to his farm labors, to stop for a visit at the parish church to pray to Our Lord Jesus Christ in the Blessed Sacrament.

Young John Vianney became a teacher to his fellow youth when still very young. His great devotion to our Lady prompted him to place a statue of God's Mother in a hollow in the trunk of a tree, as he and his sister watched over the grazing cows and sheep. There they held religious services, praying the rosary and singing hymns. This attracted neighboring children, some of whom knew nothing about their Catholic faith after years of persecution. The future priest instructed them about God and his Blessed Mother. He built an altar, and the children conducted religious processions through the fields.

Even at the age of 7 or 8, John Vianney felt a call to the priesthood. The revolution had disturbed education generally and the seminaries in particular, and so, with much difficulty, John Vianney (with the help of a good pastor) was ordained. The young priest was sent to Ars, the most undesirable parish in the diocese. The people at Ars had been without a priest for some time, had little instruction, and most did not practice their faith. The villagers were used to much drinking and carousing.

Arriving at Ars in 1821, John Vianney (the Curé d'Ars) began to preach simple sermons on the basics of the Catholic faith, going directly to the people and inviting and exhorting them to practice their faith.

At first the people did not receive the new priest well and he was an object of ridicule. This Curé d'Ars persevered and finally converted the entire village. He practiced great mortification and lived in extreme poverty. He inflicted penances upon his body in reparation and for the conversion of sinners. His devotion to the Mother of God intensified with the years, and eventually his parish was consecrated to the Immaculate Heart of God's Mother. The name of every man, woman, and child of Ars was inscribed on a wooden heart that hung from the neck of the Virgin Mother statue.

God gave great gifts to St. John Vianney, including the ability to "read souls." People began to come to this priest for confession from all over the world. The average day saw him in the confessional for at least 12 and sometimes 16 hours. He also gathered orphan children and formed a home and school for them.

For thirty-eight years this priest labored at Ars, getting little sleep and eating little food. His great sanctity became known the world over in his own lifetime. He died on August 4, 1859, and was canonized by Pope Pius XI on Pentecost Sunday, 1925.*

14. Did the nineteenth century produce any great saint concerned with the catholic education and formation of youth?

Yes. St. John Bosco, the founder of the Salesians, is the patron of Catholic youth, especially boys. John Bosco was born August 15, 1815. When he was 9 years old, his biography relates, God revealed to him how to win boys away from sin and to virtue. It was to be done not by force, but by showing them the evil of sin and the beauty of religious virtue. The Blessed Mother also revealed (the story of his life continues) that she would help him. His mother understood the message as an indication her son would become a priest.

He was ordained in 1841, and his desire to help poor boys grew ever stronger. He wanted to build a large school where boys would learn all kinds of trades to get ready for life. His brother priests shook their heads at his supposed madness.

Turin, Italy, was the place where Fr. John Bosco began his great work, but with much difficulty. Turin was a manufacturing city, and many people suffered from poverty and unemployment. Many poor boys roamed the streets. Fr. John Bosco gathered hundreds of them around himself.

This young priest was hated for his work, and some even attempted to take his life. However, the boys loved their priest and he developed them into strong Catholic men. As other priests saw the success of his work, they joined him, and he developed a religious society under the patronage of St. Francis de Sales, which is therefore known as the Salesians.

Fr. John Bosco had great devotion to Our Lady Help of Christians and built a magnificent church to her honor, laying the cornerstone in 1865. Pope Pius IX helped him, and that magnificent church can be visited to the present day.

This nineteenth-century saint had the greatest loyalty to the pope. On his deathbed he reaffirmed this loyalty, calling upon his followers to be ever "ready to accept the decisions of the Pope, not only in matters of Faith and discipline, but even in those things about which we have a right to disagree." He added: "May they follow the point of view of the Pope, even though he has expressed it only privately."

The Salesian schools of trade spread to every part of the world and their priests

---

*The life of St. John Vianney (the Cure of Ars) is found in more detail in the book *Saints & Heroes Speak* (OSV Press) by the author of this catechism.

do all kinds of pastoral work. Fr. John Bosco died January 31, 1888, and was canonized on Easter Sunday, 1934.*

15. Did God manifest his concern for mankind in any special, supernatural way in the nineteenth century?

God sent his Blessed Mother to Lourdes, France, in 1858, where she appeared to a young girl by the name of Bernadette Soubirous (according to accounts which have survived Church investigations). The Lady at first did not give her name, but later, on March 25, the Feast of the Annunciation, said: "I am the Immaculate Conception." This astounded priests and theologians, for the girl did not understand what the beautiful Lady meant. Four years earlier, on December 8, 1854, Pope Pius IX had solemnly defined it as a dogma of Catholic faith: our Blessed Lady was preserved free from original sin from the moment of her conception. The doctrine that Mary was always free from all sin is called the dogma of the Immaculate Conception.

The Lady asked Bernadette to come to the grotto every day for fifteen days. This is interpreted as in honor of the fifteen mysteries of the rosary. The Lady, on one of her visits, had Bernadette scratch the ground, from which water immediately began to gush forth. It was soon discovered that miracles began to happen when people drank the water and washed themselves with it. Some were cured of every kind of ailment. The Church finally judged that the Mother of God was truly appearing to this young girl.

Bernadette became a nun in 1866. For thirteen years she led a life of bodily suffering, as our Lady said that she would be happy, not in this world, but in the next. Pope Pius XI canonized Bernadette on December 8, 1933.†

Lourdes is known internationally and people come by the millions each year to Lourdes, France, to venerate the Mother of God and to pray as they adore their eucharistic Savior. Scientists are baffled by miraculous cures that have taken place at Lourdes.

16. What pope had a long reign in the nineteenth century?

Pope Pius IX became pope in 1846 and ruled the Church until 1878, which was the longest reign of any pope since the first pope, St. Peter. He was only 54 years of age when, as Cardinal Mastai-Ferretti, he was elected and crowned. This pope believed in giving the common people more liberty, and so he immediately placed laymen in all the important positions of the Papal States, so that the government would be more democratic. Henceforth a parliament would conduct the affairs of Rome.

---

*The life of St. John Bosco may be found in greater detail in *Saints & Heroes Speak* (OSV Press).

†A detailed life of St. Bernadette is to be found in *Saints & Heroes Speak* (OSV Press).

There were eight separate governments on the Italian peninsula at this time and a desire was developing for all of Italy to be united. Two Italian provinces, Lombardy and Venice, were under the control of Austria. Tuscany, Parma, and Modena were ruled by members of the Austrian royal family. In the south, a king ruled Naples and Sicily, who was not accepted by the people because he was supported by the Austrian army.

Despite many controversial positions among Italians, most agreed that disunity was unbearable and so everywhere there was a movement for unity. Some wanted the king of Sardinia to become ruler of all Italy.

In 1848 a revolution erupted in the Papal States, led by Mazzini, who desired to set up a republic in Rome. The pope's prime minister was murdered and the pope was enclosed in the Quirinal Palace. The Spanish ambassador helped the pope flee to Gaeta in the kingdom of Naples. In Rome, the churches were plundered, priests were killed, and there was a declaration that henceforth the treasures of the Church would belong to the people. On Easter Sunday, Mass was celebrated in St. Peter's Basilica by a disloyal priest, and Mazzini placed himself on the pope's throne.

When Pope Pius IX begged for help from Catholic powers in Europe, the Austrians and the French came to his aid, and Mazzini and his followers fled to England. When the pope returned to Rome, Austria protected the territory of the pope outside the city and the French protected the pope within the city.

17. How did the Papal States end under Pope Pius IX?

Secret societies in Italy and France plotted the overthrow of the Papal States. The king of Sardinia, through an alliance with France, forced the Austrians to withdraw from northern Italy. Napoleon III was at war with Germany in 1870 and was compelled to recall his troops from Rome.

Victor Emmanuel of Sardinia assumed the title King of Italy and the general of his army, Guiseppe Garibalid, laid siege to Rome on September 20, 1870. Pope Pius IX surrendered the city rather than have bloodshed. This ended the pope's governing of the Papal States.

All that the pope was able to keep was St. Peter's Basilica and Vatican Palace. Pope Pius IX would not accept these conditions, and until he died he remained, in protest, a voluntary prisoner in the Vatican.

A treaty of peace was not signed between the Italian government and Pope Pius XI until 1929.

18. With the temporal power of the pope crushed, how did his spiritual influence rise?

The pope was by no means occupied only with temporal problems concerning the Papal States. It was Pope Pius IX who, at the urging of bishops and laity the world over, defined the dogma of the Immaculate Conception on December 8, 1854. In the Marian Era he ushered in, the important role of God's Mother in the life of the Church would become even more evident during the next hundred years. Catholic devotion to Mary would be greatly increased.*

It was Pope Pius IX who in 1864 issued the Syllabus, a list of errors which consisted of eighty condemned propositions and was published with his encyclical *Quanta cura*. "Liberalists" were leading the world astray and confusing many Catholics' understanding of the true faith by presenting false teachings. The pope wanted Catholics to know clearly the difference between true faith and errors.†

In 1869 the bishops of the world assembled in the Bascilica of St. Peter's and the Vatican Council, which the pope had long planned, began. There were 698 bishops from around the world. Their first task was to define the Church's teaching on God and divine revelation. In an "Age of Enlightenment," it was shown that there is no contradiction between reason and revelation. True faith and right reason harmonize, for all truth comes from God.

It was Vatican Council I which in 1870 defined the dogma of the infallibility of the pope. The Catholic Church cannot err in matters of *faith or morals* when it speaks through the pope when he defines a dogma for the entire Catholic world. This position of the Catholic Church, which was always part of Catholic faith since the days of St. Peter and the first apostles, was now clearly spelled out in defined dogma. The pope is indeed the rock upon which Jesus built his Church and promised that the gates of hell would never prevail against it (Mt 16:16-19).

Vatican Council, even as it defined the spiritual authority of the Pope for the teaching Church (magisterium), was besieged by temporal powers, for at that very time Italian armies were marching on the gates of Rome. The council was interrupted and was not officially closed until the beginning of Vatican Council II in 1962.

While the temporal power of the pope was crushed in the takeover of the Papal States, his spiritual power and authoirty as supreme teacher of faith in the universal Church was more recognized and respected than ever before.

19. Did the Catholic Church expand on any newly settled continent in the nineteenth century?

Yes, on the island continent southeast of Asia, Australia. The first Catholics in the country were Irishmen under penal sentence (1795-1804). The first public Mass was offered May 15, 1803. Official organization of the Church dates from 1820, and only in March 1976 did Pope Paul VI sign a decree removing the continent from the Vatican body in charge of missions.

---

*For more information on the Marian Era, see *The Marian Catechism* (OSV Press) by the author of this *catechism of Church history*.

†The Syllabus of Pius IX was followed by the Syllabus of St. Pius X in 1907, again condemning errors of Modernism.

Today, of Australia's approximately 13 million people, about 3½ million are Catholic, or about 25 percent. (Catholics were among those who rushed to the gold mines after gold was discovered in various parts of Australia, and many remained in the country.)

The Catholic population later increased through immigration. The continent has a large Italian area and many other ethnic groups have Catholics among them. Mary Help of Christians is the patroness of Australia. As in other lands where Catholics explored and missionaries evangelized, Mary has had a major role. There is a St. Mary's cathedral in Perth and also in Armidale, New South Wales. The church at Ipswich was named St. Mary's. The name of the church at Camberwell is Our Lady of Victories.

This vast continent is as large as the continental United States and is the only continent occupied by one nation. It is the last one developed by Europeans. As for native peoples, Australia claims the Aborigines as comparative newcomers. A nomadic people, they migrated from Southeast Asia.

Australia is one of the oldest land masses in the world. Asians called it the Unknown Land long before any white man sighted it. It was explored by the Portuguese, Spanish, and the Dutch, who named it New Holland.

Greeks knew of this land mass during the second century A.D. when the mathematician Ptolemy drew a map of the known world at that time, he sketched in the known coasts of Asia, showed the Indian Ocean as an enormous lake, and placed a huge, unknown land north of it, called *Terra Incognita* (Unknown Land). Many did not believe in its existence.

The whole land seemed bleak when a Dutch explorer touched at northern Queensland in 1606. The land was considered not fit for colonizing. Botanists, however, showed interest, and in 1770 Captain James Cook anchored at Botany Bay, which was named for its botanical treasures. He returned eighteen years later and claimed Australia for Great Britain.

Another botanist, Sir John Banks, got the idea that Australia should be an island prison for the British Empire. This was accepted and convicts were sent to Australia. The prisoners were used to open the continent for colonization. On January 18, 1788, the first British fleet, with 1,030 passengers and crew, arrived at Botany Bay with 736 convicts and 200 women.

In 1818 Fr. John Joseph Therry saw a wagonload of convicts rumble through the streets of Cork. Twenty or thirty prisoners in irons were on their way to the docks, bound for Botany Bay and that faraway prison land 7,000 miles from home. The young priest, on the spur of the moment, ran into a nearby bookshop, bought a bundle of prayer books, and threw them into the cart, vowing to follow his countrymen to the ends of the earth to save their souls. That handful of books and Fr. Therry, who was the secretary to Bishop Murphy of Cork, represented early seeds of Catholicism in Australia.

Fr. Therry went to Australia at his own expense and worked among the convicts and their families for fifty years. He built the beautiful Cathedral of St.

Mary's in Sydney and is considered Australia's most famous pioneer priest and the forerunner to its Catholic social movement.

Other priests followed Fr. Therry, some becoming bishops and archbishops. The first cardinal from Australia was Fr. Patrick Francis Moran. Archbishop D. Mannix, who had been president of Maynooth University in Ireland, felt called to Australia, and there, as archbishop of Melbourne, he brought intellectual life to the Church on the continent. Bishop Ullathorne battled for prison and social reform in Australia.

Australia's Church heroine was Caroline Chisholm, who spent her life protecting and rehabilitating women who needed care. She fought for the rights of the children of convicts and paid for the education of many of them, and her piety and religious sense inspired them.

Australia in the nineteenth and twentieth centuries came far in its development from a penal colony. Devout Catholics of Australia claim our Lady had much to do with it. The convicts, who brought their rosaries with them, said them privately and publicly in community. They also had medals, pictures, and prayer cards of the heavenly Mother, who consoled them in their sorrows.

The Catholic children of the convicts grew and prospered in the large continent. They built churches and schools, naming many of them after Mary, the Mother of God and our Savior, Jesus Christ. Immigrants added to their number.

20. Summarize the reign of Pope Leo XIII (1878—1903).

Cardinal Pecci was an old man when he was elected and crowned Pope Leo XIII. People thought his reign would be short. Yet for twenty-five years he ruled the Church with great wisdom and is labeled by historians as among the greatest popes of its 2,000-year history.

Leo XIII was a pope of great intellect and spirituality. He was a great statesman, as evidenced by his settling of Church problems in Germany. The respect of nations for the Church grew tremendously under Pope Leo XIII, and even non-Catholic kings and emperors visited him.

This pope was chosen by God to guide the Church through a period of difficult changes in the world, as the style of people's lives was changed more and more by mechanical inventions, the development of factories, and growing problems for family life and the workingman. The common people suffered greatly under abuses and working conditions in the business of manufacturing. Socialists wanted governments to take over industry so that profits would not go to capitalists.

To help answer the world's questions developed by the problems of industry, Pope Leo wrote the encyclical *Rerum novarum* (On the Condition of Labor). This caused the study of social problems in the light of Christian principles to be taken seriously on all sides, and Pope Leo became known as a friend of the workingman. He spelled out the position of the state in relation to individual citizens. Writing encyclicals on social questions, he explained workers' rights and duties. He reminded employers of their obligations to the laws of social justice.

Pope Leo XIII encouraged the study of the philosophy and theology of St. Thomas Aquinas. He encouraged devotion to the Sacred Heart of Jesus and to the rosary. He urged parents to dedicate their families to the Holy Family.

Pope Leo XIII developed great Church interest in the missions. He defended the rights of the natives of colonies that were taken over by European nations.*

21. Summarize the reign of Pope St. Pius X.

Cardinal Giuseppe Melchiorre Sarto ascended the papal throne in 1903 as Pope Pius X. His principal aim was "to restore all things in Christ, in order that Christ may be all and in all." He sought to teach and defend Christian truth and law. This pope continued the spirit of the Marian Age by issuing a commemorative encyclical to celebrate the fiftieth anniversary of the proclamation of the dogma of the Immaculate Conception.

Pius X is called the Pope of the Catechism and the Pope of the Holy Eucharist. It was this pope who called for the religious education of youth under the Confraternity of Christian Doctrine. Later canonized by the Church, he called all the laity to Catholic Action, whereby ordinary baptized and confirmed Catholics would share in the work of the hierarchy by working for the conversion of souls to Christ. The work of the Church was to be a total work of all its members and not just of the hierarchy, priests, and religious.

It was Pope Pius X who on December 20, 1905, recommended the *frequent* reception of Communion. In another decree (*Quam singulari*), of August 8, 1910, he called for the early reception of the sacraments of penance and Communion by children. Children from the age of reason (about 7) should be permitted to receive these sacraments.

Following the lead of Pope Leo XIII in promoting the study of Scholastic philosophy, Pope St. Pius X also promoted it. St. Pius X also had to deal with heretical tendencies, as did Pius IX. On September 7, 1907, Pope St. Pius X, in his encyclical *Pascendi gregis*, condemned the false teachings known as Modernism which he called a "synthesis of all heresies." This movement had begun at the time of the Protestant Revolt and developed to a point at the beginning of the twentieth century that it was an agression against true religion.

Modernism, whose dangers still threaten the Church and which surfaced again after Vatican Council II (1962–1965), teaches that the Christ of history and the Christ of faith are different. Jesus Christ, it says, did not personally found the Church or sacraments; it claims these were "historical" developments. Advocates of Modernism seek freedom from religious authority and freedom of conscience, independent of the teaching authority (magisterium) of the Church. Modernism assumes that everything "modern" is more perfect than

*See *Addendum* for more detailed summary of Pontificate of Pope Leo XIII.

what had been taught and believed before it. It denies dogma, the power of the sacraments, and the authority of sacred scripture.

Pope Pius X (1903–1914) in September 1910 published the *Oath against Modernism* and required that all priests take the oath.

This same pope drew up a new collection of Church law, the *Code of Canon Law*, and extended interest in scriptural studies, establishing the Biblical Institute.

The outbreak of World War I is believed to have hastened his death, for he died August 20, 1914. He was canonized May 29, 1954.

The next pope, Benedict XV (1914–1922), wrote twelve encyclicals, dedicating three of them to the cause of peace. He avoided taking sides in the war and was therefore suspected by both sides. This pope was able to have the "Roman Question" negotiated when he arranged a meeting of Benito Mussolini and the papal secretary of state, and this marked the first step to the final settlement of 1929. In spite of suspicions, this pope did more than all other agencies to break down the barrier of hate separating the nations.

22. Summarize the reign of Pope Pius XI.

Pope Pius XI (1922–1939) was elected to the papacy on February 6, 1922, with the aim of establishing the reign and peace of Christ in society. He canonized the Jesuit Martyrs of North America. He instituted the Feast of Christ the King in 1925 to emphasize that Christ is King of Nations as well as King of Individuals and Families.

Although the World War I peace had been declared, hatred and distrust among nations still reigned. The map of Europe had been changed. A revolution in Russia had destroyed the empire of the czars and this prepared the way for the coming of communism. Relations of the Church with Mussolini's government in Italy deteriorated after 1931, when the freedom and activities of the Church were curbed. Relations also deteriorated with Germany from 1933 on, which resulted in the condemnation of the Nazis in the encyclical *Mit Brenneder Sorge* (March 1937). This pope was powerless to prevent the civil war which erupted in Spain in July 1936. There was persecution and repression of the Church by the Calles regime in Mexico and, of course, persecution of the Church in Russia. Priests and bishops in Mexico, under Communist influence, were put to death or put in prison. In 1926 there were only 4,000 priests to serve 15 million Catholics. In 1935 only 300 priests could function in all of Mexico.

Pope Pius XI settled the Roman Question, after two and one-half years of negotiations with the Italian government. The Lateran Agreement of 1929 gave the "state" of Vatican City independent status and considered Catholicism the official religion of Italy, giving the Church pastoral and educational freedom. The state recognized Catholic marriages.

The state of Vatican City became the world's smallest sovereign state, with less than 109 acres within the city of Rome. The pope would henceforth be considered the ruler of this independent territory, belonging to no foreign nation.

23. Summarize the reign of Pope Pius XII.

Eugenio Maria Giovanni Pacelli was elected to the papacy March 2, 1939, and took the name Pope Pius XII (1939–1958). He canonized the first United States citizen-saint, Francis Xavier Cabrini (Mother Cabrini) in 1946.

Before World War II started, Pope Pius XII attempted (without success) to get the contending nations to settle their differences without war. These nations included Germany, Poland, France, and Italy. He spoke out against the horrors of war and offered his services to mediate the widening conflict. He organized relief work for the victims of World War II. He obtained "open" status for the city of Rome during the war. After World War II he endorsed the principle and goal of the United Nations.

Pope Pius XII has often been called the Pope of Peace, and also the Pope of Fatima (where God's Mother appeared, appealing for peace, as Our Lady of Peace). Pius XII was an effective opponent of communism. In 1949 he decreed the penalty of excommunication for all Catholics who held formal and willing allegiance to the Communist Party and its policies.

The interest of Pope Pius XII in Fatima and his great Marian devotion are seen in a review of some of his activities. On October 31, 1942, Pius XII consecrated the world to the Immaculate Heart of Mary. On May 4, 1944, he instituted the Feast of the Immaculate Heart of Mary, the occasion being the twenty-fifth anniversary of the Fatima apparitions. On May 13, 1946, he crowned the image of Fatima through a papal legate and declared our Lady "Queen of the World." One month later, on June 13, 1946, he issued an encyclical explicitly referring to the message of Fatima.

In 1950, Pope Pius XII defined as a dogma of faith the Assumption, which states that the Mother of Jesus Christ was taken into heaven bodily by the power of God. This doctrine had always been believed by the Church, and celebrated as a feast for over 1,500 years, but now it was formally defined. On October 13, 1951, the pope closed the Holy Year for all the world at Fatima, thus demonstrating Fatima's worldwide significance.

On July 7, 1952, Pope Pius XII consecrated the Russian people to the Immaculate Heart of Mary, and on October 11, 1954, in his encyclical To the Queen of the World, Pius referred to her miraculous image at Fatima. He declared 1954 a Marian Year. On November 12, 1954, he elevated the church in Cova Da Iria, where our Lady appeared near Fatima, Portugal, to the status of a basilica. On October 13, 1956, through a papal legate, Eugene Cardinal Tisserant, dean of the Sacred College, Pope Pius XII blessed and dedicated the International Center of the Blue Army of Our Lady of Fatima, which is located behind the basilica and is dedicated to furthering the heavenly message of our Lady.

Pius XII prepared the way for the spiritual renewal introduced by his successor, John XXIII. It was Pius XII who wrote the magnificent encyclicals *On the Divine Liturgy* and *The Mystical Body of Christ*. He instituted the feasts of Mary as Queen and of St. Joseph the Worker, as well as presented the Church's teachings on devotion to the Sacred Heart of Jesus.

The first half of the twentieth century, with two world wars, offers a sad spectacle of humanity's suffering as the consequence of sin. What is especially sad is the force of destruction that occasioned the ending of the war, the dropping of atomic bombs. On August 6, 1945, an atomic bomb was dropped on Hiroshima in Japan, killing more than 100,000 people. A few days later, on August 9, the "most Catholic" city in Japan, Nagasaki, met the same horrible result. Theologians still discuss the morality of using such destructive weapons.

Summary

A review of the nineteenth century indicates that the Catholic Church is able to endure every human problem, but in no way does this lighten the burden of the cross, first laid upon the physical Christ 1,900 years ago. The Mystical Body of Christ, which is the Church, lives in the modern world, and just as Christ was mocked, spat upon, and finally crucified—but rose from the dead—the true Church of Jesus Christ would always be treated in the same manner.

The world—in transition intellectually and culturally and therefore spiritually—has been blessed in the nineteenth and the twentieth centuries with very holy popes.

We have seen how a pope had to deal with the aftermath of the French Revolution. We have seen indications that, while often it seems the Church is fighting the forces of evil without special spiritual intervention, God is nevertheless the author of salvation history and, though working invisibly, makes his presence and his power almost visible at times. We have seen God introduce his Blessed Mother, the Mother of the Church, more directly into the currents of history—something to be continued into the twentieth century.

We have seen the devotion of popes to Mary Help of Christians, and how this devotion to God's Mother blossomed in the life of St. John Bosco. We have seen how Our Lady of Lourdes intervenes in the very country that gave birth to the French Revolution, and there, to the present day, continues to baffle modern science with miracles. In a future chapter we shall see how Our Lady of Fatima, in Portugal, will warn the world, flirting with communism, that it is inviting the annihilation of nations.

During the nineteenth century the evils of communism were born, even if conceived years earlier. We shall see that the twentieth century will witness communism's growth, destroying religious freedom and overtaking one nation after another as materialism and atheism reign in the hearts of more and more men and women.

Questions for Discussion

1. Summarize Napoleon's reaction to the Church.
2. What significance do you see, in the light of faith, to the final outcome of Napoleon's efforts and the return of the pope to Rome?
3. What was the unfortunate disadvantage in the Church's having gained the image of being closely associated with the state and various governments?
4. Was the Church, in fact, on the side of personal freedom for individuals?
5. Who helped the Church revive in France?
6. Summarize the struggle for the freedom of Catholics in Ireland.
7. What great convert came to the Catholic Church in the Oxford Movement? Explain the Oxford Movement.
8. What happened in the early nineteenth century that changed society greatly? Explain how it did this.
9. What document was published in 1848 which sowed ideas which still threaten the world? What concepts does that document present?
10. What abuse spread in the nineteenth century and involved European countries' seeking control over other nations? Explain it.
11. Summarize the life of the great priest of France, who lived in the nineteenth century and is now venerated as the patron of all parish priests.
12. Summarize the life of St. John Bosco.
13. What significance does Lourdes have for the modern world?
14. What were the chief events in the history of the Church under Pope Pius IX?
15. Did the prestige of the Church and its influence suffer greatly with the end of the Papal States? Explain.
16. Which pope ascended the papacy as an old man but continued to rule the Church with great effectiveness for the next twenty-five years? What areas of Church life did he especially affect with great success?
17. Summarize the life of the Little Flower.
18. What new continent was settled in the nineteenth and twentieth centuries? How did Catholic settlements start and for what devotion were Catholics in that vast continent noted?
19. What were the outstanding features of the reign of Pope St. Pius X?
20. What was the "Roman Question" and how was it settled?
21. Explain the meaning of Modernism as condemned by Pope St. Pius X.
22. What pope reigned during World War I? Why were both sides suspicious of this pope? What did this pope issue to break down suspicions and barriers of hatred?
23. What happened to the Church in Mexico during the early part of the twentieth century?
24. Summarize the reign of Pope Pius XII, who was elected in 1939.
25. What devotion to the Mother of God particularly attracted Pope Pius XII? Explain some of his major actions in this regard.

Chapter 16
The Catholic Church in the United States of America

1. Did Catholics find freedom of religion in the English colonies in the early years of settlement?

No. The English colonies were founded at the same time the Church was persecuted in England. Virginia colonists were members of the English Church; in New England the colonists were Calvinists. Catholics were not permitted in these colonies. Catholics were excluded from the Dutch colony in New York and the Swedish settlement of Delaware also.

In 1683 James II appointed Thomas Dongan governor of New York and religious liberty was granted to all. The Jesuits built a Catholic chapel in New York City, and established a Latin school there in 1685. By 1700, laws against Catholics were again put into force. Catholics of New York had to travel to Philadelphia as late as the Revolutionary War to participate in Mass and receive the sacraments.

2. Was religious freedom permitted in Maryland?

Yes. A Catholic colony was settled in Maryland by Cecil Calvert in 1634. A church and school were built as Catholic settlers arrived, accompanied by Jesuit priests. They permitted religious freedom to others and, as a result, Protestants obtained control of the colony. The English Church was then established and Catholics were denied their right to vote. The religious freedom of Catholics in Maryland was then restricted until after the Revolutionary War.

3. Were Catholics given freedom in Pennsylvania?

Yes. Under William Penn, the Quakers in Pennsylvania permitted Catholics to practice their faith. In 1730 the Church was given greater security when a

Jesuit, Fr. Joseph Greaton, settled in Philadelphia and had St. Joseph's Church built. When Catholic emigrants came from Germany, they too built churches. By the end of the French and Indian War there were only 7,000 Catholics in the English colonies. Most of them lived in Maryland and Pennsylvania.

4. Summarize the development of Catholicism in other parts of the New World.

The Capuchins built a chapel in New Orleans in 1721, just three years after the city was founded. They opened a school for boys. The French king gave the Ursuline sisters permission to settle in New Orleans and they opened the first convent in the United States. They built a hospital, an orphanage, and a school for girls.

Fr. Pierre Gibault left the seminary at Quebec, Canada, and came to labor for the Church in Vincennes, Mackinac, Detroit, and Peoria. This priest blessed the first church in St. Louis in 1770. He made it possible for George Rogers Clark to gain possession of the great Northwest for the United States, which included what is now Indiana, Ohio, Illinois, Michigan, and Wisconsin.

Attempts to colonize Florida failed at first because of the hostility of the Indians. Early missioners did not succeed, even though as early as 1528 Fr. Juan Juarez, a Spanish Franciscan, was appointed bishop of Florida. He disappeared mysteriously. In 1549 a group of missioners landed near Tampa Bay and within a few days all were savagely killed by the Indians.

Philip II in 1565 sent Admiral Pedro Menendez de Aviles, a leading naval leader of the Spanish Empire, to establish a colony in Florida. Twelve Franciscans and four Jesuits went with him to convert the Indians. Sailing along the Florida coast on August 28, 1565, Admiral Menendez saw an ideal peninsula and ordered the boats to drop anchor. On September 8 he proclaimed the founding of St. Augustine because the peninsula was found on the saint's feast day. Missioners spread out from St. Augustine to convert the Indians, with many priests losing their lives as the new, advancing civilization was resisted by the Indians.

Missionaries were determined to bring Christianity to Florida and so the priests who lost their lives were always replaced, and gradually St. Augustine developed and the colony grew. The countryside became peaceful as missions and monasteries were founded throughout Florida and most of the Indians north of the Gulf of Mexico and east of the Mississippi River converted to the Catholic Church.

The French Huguenots then appeared and raided Spanish Catholic Indian settlements. Missionaries and the faithful were put to death with extreme cruelty. The British, who had been colonizing in the north, also began to destroy Spanish gains.

Governor Moore of South Carolina in 1704 directed a raid of the Apalachee Mission, valuable for food supplies. Franciscan missionaries were put to death;

1,400 Indians were taken into slavery by the English governor and 800 Catholic Indians were killed.

Weakened, the Spanish signed the Treaty of Paris with England in 1763, ceding Florida to the British. The Catholic faith in Florida was then even more suppressed. At the end of the American Revolution, however, the United States government returned Florida to Spanish control. In 1821 Florida was purchased as part of the United States.

In 1598 Don Juan de Onate led an expedition to establish a colony in New Mexico. It consisted of 400 soldiers, 10 missionaries, 83 supply wagons and carts, and 7,000 head of stock. Onate went as far as Wichita, Kansas, and California. Onate's expeditions to New Mexico became an economic drain and the victory of New Spain assigned Pedro de Peralta to build a new capital and to colonize. This was done. He named a site, Royal City of the Holy Faith of St. Francis, known today as Santa Fe (Holy Faith). Santa Fe was founded in 1609 and became the headquarters for future missions in New Mexico. By 1625 there were forty-three missions and 34,000 Christian Indians.

A Jesuit priest, Fr. Eusebio Francisco Kino, labored in the Upper Pima country, which is now the Mexican state of Sonora and southern Arizona. Fr. Kino has been called "the most picturesque missionary pioneer of all North America—explorer, astronomer, cartographer, mission builder, ranchman, cattle king, and defender of the frontier." His maps were the most accurate of the time, winning fame in Europe.

Fr. Kino's mission of San Xavier del Bac, not far from what is Tuscon, Arizona, is now a national monument while still the parish church for the Pima Indians. It is the finest example of Spanish Renaissance architecture in the United States.

Fr. Kino traveled thousands of miles on horse, ever anxious to convert souls. Some of his trails became roads, and he kept journals of his extensive travels. His papers are preserved in the Huntington Library in San Marino, California. While Fr. Kino won the faith of the Pima Indians for Jesus Christ, he was always sad that he did not succeed in converting the Apache Indians.

Fr. Kino died on March 15, 1711, in poverty, as he had lived. He is venerated as a great American pioneer.

The cause for canonization of Fr. Antonio Margil, who developed missions in Texas, has been introduced. One of the missions he founded near San Antonio (San Antonio de Bexar Mission) is still used as a parish church and has been declared a National Historic Site by both the state and nation. Margil is compared to Kino and Serra as among the greatest of Spanish missionaries.

The Spanish came to Texas first but met competition from the French, who came down the Mississippi River from Canada. La Salle built Fort Prudhomme in Tipton County and Fort St. Louis in Victoria County.

Besides San Antonio, the Spanish built the missions of San Saba, San Luis, and San Francisco de los Tejas (now a lost site). The Spanish built their missions not simply as churches for worshipers but to become self-sufficient communities with farms, cattle and ranches, and homes for Indians who worked at the mission—also homes for teachers, nurses, and guards. They built hospitals, schools, and guard posts as protection from Apache and Comanche Indians.

The Spanish crown withdrew support and in 1793 the mission of San José de Aguayo was suppressed by the Mexican government. The Franciscans had to leave when the new Mexican government took over the missions in 1824, and with the passing of years the mission was neglected. San José, which had earned the name Queen of the Missions, began to be restored to its former beauty in 1912 when the archdiocese of San Antonio began a restoration program. In 1941 arrangements began whereby it was named a National Historic Site.

Fr. Junipero Serra, the great missionary of California, has been named to the Statuary Hall of our nation's capitol for the state of California. Fr. Serra arrived in the harbor of Veracruz, Mexico, on December 6, 1749, with a group of Franciscan missionaries assigned to evangelize the Indians of northern Mexico.

The Franciscans were welcomed in the New World missions. They avoided politicizing. The viceroy of Peru wrote to King Philip II: "They are the ones who preach the doctrine with the greatest care and example, and the least avarice." This was especially true of Fr. Junipero Serra.

Fr. Junipero was known for his great oratory, and his keen philosophical mind gave him a reputation among scholars. Nonetheless, he requested an assignment as a missioner. He said: "I have wanted to carry the Gospel teachings to those who have never heard of God and the kingdom He has prepared for them."

His real missionary work did not begin until he was 56 years old, after he spent nine years among the Toltec Indians in Serra Gorda and seven years as an itinerant preacher from San Fernando College in Mexico City.

Learning of California and the needs of its Indians moved him. He then received permission to begin mission work there. His motto was "Always forward, never back."

Fr. Serra walked whenever possible, in spite of poor health. He carried on a most heroic conquest of America for Christ from 1750 until his death in 1784, with no other weapon than a crucifix and the love of God. He converted the solitudes of California into an earthly paradise—where formerly fierce Indian tribes attempted to annihilate each other in cannibalistic battles.

Fr. Serra founded nine important missions in California. His successors founded twelve more. The cities of California grew around these missions. San Diego, Carmel, San Gabriel, Santa Clara, San Luis Obispo, Ventura, Capistrano, San Francisco—all missions of Fr. Serra—became centers of colonization and development in California.

Fr. Junipero Serra was always on the move, back and forth between his missions, urging all to greater charity and zeal and encouraging new converts. Not satisfied with simple conversion to the Catholic faith, this great Franciscan priest and missionary taught the Indians a better life by teaching them how to sow and harvest. He led in the development of farmlands and wine presses and helped build, with his own hands, forges, mills, and slaughter houses.

Fr. Serra once walked 2,400 miles to Mexico City to get retribution from the viceroy when a commandant of the Spanish military practiced cruelty to the Indians. His death at Carmel Mission, on August 28, 1784, marked the end of Spanish extension in the United States in the pioneer missionary era.

5. Did religion continue strong in the hearts of people after the early pioneer days?

To some extent it did, but once the hardships of the pioneer days were over and the descendants grew wealthy from trade and agriculture, the old religious spirit weakened among Protestants. The spirit of the Enlightenment overtook them and Rationalism dominated in too many cases, as many depended more on themselves than on God.

Thomas Paine, a leader of the revolutionary spirit, resembled in some respects the infidelity of Voltaire. Thomas Jefferson, who wrote the Declaration of Independence, was a deist who sympathized with the Freethinkers of France.

Catholics were blessed with heroic and saintly missionaries. Their faith continued to spread. There were three Catholics among those who signed the Declaration of Independence and the Articles of Confederation: Thomas Fitzsimmons, Daniel Carroll, and Charles Carroll of Carrollton.

The Carroll family of Maryland played a great role in the foundation of our American nation. One of the great Carroll family became a priest, namely John, who was born in Maryland on January 8, 1735. On July 1, 1784, Fr. John Carroll was appointed superior of the Catholic clergy in America. In 1789 Monsignor Carroll was appointed bishop, and was consecrated bishop of the United States in 1790, with his see at Baltimore.

When Bishop Carroll returned from England (where he was consecrated), he took a survey of his vast church. The first national census showed that in 1790 there were approximately 30,000 Catholics in a population of 3,200,000. There were fewer than thirty priests for the widely scattered Catholic population. More than half the Catholics, about 16,000, lived in Maryland; 7,000 lived in Pennsylvania; 3,000 around Detroit and Vincennes; and 2,500 in Illinois.

6. How did the first bishop of the United States prosper in ruling the Church?

Bishop John Carroll was later named archbishop and he directed the Catholic Church in America for twenty-five years. He called the first Synod of Baltimore, which set up rules and regulations that have governed the Church until the present day. He founded Georgetown University, and when the Jesuit Order was restored in 1801, he asked the Jesuits to take over Georgetown.

Bishop Carroll influenced the Sulpicians to come to Baltimore and open the first seminary in the United States, which was named after the Blessed Virgin

Mary. He invited Augustinians, Dominicans, Carmelites, Visitation nuns, and the Sisters of Charity to come to America to work.

Catholics began to emigrate to the United States by 1807. There were 14,000 Catholics in New York City, compared with less than 100 seventeen years previously. The French Revolution drove many priests from France and they came to the United States and assisted Bishop Carroll.

In 1808 the Holy See elevated Baltimore to an archdiocese and created four new dioceses: Boston, New York, Bardstown, and Philadelphia.

When Archbishop Carroll died in 1808 at the age if 81, there were 200,000 Catholics in the United States and the Church showed signs of growing stability. Archbishop Carroll is attributed with being the spiritual father and founder of the Catholic Church in the United States.

7. Did the early Catholics of the United States prove themselves loyal Americans?

Yes. When the Revolutionary war came they rallied to the cause of the patriots. At the time of the American Revolution, Catholics were only about 1 percent of the population of the colonies but they made great contributions.

Some Catholics rose to high positions, such as Commodore John Barry, who became Father of the American Navy. Many Catholics enlisted in the Continental army and the navy and a regiment of Catholic Indians came down from Maine. Catholic generals even came from Europe to help the War for Independence.

General Washington wrote to Monsignor John Carroll that he recognized the important aid given by Catholics and "a nation professing the Roman Catholic Faith" in the establishment of our government.

The loyalty of Catholics to their country, America, has been in evidence from the very early days and during its more than 200 years of history.

8. Did Catholics in the early years of the United States labor to establish schools?

Yes. From the beginning, Bishop Carroll and other bishops of the country labored to provide schools for Catholic children. The bishops met in Baltimore in 1829 and held the First Provincial Council. They declared: "We judge it absolutely necessary that schools should be established in which the young may be taught the principles of faith and morality while being instructed in letters."

Priests who escaped France during its revolution and came to the United States established missions, opening Catholic schools wherever possible.

9. Who was the Apostle of the Alleghenies?

Prince Demetrius Gallitzin was ordained in 1795 by Bishop John Carroll. His father was the Russian ambassador to Holland and he was born at the Hague in 1770. Demetrius had been prepared for a military career by his father, who scoffed at religion as he was an admirer of Voltaire. The elder Gallitzin kept religion from his son and even destroyed his wife's faith. In danger of death, the mother of Demetrius, when he was only 16, repented, called for a priest, and was reconverted. Upon her recovery she prayed to St. Monica, who in her own time had prayed for the conversion of her son, St. Augustine.

Amazed at his mother's conversion, when he had been taught to ridicule religion and revelation, Demetrius told how his curiosity was stimulated. "I soon felt convinced of the necessity of investigating the different religious systems, in order to find the true one. . . . My choice fell upon the Catholic Church, and at the age of seventeen, I became a member of that Church."

After his conversion Demetrius continued his interest in military pursuits. Circumstances led him to come to America to offer his services to the infant army, but instead he became aware of the shortage of priests and offered himself to Bishop John Carroll to study for the priesthood. He entered the seminary at Baltimore.

After his ordination to the priesthood, he traveled westward and settled in the Alleghany Mountains. He labored among the people of western Pennsylvania for forty-one years. He labored for the Church both by the spoken and written word in the cause of truth. He defended the Church by writing, while all the while concealing the fact that he was a Russian prince.

Fr. Gallitzin built a mission center at Loretto, Pennsylvania, which grew to ten churches and three monasteries. His work covered the present dioceses of Pittsburgh, Harrisburg, Greensburg, and Erie.

10. Relate the founding of seminaries in Kentucky and Missouri.

The first bishop of Bardstown was a Sulpician, Bishop Flaget. In 1811 he and another Sulpician, Fr. John David, founded a seminary in Kentucky which consisted of a couple of log cabins, with the bishop living in one and the seminarians in the other. Later they made bricks and cut wood to build a church and seminary building.

In 1817 the Vincentian fathers started a log-cabin seminary in similar manner west of the Mississippi in Missouri. It became Kenrick Theological Seminary of St. Louis.

11. What were other significant establishments for the early Church in America?

The diocese of Cincinnati originally included Ohio, Michigan, and the Northwest Territory. Its first bishop was Edward Fenwick, a Dominican who was appointed bishop in 1822. He established Athenaeum Seminary, which later became known as Mt. St. Mary's Seminary of the West.

Fr. Sorin and six lay brothers of the Congregation of the Holy Cross came to northern Indiana in 1841. They founded a college which was dedicated to Our Lady, and is still known as Notre Dame du Lac.

In 1792 the Poor Clares came from France to open a monastery at Frederick, Maryland. In 1801 they opened an academy at Georgetown, which later was taken charge of by the Pious Ladies, a religious order founded in the United States in 1799. This society later became part of the Visitation Order.

12. What made the great growth of the Catholic school system in the United States possible?

The self-sacrifice of good Catholic parents and religious brothers and sisters who labored for little, under a vow of poverty, made the Catholic school system possible. The early American Catholics desired to provide education for their children, whether from rich or poor families. Laws were passed by American churchmen commanding parents to send their children to Catholic schools whenever possible; and schools were established in all the states.

Many in the public school system were affected by the false spirit of the Enlightenment in Europe and they did not want the churches to have any influence in the public school system. Catholics came to the support of their bishops and built schools of their own, building one of the greatest Catholic school systems in the entire world. The sacrifice was great because most Catholic parents were poor and they received no help from the state. Instead, they had to help support, through taxes, the public school system.

Young men and women, dedicated to Christ and reared by good Catholic parents, left the world to join religious orders. These people became the backbone for the education of future Catholics in the United States Catholic school system.

The Christian Brothers, the Brothers of Mary, the Marists, the Xaverian Brothers, and the Brothers of the Holy Cross worked for the Catholic education of boys. Communities of nuns multiplied for the education of girls, and in many cases labored for the Catholic education of boys *and* girls.

Largely, it was a strong Catholic school system which assisted the Catholic Church in the United States to grow strong, with millions of devout Catholics.

13. Was the Catholic press an important organ for spreading the true faith in the early years of our country?

There were some earlier attempts, short-lived and without much success, but the first strictly Catholic newspaper in the United States was founded by Bishop John England of Charleston. In 1823 he founded the *United States Catholic Miscellany*. Thereafter other papers appeared under Catholic sponsorship. The oldest still-existing Catholic publication in the United States is *The Pilot*.

In 1833 Fr. John Martin Henni of Cincinnati, who later became the first archbishop of Milwaukee, founded a German weekly. A convert to the Church, Orestes A. Brownson became a great defender of Catholic truth when in 1844 he began publishing *Brownson's Review* every three months. *The Catholic World,* a magazine, began publication in 1865 under the Paulist fathers, founded by Fr. Isaac T. Hecker in New York City in 1858. Also in 1865, Fr. Sorin began to publish *Ave Maria* at Notre Dame. Although not strictly under official Church auspices, *Der Wanderer* was founded by the German Matt family in 1867 and has continued as an English edition since 1931, *The Wanderer.*

In more modern times, Monsignor Matthew Smith founded the *Denver Catholic Register,* later called *The Register* and currently called *The National Catholic Register.* The national edition of *The Register* began in 1924, although this paper had already existed for many years. Under Monsignor Smith it grew to a circulation of about 1 million, with the powerful pen of the monsignor campaigning for fair treatment of migrant workers, battling the bigoted Ku Klux Klan, promoting the rights of Mexican minorities, and promoting the Christian reunion movement. Monsignor Smith defended Catholic truth with his straightforward presentations in Catholic apologetics.

Another crusading Catholic journalist was John F. Noll, born in Ft. Wayne, Indiana, in 1875. Ordained June 4, 1898, Fr. Noll from the beginning was interested in helping Protestants to better understand Catholicism. He felt that, if truth was known, bigotry would disappear. He began by publishing the *Parish Monthly,* which grew into a magazine. The little magazine grew to include neighboring parishes.

When Bishop Noll became aware of new and growing anti-Catholic forces against the Church (from publications such as *The Menace, The Peril,* and *The American Defender*) and that socialism, with its materialism, was gaining political strength, he attempted to gain the support of the laboring class, to which Catholics largely belonged. Fr. Noll enlarged his paper and named it *Our Sunday Visitor.* In less than a year it had a weekly circulation of 200,000 and eventually 1 million.

The Catholic press in the United States, like the Catholic school system, grew to be the best in the world and had great influence on not only the defense but also the growth of authentic Catholicism.

14. Did the Catholic Church in the United State show interest in the Indians and black people?

The abuse of the Indians by the white man mars the pages of American history, as does the abuse of black people as slaves. While the new American civilization was in many ways an enemy to the Indians' nomadic manner of life, the Church befriended the Indian tribes from the very beginning. Many historical accounts could be given of "Blackrobes" helping the Indians, and significant examples are the following.

The Cheyenne were sent to reservations chosen by the white conquerors. Massacres took place. Wherever the Cheyenne went, priests were there to administer to their spiritual needs and seek justice for them. These included the Jesuits, the Edmundites, and the Capuchins.

The Navajos, who roamed the Southwest, were a talented tribe who learned the Spanish language as they were Christianized by the first Spanish missioners; Franciscans first preached to them. Fr. Bernard Haile O.F.M. made the first alphabet for the Navajo. His dictionary and anthropological works are still chief sources for knowledge about these people. The government tried unsuccessfully to remove these people to reservations in Okalhoma.

In Indiana, the Potawatomi Indians were under pressure of the government to be removed to Kansas. When Chief Menominee refused, the Indiana governor ordered them removed by force. The attack came on a Sunday morning, while the Indians, converted to Catholicism, were at Mass.

In South and North Dakota the Benedictines have labored long for the Indian people, as have other missioners. The Benedictines still labor in the Dakotas, from their chief monastery, Blue Cloud Abbey, at Marvin, South Dakota.

In 1824 the Jesuits opened a school for Indian boys at Florissant, Missouri, while the Ladies of the Sacred Heart opened a school for Indian girls there. Later the Vincentian fathers took charge of the Indian missions on the Mississippi River. The Jesuits took charge of those on the Missouri. In 1840, Fr. John de Smet established missions among the Indians west of the Rocky Mountains.

In 1842, in New Orleans, Bishop Blanc founded the Sisters of the Holy Family to take care of black people, especially orphans and the aged.

In 1866 the Second Plenary Council of Baltimore met, with the bishops urging priests "as far as they can to consecrate their thoughts, their time and themselves, wholly and entirely if possible, to the service of the colored people."

A large congregation of Negro Catholics formed St. Francis Xavier's Church in Baltimore, when in 1871 four young priests who had studied for the missions in England were put in charge. This marked the beginning of St. Joseph's Society for Colored Catholics—the Josephite Fathers. As the society grew, missions for black people spread throughout the South.

Mother Catherine Drexel founded a new order of nuns in 1889. They called themselves the Sisters of the Blessed Sacrament and devoted themselves to spreading the Catholic faith to the blacks and Indians of the United States.

To the present day there are Catholic missions among the colored people and the Indians. The Commission for Catholic Missions reported in the 1970s that missions are located in twenty-five states: 157 in the Southwest, 63 in the Northwest, 60 in the Dakotas, 45 in Alaska, 36 in the Great Lakes area, and 40 in other states.

15. Has the Catholic Church admitted black people to the hierarchy in the United States?

The first black bishop in United States Catholic history was Bishop James A. Healy. He headed the diocese of Portland, Maine, from 1875 to 1900, and suffered much because of his mixed ancestry. Born in Macon, Georgia, on April 6, 1830, Bishop Healy was the son of an Irish immigrant plantation owner and a mother who was a slave. The bishop's brother was Jesuit Fr. Patrick F. Healy, who became the twenty-ninth president of Georgetown University in Washington, D.C. Another brother was Monsignor Sherood Healy, who became rector of Boston's Holy Cross Cathedral. Two sisters of the Healy family (of ten children) became nuns.

Bishop Healy studied for the priesthood in Sulpician seminaries in Montreal and Paris, and was ordained in Paris in 1854. In his diary for the year 1863, commenting on the Emancipation Proclamation, which ended slavery in the rebel states, Fr. Healy noted "there were going to be terrible problems for all the freedmen to make their way."

In 1977 Pope Paul VI established a new diocese of Biloxi, Mississippi, and named Bishop Joseph L. Howze the first black bishop to head a diocese— appointed in the twentieth century in the United States. Bishop Howze had been auxiliary bishop of Natchez-Jackson in 1972 but in 1977 was named head of the Biloxi diocese, formed from the diocese of Natchez-Jackson which had included all of Mississippi. In 1972 he was only the third black person to become a Catholic bishop in the United States. In 1975 the Holy See named Josephite Fr. Eugene A. Marino, auxiliary bishop of Washington and the fourth black bishop in United States history.

By the 1970s the number of black Catholics was estimated to be more than 900,000, in a total black population estimated to number more than 22 million. There were 666 Catholic parishes that were entirely or predominantly black. These parishes were served by 1,014 pastors or assistant pastors of missions and parishes. Also, the black population in more recent years has moved from the Southern United States, until nearly two out of three Catholic Negroes now live in the largest Eastern, Midwestern, and Western cities.

16. Did Catholics find freedom from bigotry after the Constitution guaranteed religious liberty?

In many cases, no. The idea that one could not be a good American and a good Catholic at the same time was introduced to this country from Europe. Unscrupulous politicians used it to their advantage in appealing to hatred of the Catholic Church.

In 1837 an organization was formed, Native Americans, that apparently forgot that the Indian people are the natives. This organization developed into the Know Nothing Party, and when a papal representative came to the United States in 1853, he was mobbed by its members in Cincinnati.

Persecution of Catholics resulted all over the country, and Catholic churches were destroyed. A Jesuit priest was tarred and feathered in Bangor, Maine. Riots broke out in cities like Louisville and St. Louis, and blood was shed. A movement was on to keep Catholics from holding public office and having the right to vote.

Archbishop John Hughes, who was made bishop of New York in 1842, did everything he could to defend the Church from this bigotry and intolerance. At first he tried to win public support for Catholic schools. Realizing he was defeated and that, unjustly, Catholics had to pay taxes for education from which they did not benefit, he worked hard to build and staff a Catholic school in every parish.

Archbishop Hughes, the first archbishop of New York, continued to fight the Native Americans and the Know Nothing Party, at the same time demonstrating great patriotism for America. He eventually won support from fair-minded Americans who were not Catholic, but bigotry has never entirely disappeared from the American scene.

17. What was the bigotry represented by the Ku Klux Klan?

The Ku Klux Klan was a bigotry movement that was anti-Catholic, anti-black, anti-Semitic, and anti-alien. The American Protective Association (APA) first appeared in 1887; it spread throughout the country but its main strength was in the Midwest. It sought to repeal naturalization laws, to forbid teaching of foreign languages in public schools, and to tax Church property. This movement was followed in 1915 when thirty-four men, meeting under a blazing cross on a mountaintop near Atlanta, Georgia, pledged loyalty to the "Invisible Empire." This was the origin (in modern days) of the Knights of the Ku Klux Klan.

The Ku Klux Klan used murder, beatings, and tar and feathers as they spread hatred and misunderstanding. Membership was placed at 1,200,000 by 1922. In 1925 it claimed 5 million members, living in every state, the Canal Zone, and Alaska. Its symbols became the burning cross and hooded white figures. Burning crosses were sometimes placed in front of Catholic churches. In Pennsylvania, a court trial produced evidence of Klan-inspired riots, floggings, kidnapings, and even murder.

The Klan gained strength in the Democratic Party and is considered to have played a large role in the prejudice that hindered Governor Alfred E. Smith, the first Catholic ever nominated, from being elected president of the United States in 1928. His presidential campaign stirred prejudice that brought wild anti-Catholic emotions into the open. Among the extreme methods was circulation of a false oath, purported to be the secret Knights of Columbus oath.

The 1960 presidential campaign of John F. Kennedy, the first United States president who was Catholic, was an occasion for anti-Catholic prejudice again to surface. While the prejudice was not as severe as in 1928, the bogus Knights of Columbus oath again appeared, sermons were preached against a Catholic president, and false accusations were again circulated.

18. Does anti-Catholic bigotry still continue?

Yes. Protestants and Other Americans United (POAU) has spread much anti-Catholic sentiment in recent years.

Evidence that anti-Catholicism is not dead was seen in May 1973, when need for a Catholic League for Religious and Civil Rights was noted. Patterned after the Jewish Anti-Defamation League and the National Association for the Advancement of Colored People, it seeks to champion the rights of Catholics and other religious minorities as expressed in the Declaration of Independence and the Bill of Rights. It seeks to make public exposure, where necessary, of anti-Catholicism and to negotiate anti-Catholic prejudices with offenders.

19. What canonized saints did the United States produce in its first 200 years of history?

Mother Frances Xavier Cabrini (1850–1917) was the first American citizen to be canonized (in 1946). Born in Italy, she founded the Missionary Sisters of the Sacred Heart in 1877, settled in the United States in 1889, and became an American citizen at Seattle in 1909. St. Frances Xavier Cabrini labored among Italian immigrants.

Mother Elizabeth Ann Seton was canonized as the first native-born citizen of the United States in 1976, when America celebrated its 200th birthday as a nation. St. Elizabeth Ann (1774–1821), a convert to the Catholic Church, founded the Sisters of Charity in the United States.*

Bishop John Nepomucene Neumann, who was born in Bohemia in 1811, was ordained a priest in New York in 1836. He became a missionary among Germans near Niagara Falls, then joined the Redemptorist Order. In 1852 he became the bishop of Philadelphia. Canonized in June 1977, John Neumann was the first United States bishop to prescribe Forty Hours devotion to our Lord (in the Blessed Sacrament) for his diocese.*

20. Have Catholics demonstrated their patriotism whenever the United States has been at war?

Yes. During World War I, although Catholics at that time were about 17 percent of the population, it is estimated that between 25 and 35 percent of the army and about 50 percent of the navy were Catholic. This is attributed to the fact that our Catholic schools have always taught patriotism. During this war, Catholic priests became outstanding as chaplains, the best known being Fr. Francis P. Duffy of the famous Fighting Sixty-Ninth.

One of every four members of the armed forces was Catholic in World War II. Again, at least half of the navy was Catholic, as was a high percentage of the Marine Corps. Many Catholics received the Congressional Medal of Honor, the nation's highest decoration for heroic service beyond the call of duty.

In the various wars of the United States, the loyalty and contributions of Catholics have been obvious. Catholics again showed their loyalty in the Ko-

---

*Detailed lives of St. Elizabeth Ann Seton and St. John Neumann may be found in *Saints & Heroes Speak* (OSV Press), by the author of this catechism.

rean and Vietnam wars. The manner in which the Vietnam War was fought proved very controversial, although its anti-communism aim was worthy.

Patriotism, which is love of one's country, was taught by Christ, who said we should give our country its due. St. Paul wrote that we should be obedient to just authority. Patriotism is related to justice and an ally of charity, which requires us to love our fellow countrymen. The Church, however, does not teach blind patriotism or excessive and inordinate affection for one's country, to the detriment of the rights of other nations. This is nationalism, which is opposed to the unity of the human race. In modern times, nazism, fascism, and communism are disguised and extreme forms of nationalism.

It is true that there have been many cases of great patriotism and heroism among non-Catholic chaplains, but it's a fact that only four chaplains have received the nation's highest decoration, presented in the name of Congress for "conspicuous gallantry and intrepidity at the risk of life above and beyond the normal call of duty." All four were Catholics.

21. Has the Catholic Church in the United States had a record of befriending the rights of the workingman?

Yes. Catholic immigrants made a large proportion of the working force in the United States and their bishops have long worked for social reform and justice in the conditions of labor. In the development of the labor movement, the Catholic Church has worked to protect the rights of the laboring man while, at the same time, protecting him from capitalistic abuses and exploitation by socialistic and atheistic forces. Communist forces have long sought to gain the favor of the workingman by deceit.

As socialistic groups attempted to take over the labor movement for their own ends, the Church has sometimes found itself in delicate positions, working to defend the social rights of the laboring force while not condemning labor organizations. Attempts were made, however, to make the Catholic Church appear to be a friend of the powerful rich and the enemy of the helpless poor.

Cardinal James Gibbons (1834–1921) won the support of another champion for the rights of labor—Archbishop John Ireland (1839–1918) of St. Paul and two other bishops. These bishops prepared a special document, examining the Knights of Labor to forestall any misunderstanding that the Church was condemning the right of labor to organize for their rights and against abuses. Cardinal Gibbons took the document to Rome with him in 1887, when he received the "red hat" for his cardinalate.

This effort won an official Church position that saved the workingman for the Catholic Church in the United States, and had great influence on Pope Leo XIII. In 1891 this pope issued his historic encyclical, *Rerum Novarum*.

22. What did the encyclical "Rerum Novarum" concern and how did the Church follow its teachings?

Rerum Novarum, by Pope Leo XIII, dealt with the conditions of the working class and laid down the principles of social justice. After this great, progressive encyclical, Catholic social doctrine has steadily presented successive authoritative documents.

An outstanding encyclical after Rerum Novarum is Quadragesimo Anno by Pope Pius XI, issued in 1931—forty years after the first great social pronouncement of the Church. These were followed by Mater et Magistra (Christianity and Social Progress) and Pacem in Terris (Peace on Earth), by Pope John XXIII in 1961 and 1963. In 1967 Pope Paul VI issued Populorum Progressio (Development of Peoples).

In 1965, Vatican Council II issued the Pastoral Constitution on the Church in the Modern World, which deals with the dignity of the human person, the problem of atheism, the community of mankind, etc. It also deals with the nobility of marriage and the family, culture and socioeconomic life, the political community, and the fostering of peace.

In America, in particular, the Catholic Church has best identified itself with the welfare of the laboring man, as leaders pioneered paths for social justice. Many Catholic bishops ard priests have labored to implement the Church's social doctrines, outlined in official Church documents. Too frequently, however, the social doctrines of the Church have not been properly taught or implemented.

23. How did the bishops of the United States coordinate their efforts in a young and growing country?

The bishops of the expanding dioceses met at Baltimore for seven provincial councils between 1829 and 1849. In 1846 they named the Mother of God, under her title the Immaculate Conception, patroness of the United States. This was eight years before the dogma was proclaimed by the universal Church.

The first of three plenary councils of Baltimore was held after the establishment of the archiocese of Oregon City in 1846 and the elevation to metropolitan status of St. Louis, New Orleans, Cincinnati, and New York.

Archbishop Francis P. Kenrick of Baltimore served as papal legate at the first plenary assembly, which convened May 9, 1852. Regulations were drawn up concerning parish life, liturgical ritual and ceremonies, administration of funds, and the teaching of Christian doctrine.

The second plenary council met from October 7 to 21, 1866, and was presided over by Archbishop Martin J. Spalding. It dealt with current doctrinal errors, norms for the organization of dioceses, the education and conduct of the clergy, the management of church property, parish duties, and general education.

The third plenary council, held from November 9 to December 7, 1884, was called into session by Archbishop James Gibbons (who was later named a cardinal of the Church). It provided for preparation of a line of "Baltimore catechisms" which have served (even to the present) as a basic means of religious education. It called for building Catholic elementary schools in all parishes, establishment of the Catholic University of America in Washington, D.C. (in 1889), and the six Holy Days of Obligation for the United States.

The Holy See established an apostolic delegation at Washington, D.C., on January 24, 1893.

24. What system of coordination have the Catholic bishops of the United States used in modern times?

In 1917, under the title National Catholic War Council, the bishops mobilized the Church's resources. Several years later it changed its name to National Catholic Welfare Conference. Its objectives were to serve as an advisory and coordinating agency of American bishops for advancing the works of the Church in social action, education, communications, immigration, legislation, and youth and lay organizations.

The organization of American bishops was renamed the United States Catholic Conference (USCC) in November 1966, when the hierarchy organized itself as a territorial conference under the title National Conference of Catholic Bishops. USCC carries on the work of the former NCWC.

The National Conference of Catholic Bishops elects one of its members as president for a term of three years. In many respects, the president of the NCCB becomes a chief spokesman for the Catholic Church in America, but he must work in harmony with all the American bishops.

25. What have American Catholics done to demonstrate their devotion to the Mother of God as their patroness?

To demonstrate their dedication to the Mother of God, American Catholics in 1914 launched the project for the National Shrine of the Immaculate Conception at Washington, D.C., in the nation's capital. The shrine, dedicated November 20, 1959, is the seventh largest religious building in the world, with normal seating capacity for 6,000 persons and up to 8,000 persons in attendance on occasion. Each year, approximately 1 million persons visit the shrine, which is adjacent to the Catholic University of America. The huge undertaking was financed by contributions from Catholics throughout the country.

The National Shrine of the Immaculate Conception's many chapels are dedicated to, and depict, God's Mother under her various titles.

Summary

This chapter has taken us from the early days of the English colonies, when the rights of Catholics were not respected, to the end of the nineteenth century, when great churchmen fought for the rights of the laboring man, who, with his family, made the Catholic Church grow from 30,000 souls in 1790 to over 50 million by the latter part of the 1970s. The chapter has also introduced us to the present era.

Catholics in the United States have often had to fight against bigotry. Although, in the present day, Catholics are the largest single Christian body, much prejudice against the Catholic faith still remains, though it is not as violent as it was in the first two centuries of our country. The celebration of the country's bicentennial in 1976 found America beginning its third century with much residual, if more sophisticated, bigotry.

Catholics have suffered when their rights have been suppressed. A minority among Protestants, who represented hundreds of differing religious communities in the United States alone, Catholics have not always fought for their rights as well as they could have. At the same time, the struggle of Catholic leaders, among both the clergy and laity (as in the case of labor), has greatly enhanced the human rights of the entire country.

The Catholic Church has made great contributions in the United States in many areas—in its schools, its hospitals, and vast charitable works. Catholics have also made significant contributions to science in the United States. They have been part of the exploration of space, just as they were in exploring the New World after the discovery of America. Catholics have also made significant contributions in the United States in literature, the arts and social justice.

Questions for Discussion

1. Describe the kinds of restrictions Catholics met in the English colonies.
2. What happened to the freedom of Catholics in the colony that was founded to give Catholics freedom?
3. What Catholic family played a great role in the foundation of our country? Which member of this prominent family held an important position in the early Church in the United States?
4. What did the first bishop of the United States do to help the Church prosper?
5. What did the early Catholics in the United States do about schools?
6. Relate the story of the prince who became a priest in the United States.
7. What made possible the great growth of the Catholic school system in the United States?
8. Did the Catholic press have any influence on Catholic life during the first 200 years of our nation? Explain.
9. Has the Catholic Church done anything for the Indians and black people in the United States? Explain.
10. What did the Know Nothing Party try to do?
11. Explain the purpose and activities of the Ku Klux Klan.
12. Has religious bigotry ceased in the United States? Explain.
13. Who were the first three canonized saints among American citizens?
14. Has the history of Catholics proved to be one of patriotism toward their country, the United States? Explain with examples.

15. What has been the relationship of the Catholic Church to the working class in the United States?
16. What could have been the outcome of the relationship of the laboring people to the Catholic Church in the United States if leaders among our bishops had not developed deep insights to the problems of working people and thus kept the pope correctly informed?
17. What have Catholics in the United States done in the past century to manifest their love and devotion for the Mother of God?
18. Why was the Catholic faith so strong and why did its membership grow so rapidly during the first 200 years of our country?

Chapter 17
Russia, Communism, and the Future of the World

1. Give a brief history of Russia before the Revolution of 1917.

Not until the seventeenth century was Russia considered a part of Europe, but rather part of Asia. Seldom was it involved in the affairs of Europe. When Peter the Great became czar in 1682, he desired to Westernize this giant country. He moved the capital from Moscow to St. Petersburg, which was nearer Europe. It played a part in the Wars of Napoleon and, in the nineteenth century, was very much a part of European affairs. Yet the culture of Russia was somewhat different. The people were predominantly Christians of the Russian Orthodox Church, which resembles Catholicism in most of its faith and morals but broke in schism from Rome several centuries previous.

The Industrial Revolution did not affect Russia as soon as it did the various countries of Western Europe. The czar ruled as an absolute monarch and most of the people were peasants. The czar was a dictatorship with a huge army. The people were satisfied for the most part under this form of government.

Universities are often places for the development of new ideas, and when Liberalism reached Russia, it became popular in the universities. While Czar Alexander II had begun some needed reforms, he was assassinated in 1881 by a bomb which exploded in his carriage. His son, Alexander III, increased police power and did not continue the reforms.

Revolutionary ideas spread in Russia. Nikolai Lenin was a leading personality for the revolution. His name had been Vladimir Ilyick Ulyanov, but as a Communist alias he took the name Nikolai Lenin. He made no secret of his atheism. In 1905 a Communist-inspired revolution broke out in Russia but was crushed, and Lenin fled to Switzerland. Nicholas II set up a parliament and from 1906 to 1914 the country fared well, and it seemed revolutionary ideas were forgotten.

Then came World War I, and millions of Russian soldiers were killed. During World War I Nicholas II ruled Russia. Almost every Russian family was affected with losses and the country was demoralized. Because the government of the country was unpopular, talk of revolution again became widespread.

By March of 1917 there was rioting in the streets of St. Petersburg and disorganized revolution, with conflicting groups attempting to get control of the country. Alexander Kerensky and his followers succeeded in taking over, and the Mensheviks ruled as Liberals and Socialists. They were *not* Communists. The royal family was arrested, as the Mensheviks continued the war.

Lenin, who had earlier been driven into exile, watched for his opportunity to return to Russia to put the Communist Manifesto of Karl Marx into practice. Lenin got in touch with the government of Germany, promising that if it helped him get safely back into Russia, he would take over the government and see that Russia withdrew from the war. The German kaiser aided this plan.

Josef Stalin welcomed Lenin when he arrived in St. Petersburg on April 16, 1917. Lenin took charge of the most revolutionary groups that wanted to dominate the country, namely the Bolsheviks. This group intended to dominate the people. Through lies, and false promises of peace, bread, and land, they won the support of many people. They claimed that property and wealth should be taken from the minority, who owned it, and divided among the common people. However, the Communists' real goal was that the people would have *no* property and *no* freedom and the state, in effect, would become *god*.

The Bolsheviks became well organized, and by June the Mensheviks were weakening. The Bolsheviks infiltrated various posts of the government. On November 7, the Bolsheviks seized banks, power stations, bridges, telephone exchanges, and railroad stations. Soldiers in the capital supported the Bolsheviks. Kerensky's followers were left with only the former palace of the Czars, and by early morning the next day the Red Guards had control of the palace and the "Kerenskys" were taken prisoners. On November 8, Communists met under the leadership of Lenin. They declared an end to their participation in the war, seized all private property, and declared Lenin head of the new Communist government.

By November 18—though only a relatively small number of Russia's people were Bolsheviks—the 175 million people of Russia were under their control and representative government, which had been promised, was not to be. The Communist insurgents took over all newspapers and henceforth only the Communist line could be publicized.

2. What was life like in Russia, after Lenin and his Communists took over?

Russia was renamed the Soviet Union. When the people realized the Communists' promises had been lies they refused to cooperate, as everything belonged to the government. Farmers grew only what they needed, since all surplus went to the Communist state. Factory workers went on strike and refused to work, so that production fell far below their previous output. Events proved that communism, according to the atheistic ideas of Marx and Lenin, is contrary to human nature and justice. Lenin was thus forced to ease up somewhat, but before he came to grips with the immediate problems, at least 5 million Russians died of starvation.

Religion and family life suffered greatest in Russia after the Communist takeover. Religion was considered an enemy of the Communist state; children could not be taught religion nor could religious literature be published. Many bishops, priests, and religious were murdered or jailed. Schools, seminaries, monasteries were closed. Children were encouraged to spy on their own parents and report them to the Communist police if they practiced religion in the home or held ideas contrary to Communist indoctrination in the state schools. Respect for the sacredness and indissolubility of marriage was disregarded and easy divorce was made possible. A couple simply signed a governmental paper to get married or divorced.

The Communist International was organized by Lenin and spread throughout the world, with the aim of world domination by Communists. When Lenin died in 1924, Josef Stalin took over as Communist dictator, without any voice by the people in this decision. In 1928 Stalin started the first of his infamous Five-Year plans, aimed at industrializing Russia and making the country more economically productive. The peasants *had* to work on "collective farms," owned by the Communist state, or in factories. Some who attempted to work their own farms and resist their Communist takeover were either shot to death on Stalin's orders or transported to Siberia for slave labor in prison camps.

Great suspicion of Communists toward other Communists developed, so that no one trusted anyone else. Purge after government purge ensued, to "purify" the Communist Party of "undesirables." If Stalin even suspected an individual Communist, the result was usually execution. With everyone spying on everyone else in the Communist Soviet Union, workers could report each other, so that a fellow worker could be done away with when resentment developed.

3. Describe how the Communists took over Catholic Spain and how the Spanish people threw off their yoke.

During the early part of the twentieth century an unstable Spanish government provided the opportunity for other parties to take over. (Communism looks for unrest and unsettled conditions to make big promises, deceive the people, and then rule by force.) In 1931, atheistic and anti-Catholic forces gained power in Spain. Even though *traditionalists* won the greatest number of votes in 1933, the "liberal," atheistic parties still held control. Communists worked their way into complete control of the government. Churches were destroyed, thousands of priests and religious were killed. As Spain moved toward civil war, violence and disorder reigned.

Opposing forces struggled in Spain. There were forces for religion and those opposed; forces for private property and those for state ownership, under the Communist plan; those who defended the rights of the individual and those who fought for the supremacy of the government, with no rights for citizens.

Two army generals, Francisco Franco and Emilio Mola, rose against the Communist government. Franco called for the uprising on July 18, which became known as a "crusade" because it was a fight against the enemies of Christ and for religious freedom. Many rallied to the support of Franco, and by July 20 the north of Spain was controlled by the Nationalists—Franco, Mola, and their followers. The south of Spain, including the capital, Madrid, remained in Communist control. The Communist forces were known as Republicans or Loyalists, but were in reality leftists and Marxists.

By July 22 Spain was in a full-scale civil war and the Soviet Union was aiding the Communist forces within Spain. Italy and Germany came to the aid of the Nationalists. Great heroism on the part of the Nationalists aided their fight against the Communist forces. Their defense of the Alcazar, a fort at Toledo, inspired courage, as reports of resistance against the Communists spread throughout Spain. To resist to death for the cause of religion and the personal freedoms of living in a free country became the wartime principle of the traditionalists.

The Spanish Civil War lasted about three years. Franco marched into Madrid in March 1939. He restored peace to the country, after defeating the leftist Loyalists. Order and prosperity also were restored to Spain under Franco, who ruled as a dictator but as one concerned for the religious freedom and material welfare of the people. Franco was often misunderstood and misrepresented outside his country. He ruled the country until 1976, when King Carlos and others restored democracy to Spain.

4. What national monument did Spain erect to honor those who fell in the Spanish Civil War for the defense of freedom and true religious principles?

The magnificent Monument of the Holy Cross in the Valley of the Fallen was built in the geographic center of Spain to emphasize the fact that it is a monument to all Spaniards. It can well be considered one of the wonders of the world, but it is not well known in other countries, perhaps due to the unjustified prejudice against General Franco, who conceived the idea of the monument and chose the site for it.

The monument consists of a great church dug inside a huge mountain and surmounted by a great cross, the predominating feature. It rises 150 meters from its base and stands 300 meters above the esplanade (measured from the entrance to the crypt). The arms of the Cross are 46 meters in length. The cross "ensemble" consists of three principal parts: a large base, on which stand the figures of the four evangelists, surmounted by a smaller base from which the shaft rises, and at the four corners are figures of the four cardinal virtues. The first base is 25 meters high, the second 42. From these two bases, the giant cross soars into the sky.

Visitors who are unaquainted with this monument at first think the cross atop the mountain is the totality, but discover that inside the mountain, upon which it stands, is a giant basilica with magnificent statues, a choir section, central nave, main altar, crypt, and magnificent mosaics in the cupola ceiling, which crowns the transept.

This national monument also houses the Center of Social Studies, which works for knowledge and peace among men, based upon *Christian social justice*. The center pursues up-to-date social thought and strives to implement the social doctrines of the popes and Catholic thinkers.

The communists, having taken over Spain, were nevertheless defeated. Thus Spain, in freeing itself of Communist control, is a unique country. And thus the monument deserves to become a greater worldwide symbol of resistance to atheistic communism. Concerned and aware Christians (especially in Spain) know, however, that Communists await every opportunity to seize control.

5. Has Communism taken over other nations?

Almost half the world is under the hammer and sickle of atheistic Communist control, thus forgoing human freedoms. The Russian peoples themselves are unwilling subjects of their atheistic government, and only a minority belongs to the Communist Party. The Russian Church, in the years immediately following the revolution, lost over 80 million members. Of the 79,767 churches and chapels in Russia in 1914, only 7,500 remained in 1973 and these were under restrictions. In the huge city of Moscow, only 26 churches remained open, and these were mostly show places for tourists and attended mostly by older people.

Since 1917, tens of thousands of priests, religious, and faithful in the Soviet Union have been murdered for their faith. Of the numerous Catholic seminaries in Russia, Estonia, Latvia, and Lithuania before World War I, only one still exists—in Lithuania.

Some of Finland's territory was annexed by the Communist Soviet Union in 1940. Estonia was annexed in 1940, as were Latvia and Lithuania. Prussian territory was annexed in 1945. Poland was partitioned by the Nazis and Communists in 1939. East Germany became a Communist satellite in 1949, and Czechoslovakia in 1948. Hungary had met the same fate in 1945. Rumanian territory was annexed in 1949; Bulgaria and Albania became satellites in 1944. China fell to the Communists in 1949, with the former rulers being driven to Taiwan, then called the Republic of China. North Vietnam fell in 1954. A long, bloody war was fought against the Communists in South Vietnam with the help of United States soldiers and supplies, but the United States pulled out in

1975. Then the South also fell to the Communists. The United States also fought a war in Korea from 1950 to 1953. (North Korea became a Communist state on May 1, 1948, in the wake of Soviet occupation.)

Yugoslavia was proclaimed a socialist republic in 1945. Repression of religion, as in other Communist takeovers, became government policy. Between May 1945 and December 1950, two-thirds of Yugoslavia's twenty-two dioceses lost their bishops, about 348 priests were killed, and 200 priests were put under house arrest or in prison. Twelve of its eighteen seminaries were closed. Three hundred religious houses and institutions were confiscated and their nuns and other religious were driven out. All Church property was taken over by the Communists. Cardinal Stepinac, arrested by the Communists in 1946, became a symbol of the Church under persecution in Yugoslavia until he died (February 10, 1960).

Cardinal Jozsef Mindszenty, who became primate of Hungary on October 2, 1945, was sentenced to life imprisonment by the Communist Hungarian government on February 8, 1949. During the Hungarian uprising against the Communist government in October 1956, this cardinal-archbishop of Esztergom and primate of Hungary escaped to the United States embassy in Budapest and remained there until October 1971, when, through negotiations between the Communists and the Vatican, he was permitted to leave for the free world. Until his death in 1975, Cardinal Mindszenty was a major inspiration to peoples in the free world, everywhere fighting against the attempts of Communists to dominate the world.*

St. Michael's Priory in Orange, California is a constant reminder of the Communist suppression of freedom in Hungary. There slowly grows a religious foundation of the Norbertine Fathers in the foothills of Saddleback Mountain. The religious community with its seminary and boys school was named after a former Roman Catholic abbey in the Hungarian village of Csorna near the Austrian border.

When St. Michael's abbey in Csorna was seized by Communists in 1950, seven priests risked death to flee across the border with hopes to rebuild their lives and the Csorna abbey in the free world. The Norbertine Fathers in Hungary had produced the likes of Cardinal Mindszenty who visited St. Michael's in Orange not long before his death. The talks Cardinal Mindszenty gave at the new Csorna priory in the free world were later beamed across the iron curtain.

In their diary known as *The Cross & the Flag Against the Hammer & the Sickle*, which began July 11, 1950, the seven Founding Fathers of St. Michael's in Orange, California report how their numbers have grown with the ordination of native American young men.

Thus the Hungarian mother abbey, which has been converted into a Com-

---

*For a detailed treatment of the life of Cardinal Mindszenty by the author of this book, see *Saints & Heroes Speak* (OSV Press).

munist government headquarters now continues in the United States through the seven priests who have established the new Norbertine priory in memory of their centuries old abbey in Hungary and American young men who have answered the call to the holy priesthood to succeed them.

Cuba, only 90 miles from America, fell under Communist rule when Fidel Castro took control of the government on January 1, 1959. In 1961, after Cuba was officially declared a socialist state, 350 Catholic schools were nationalized and the University of Villaneuva was closed. One-hundred-thirty-six priests were expelled and the Church has ever since been severely restricted, with many people discontinuing the public practice of their Catholic faith.

Since 1917, entire countries (or parts of them) have been absorbed into the Red orbit. As early as 1960, it was estimated that 900 million persons, or more than one-third of the world's population, were dominated by Communist regimes. In China, many millions were killed who resisted the Communist takeover. Communists control several African nations (e.g., Angola), and South American nations, stirring up unrest while working to take over.

Communists in 1974 and 1975 came close to taking over Portugal, but the faith of the people caused them to rise up in resistance. The Communists look to Taiwan, Japan, the Philippines, Italy, France, where they have made great inroads in various elections. Infiltration of our own United States is considered by many experts to be far greater than many like to think.

6. Has the nature of communism changed over the years?

No. Even Catholics in traditionally Catholic countries, such as Italy, have been deceived at times into thinking that Communist parties in other countries have goals other than those of the Russian Communists or that the nature of Communist parties differs. In 1977, Cardinal Josef Hoeffner (of Cologne, Germany) reported that the nature of communism remains unchanged. Moreover, the popes have repeatedly condemned it, such as Pope Pius XI in his encyclical on atheistic communism, issued forty years earlier.

Cardinal Hoeffner called the world's attention to "the conspiracy of silence" in the press, when millions were slain in Russia under Stalin and in Mexico. He examined the fundamental principles of communism, beginning with its materialism, "which leaves no room for God, for a spiritual principle of life or for a life after death." He stated that the same Communist principles are in force in this latter quarter of the twentieth century, which "explains the hostility to the Church and to religion in Communist countries today."

Cardinal Hoeffner, one of the Church's outstanding spokesmen against communism, said that the most fundamental error of the system "is to create the idol of self-redemption." The Communist claim that human rights are rooted in the state or in a social process leads to denial of individual freedoms. The history of communism "is an uninterrupted chain of violations of fundamental human rights. . . . Communism makes man the object of an historical process. Its goal is not to create a new social order, but a new type of man, a man without faith, hope, love, liberty or personal responsibility. . . . The Communist ideal of collectivism destroys personal liberty and changes it into a simple compliance with social necessity."

Community welfare does not govern rulers in Communist countries. The only rule is that of the party, or the "dictatorship of the proletariat." The atheistic rulers of communism still look forward to one world under communism.

In 1977 Cardinal Yu Pin, president of the Chinese Catholic Bishops Conference in the Republic of China, toured the United States, contacting congressmen, the President, and all Catholic bishops of the United States (and everyone else he could), urging that the Republic of China (Taiwan) not be abandoned in favor of full diplomatic relations with Communist China. He said that 16 million people in the Republic of China would then be killed or enslaved. His experience and suffering under Communist persecution on the China mainland led him to claim that such a Communist takeover would affect Japan, the Philippines, the other nations in the area, and eventually the United States.

7. What does "communism" really mean?

In the literal sense, it means common ownership of all material property. There is no private or individual ownership of wealth, property, or productive goods; everything is owned by the community. In a sense, religious orders strive to practice communism in a *Christian* way, but as conceived by Karl Marx, communism is the most extreme form of socialism. It is based on a "world view" called "dialectical materialism," which puts all emphasis on matter and denies the existence of God. It is materialistic and deterministic.

The social order, according to theories of Marx, "evolves" through economic struggles between the classes in the direction of a violent revolution, followed by a society which substitutes private ownership for ownership of all things in common.

The Church's opposition to communism is not based on the *true* nature of communism, of "all things in common," for many religious orders follow it. The Church opposes Marxism, which is atheistic communism, because it denies God, replacing the Almighty with material things held not in common, but by the government, and betrays human rights, including the right to own private property.

Communism puts the state above the individual and the family, as we have seen. It teaches that there is no life after death; there is no moral law or personal liberty. Under Marxism, no man has rights over material things or the means of production. Marriage and the family are "artificial institutions" and the primary responsibility for the education of children, according to Marxism, belongs to the state.

8. What do Marxist Communists hold about matter?

This form of communism holds that matter is autodynamic or self-creating, and so it promises to bring about an earthly paradise by a Communist society. When the "perfect society" evolves, there will be no state, no family, no morality, and man will thus have no unhappiness, ill health, or neuroses. There will be lasting peace. The concept is contrary to reason, experience, and divine revelation.

The first stage in developing this perfect Communist society is to extend the world Soviet dictatorship and world socialism, which is to be accomplished in each country by guile and then by violence. For the Communist there is no such thing as truth, as in the Christian conscience. "Truth," for atheistic communism, is whatever will help the Communist cause, even if it is false.

The proper name for the system of atheistic communism is really *Marxism* or *Soviet fascism,* for all power is held in the hands of a few persons. It is extreme socialism that deifies matter and the state. The only reality is matter, which is in constant motion, evolving into new forms.

9. What is Marxism?

This political-economic system gets its name from Karl Marx, who wrote *Das Kapital* and the Communist Manifesto in cooperation with Frederick Engels. Born in Germany in 1818, Marx died in 1883. Engels was born in 1820, died in 1895, and as the son of a wealthy textile manufacturer, he contributed financially to Marx's goals.

10. Summarize "Das Kapital."

It consists of three volumes, the first completed in 1867, and is considered the bible of Marxism. It relates the history of the "class struggle" through the ages and posits "class warfare" between workers and "oppressors." The oppressors are capitalists or those who employ workers. *Das Kapital* is based on the philosophy of Marx, namely *dialectic materialism,* as he presents his economic theories.

11. Summarize the Communist Manifesto.

Written by Marx in 1848, it develops hatred for capitalism and presents the strategy for the world's workers to take wealth and industries from the middle and upper classes, called the *bourgeoisie,* and give them to the workers, who are the *proletariats.* In fact, the system results in dictatorship *over* workers.

12. Why do Communists speak of materialism as "dialectical"?

Their faulty concept of matter as the only reality, with their denial of God, the soul, and anything spiritual, making matter itself god, its self-creator, is "explained" by the *dialectic* (the method by which Marx explained his theory of materialism). The dialectic rules the laws of nature, society, and man's thinking. *Marx held that every idea contains, within itself, its own opposite or denial.* This is called an operation of *thesis*, antithesis, and synthesis.

At the present time, according to dialectical materialism, the thesis (or ruling class) is the bourgeoisie. The antithesis is the proletariat. The synthesis is the dictatorship of the proletariat or socialism, which is the first stage of communism. In reality, however, the proletariat is the dictatorship of the Communist Party, which is controlled by a few men.

13. How does the Communist system relate matter and motion?

Matter and motion are inseparable in this theory. The constant motion in matter, in nature, in the history of mankind, is always a motion of conflict, a debate which they call "dialectical motion."

Making much of motion, the theory never answers the question *who* is the First Mover. St. Thomas Aquinas, in one of his five proofs for the existence of God (none of which the Communists can refute), demonstrates conclusively that motion in matter proves the existence of the First Mover, whom we know as Almighty God.

Engels admitted that the Communists have no knowledge of the origin or source of the motion and look forward to the day when science can find the answer.

14. How does Marxism-Leninism explain dialectic motion in society?

Lenin, who developed the theories of Marx and Engels, reaffirmed the basic atheistic materialism of Marx and added the "necessity" for the final violent overthrow of all nonsocialist governments. He said that this applies to the governments of the United States and Great Britain, which must "inevitably" be overthrown.

Marxism-Leninism developed the theory that originally there was primitive communism, then the slave state, then feudalism, then capitalism. After this must come socialism, or the dictatorship of the proletariat.

Many falsehoods can be proved in this interpretation of the development of historical materialism. For example, the Catholic hurch—with its unchangeable, true faith through the centuries, since the days of Jesus Christ and the apostles—has existed though all the periods of the slave state, feudalism, and capitalism, and we know by divine faith that neither communism nor any other evil will ever destroy the Catholic Church.

15. Can a country rely on negotiations with Communists?

No. We must remember how the Communists regard truth. Their word is of no value, unless an agreement will help their cause, which ultimately is worldwide control under an atheistic dictatorship. There is an international Communist conspiracy, and their negotiations with the free world are conducted with the intention of bringing about the defeat of the free world.

Rulers in the free world, and even some churchmen, sometimes find it difficult to remember or to grasp the nature of Communist thinking, and imagine that Communists can be trusted. They are masters of deceit who stir up wars, or misunderstandings, between individuals and countries—all to their own advantage.

16. Give an example of how communism seeks to destroy the Church.

The effort of communism to destroy the Church was clearly stated in a Communist document, *The Catholic Church in Cuba: A Program of Action*. The same manifesto had been used successfully against the Church in China where millions were murdered. Printed in China by the Foreign-Language Press of Peking, it states:

1. If the Peoples' Democracies are to continue . . . they must first and foremost put an end to the influence of the Catholic Church and its activities.
2. When the political struggle and the productive forces have reached a certain level, we shall then be in a position to destroy the Church.
3. The first line of action to be followed consists in educating, persuading, convincing the Catholics to participate in study circles and political activities.
4. We shall progressively replace the religious element by the Marxist element.
5. The Church must not be allowed to preserve its supranational character. . . .
6. By making the Church subject to the processes of democratic centralism we open the way, via the masses, to patriotic measures that will weaken the Church and undermine its prestige.
7. The next step is to destroy the link existing between the Church and the Vatican.
8. Once the separation of the Church from the Vatican is complete, we can proceed to the consecration of Church dignitaries chosen by ourselves.
9. It is notorious that when the practice of religion has simply become a matter left to the individual's sense of responsibility, it is gradually forgotten.
10. The rising generations will succeed the older, and religion will become merely an episode of the past.

17. Have the popes of the Catholic Church condemned communism?

Yes, repeatedly. Pope Pius XI issued an encyclical letter, *Divini Redemptoris*, on atheistic communism on the Feast of St. Joseph, March 19, 1937. (St. Joseph is a model for workingmen.) His Holiness spoke of the "trickery in various forms" used by Communists. He wrote to the world's bishops: "See to it, Venerable Brethren, that the faithful do not allow themselves to be deceived! Communism is intrinsically wrong, and no one who would save Christian civilization may collaborate with it in any undertaking whatsoever."

As early as 1878, Pope Leo XIII defined communism this way: "the fatal plague which insinuates itself into the marrow of human society, only to bring about its ruin."

Even before Pope Pius XI issued his famous encyclical on atheistic communism, he had written nine official documents on its evils. Succeeding popes—Pope Pius XII, Pope John XXIII, Pope Paul VI—have also condemned communism. Pope John Paul I who reigned but 34 days (August 26—September 29, 1978) was immediately recognized as strongly opposed to communism. Pope John Paul II in his first encyclical to the world spoke of those who give "only atheism the right of citizenship in public and social life."

Pope Pius XII, in addition to opposing and condemning communism in 1949, decreed the penalty of excommunication for all Catholics who hold formal and willing allegiance to the Communist Party and its policies. This pope, sorrowfully, saw some fifteen countries fall under the hammer and sickle and religious and other freedoms thus destroyed.

18. What, in summary, is the reported message of our Lady regarding Russia and communism, which God's Mother gave the three Fatima children in 1917?

According to accounts judged by Church authorities as authentic in apparitions of God's Mother on six occasions (the thirteen of each month, May through October 1917), the Mother of God, known as Our Lady of Fatima, appeared near the town of Fatima in a deserted area known as the Cova da Iria in central Portugal. The Lady, who mentioned Russia by name, foretold the end of World War I. Our Lady also stated that if her call for special prayer and penance, especially *eucharistic reparation,* is not heeded, "Russia will spread her errors throughout the world, promiting wars and the persecution of the Church. The good will be martyred, the Holy Father will have much to suffer, and various nations will be annihilated. . . . " Both predictions—the end of World War I, followed by another more terrible war if men did not repent—are now matters of history.

Each time the Mother of God appeared in the Cova, she asked that the rosary be prayed *daily.* She also called for the *proper* praying of the rosary, which consists of meditating on the mysteries which concern the *word of God,* relating the chief events of our salvation.

Scholars who have studied the Fatima message in depth relate that our Lady taught the children as a catechist, and the message is rich in doctrinal content. The basics of the Catholic faith are to be found in the Fatima message. The message also called for the consecration of individuals, families, and nations—

and Russia in particular—to the Immaculate Heart of Mary. The consecration of Russia was to be accomplished by the pope *in union with the bishops of the world.*

Wars are caused by sin, according to the Fatima message, and so our Lady called all people back to her Son, Jesus Christ, in the daily living of an authentic Christian life.

The Fatima message is often misunderstood, oversimplified, or misrepresented. It is a profound message, yet easy to grasp by those with pure and open minds, desirous of union with God.

The promise of the message is not pessimistic but optimistic. Our Lady of Fatima promised that ultimately Russia will be converted and a time of peace will be conceded to the world. For this to happen, scholars of Fatima hold, a sufficient number of people throughout the world must *live* the message of Fatima.

The events of Fatima reached a climax with the spinning-of-the-sun miracle on October 13, 1917. Fatima received official approval in 1930.

19. Of what does "living the message of Fatima" consist?

The message requires accepting all the teachings of the Church and loyalty (in obedience) to the pope, the chief Vicar of Jesus Christ upon earth. The message also requires *living* the faith. Pope Pius XII, who knew the Fatima message well and was devoted to it, called Fatima the "reaffirmation of the Gospels." He said: "The time for doubting Fatima is past. Now is the time for action."

The Fatima message, properly interpreted, places Jesus in the holy Eucharist as *central* to our religious practices. Fatima is essentially eucharistic reparation, offered primarily through the *sacrifice of the Mass,* for the glory of God and the conversion of sinners. But "eucharistic reparation" includes other forms of devotion to the Real Presence of Jesus Christ in the Blessed Sacrament, namely, visits to the Blessed Sacrament and all forms of eucharistic adoration, such as Benediction of the Blessed Sacrament, Holy Hours, Night Vigils, etc.

In the July 1917 apparition, Our Lady of Fatima asked for *First Saturday* "Communions of Reparation" and promised: "I shall come to ask for the consecration of Russia to my Immaculate Heart, and the Communion of reparation on the First Saturdays."

Our Lady kept her promise of coming again to request the First Saturdays, according to the official accounts, on December 10, 1925, when she appeared to Lucia at Ponteverdra, Spain, where Lucia was a Dorothian nun. The Child Jesus was by her side, on a cloud of light. The message, subsequently approved by the bishop of Leiria-Fatima for promulgation, goes like this:

"Have pity on the heart of your Most Holy Mother. It is covered with the thorns with which ungrateful men pierce it at every moment, and there is no one to remove them with an act of reparation" (words of the Child Jesus).

Then our Lady spoke to Sister Lucia:

"My daughter, look at my heart, surrounded with the thorns with which ungrateful men pierce it at every moment by their blasphemies and ingratitude. You, at least, try to console me, and say that I promise to assist at the hour of death, with all the graces necessary for salvation, all those who, on the First Saturday of five consecutive months, go to confession and receive Holy Communion, recite the five decades of the rosary, and keep me company for a quarter of an hour while meditating on the mysteries of the rosary, with the intention of making reparation to me."

Those who explain the First Saturday message stress that four things must be done, and each is to be offered in reparation: (1) confession, (2) Communion, (3) the rosary, and (4) meditation on the mysteries of the rosary for at least fifteen minutes.*

20. Has the Church continued to approve of Fatima since the 1917 events?

Yes, each pope has endorsed the Fatima message. Shortly after the Fatima events, the Fatima diocese was restored by Pope Benedict XV, on January 17, 1918. On October 31, 1942, Pope Pius XII consecrated the world to the Immaculate Heart of Mary; then, on May 4, 1944, he instituted the Feast of the Immaculate Heart of Mary, and on May 13, 1946, at Fatima, through a papal legate crowned her Fatima image, proclaiming her Queen of the World. In the following month (June 13, 1946) he issued an encyclical explicitly referring to the message of Fatima. Also, the pope chose Fatima (October 13, 1951) to close the Holy Year for all the world.

On July 7, 1952, Pope Pius XII consecrated the Russian people to the Immaculate Heart of Mary, as requested by Our Lady of Fatima; however, he did not do so in conjunction with the bishops of the world. On October 11, 1954, Pope Pius XII referred to her miraculous image at Fatima in an encyclical, *To the Queen of the World.* On November 12, 1954, he elevated the large church in the Cova da Iria to the status of a basilica, and on October 13, 1956, through a papal legate (Eugene Cardinal Tisserant, dean of the Sacred College), blessed and dedicated the International Center of the Blue Army of Our Lady of Fatima (which is near the basilica). The Blue Army exists in 110 nations for the purpose of spreading the message of Fatima. Since May 23, 1975, it is inscribed at the Vatican by the Council of the Laity.

On December 13, 1962, Pope John XXIII instituted the Feast of Our Lady of the Rosary of Fatima. On November 21, 1964, Pope Paul VI renewed the consecration to the Immaculate Heart of Mary, first made by Pius XII, and he did so in the presence of the bishops of the world, gathered for Vatican Council II.

On May 13, 1965, Pope Paul VI, through a papal mission, presented a golden

---

*Detailed accounts of the Fatima messages may be in the lives of Lucia, Jacinta, and Francisco, in *Saints & Heroes Speak* (OSV Press) by the author of this book.

rose to the shrine at Fatima, confiding "the entire Church" to her protection. When the pope presents a golden rose to a Marian shrine it is a sign of special papal approval.

On May 13, 1967, Pope Paul VI personally went to Fatima as a pilgrim and called all the world to renew consecration to the Immaculate Heart of Mary. Arriving in Portugal, he announced that he had come to Fatima to pray to our Lady for peace in the Church and in the world.

21. Summarize the doctrinal content of the Fatima message.

Many who have missed its theological richness and genuine program of spiritual life have reduced the message to a request of our Lady to say the rosary each day so that Russia will be converted. The message, however, is far richer in content.

The message contains the Mystery of the Blessed Trinity. Divine providence, as God directs and governs the world and human history. God is all knowing and all powerful. He knows future events and can, on occasion, intervene with extraordinary signs (miracles) to prove the truth of his supernatural messages. God rewards the good and punishes evil. Still, God is infinitely merciful toward repentant sinners.

Heaven, purgatory, and hell are realities. Guardian angels exist. (A fact that is new in the history of apparitions: *nations* have guardian angels.) The Real Presence of Jesus Christ in the Eucharist. Holy Communion, which is the Body, Blood, soul and divinity of Jesus Christ, our Lord and Savior, is necessary and of great value to the spiritual life. True happiness requires sanctity on earth and for eternity. Growth in grace is the result of divine action first and then the cooperation of the human will.

Sin is an offense against God. Punishment in hell for all eternity for nonrepentent sinners. Sin is also an offense against other members of the Communion of Saints, especially the Sacred Heart of Jesus and the Immaculate Heart of Mary. Flight from sin and amendment of one's life are indispensable to the life of grace.

The unity in Christ of the Church, Christ's Mystical Body, with the Communion of Saints. God's Mother as the Mediatrix of Grace (a title used by Vatican Council II). The necessity and value of prayer and penance, both of petition and reparation. The *personal* love of God for all men and each individual, as expressed in the Sacred Heart of Jesus, and the personal love of the Mother of the Church, through her Immaculate Heart.

The importance of Marian devotions and the efficacy of the rosary when prayed while meditating on the word of God (i.e., the mysteries of the rosary). Consecration to Mary's Immaculate Heart as a more perfect way of living the Christlife, with Mary as model. The action of grace, which transforms souls, as in the case of the Fatima seers. Christianity is not just an "adult religion" but also a religion for children.

The power of Mary's intercession, eventually to bring about the conversion of an entire people, namely Russia, which is both the scourge of God through the spread of its errors and, at the same time, an object of God's mercy. The necessity of the sanctification of the family for the sanctification of society.

Loyalty to the pope, who suffers much at the disobedience of Christians and those who reject or distort true teachings. The necessity of purity and modesty (which is not seen strictly in the apparitions themselves but in the wisdom of the children, especially Jacinta, who was spiritually transformed).

Good always triumphs ultimately and evil always fails in the end. Also seen in the promise is the final triumph of the Immaculate Heart of Mary, which is inseparable from the Sacred Heart of the God-Man, the Redeemer and Savior.

Summary

The plan of communism, instigated over a century ago, calls for a violent overthrow of existing society. Some have thought the Communist goal has changed in recent decades, when Communists have sometimes used sophisticated methods. Also some have erroneously thought the *nature* of communism has changed. Too often, new generations have grown up not knowing what communism really is.

It was Lenin (Russia) who first applied the vicious principes of communism to modern society. He carried out the first successful Communist revolution, which began in Russia in March 1917 and ended with the overthrow of the provisional government in November 1917. *Between those very months, our Lady appeared six times at Fatima, telling us what communism, "the errors of Russia," holds for the world.*

In 1923, six years later, Lenin said: "First we will take Eastern Europe, then the masses of Asia; then we will encircle the United States, which will be the last bastion of capitalism. We will not have to attack. It will fall like overripe fruit into our hands."

Lenin died in 1924. Then Stalin, through brutality, murder, deceit, and a reign of terror, enlarged communism's power, establishing control in Russia and spreading its atheistic evils to other countries.

Between 1939 and 1953, Stalin took advantage of disturbed world conditions during and after World War II. He started on world conquest, in whole or part annexing such areas as eastern Poland, Estonia, Latvia, Lithuania, Finland, Czechoslovakia, and Roumania. Then he created a Soviet orbit, embracing Yugoslavia, China, Poland, Hungary, Bulgaria, North Korea, Czechoslovakia, Roumania, East Germany, Albania, Tibet, Outer Mongolia, and North Vietnam.

Lenin had said it would be necessary first to secure Eastern Europe and the land masses of Asia. This was accomplished for the most part. When Krushchev was the chief Communist he said: "We will never go against the program of

Lenin, and will follow it in the future." Speaking to American diplomats in November 1956, he said: "We will bury you!"

China is an example of what communism has done in countries it has taken over. The last official statistics on the Church in China, published by the Vatican Congregation for the Evangelization of Peoples, recorded that as of June 30, 1947, there were 3.2 million Catholics in China. They included 96 bishops, 5,588 priests, 1,077 brothers, 6,753 sisters, 803 major and 2,900 minor seminarians. Chinese priests and sisters in Hong King, who were allowed to visit relatives in China in November 1973, reported that the Catholic Church was no longer visible in Communist China. Some church buildings were still standing, they reported, but they were used for other purposes. In Peking, only one church was open for Mass, and only once per week. These visitors to China could find no trace of the bishops and priests who were there before the Communist takeover. There were reports that some Catholics still exist in mainland China, practicing their religion underground.

At the close of 1978 President Carter surprised the world by announcing that the United States woud recognize the communist government of mainland China. Controversies immediately developed.

On New Year's Day, 1979 Peking and Washington celebrated "normalization" of diplomatic relations. In Washington the activities took place in China's liaison office on Connecticut Avenue. Vice President Walter Mondale rejoiced over "the dawn of a new and bountiful era" and hailed China as "a key force for global peace." Ch'ai Tse-min, head of the Chinese mission, in response said that the new Sino-American ties would serve to "combat the expansion and aggression of hegemonism"—a reference to the Soviet Union.

In another part of the capital, the derecognized Republic of China (Taiwan) was in anguish in its former embassy as a disconsolate crowd of about 300 people gathered, as many actually were crying, and watched the flag of Taiwan lowered for the last time. Demonstrations, pro and con, were held in major cities of the United States.

In the early months of 1979, Catholic missionary groups were among American church organizations which claimed settlements for millions of dollars after the communist government took over China 30 years before.

In February 1979 China agreed to pay $80.5 million over five years to American businesses, churches, non-profit institutions and individuals against claims of some $197 million.

The 9th and 10th greatest claims were requested by two provinces of the Vincentian Fathers, with claims of more than $3 million each. In all, eight Catholic religious orders were slated to receive about $3.6 million.

China agreed to pay the $80.5 million in settlements when the United States agreed to unlock an identical amount of Chinese assets frozen in the United States after China entered the Korean War in December, 1950.

Father Frank Harden, treasurer of the Vincentian province based in St. Louis, said that the order would invest the money it received and use the income to support its mission activities, including those in Taiwan.

The Vincentians and other religious orders hoped that the diplomatic relations would open the doors for Catholic missionaries to work once again in China where the Church had been driven out.

Questions for Discussion

1. Are the common people of Russia Communists?
2. What does the takeover of Russia by communism teach us about our own nation's possibly falling to communism?
3. What kind of war was the Spanish Civil War in reality?
4. What is the meaning of the Spanish Monument of the Holy Cross in the Valley of the Fallen?
5. List the nations which are now living under atheistic communism.
6. Cuba, ninety miles from America, fell to communism. What do you think this says about the awareness of the United States to the dangers of communism in our hemisphere?
7. Is communism today essentially the same as that conceived by Marx, Engels, and Lenin, and which began worldwide domination under Stalin? Explain.
8. Summarize the meaning of communism according to Karl Marx.
9. What does the Communist theory hold regarding matter?
10. What is the meaning of Marx's Communist Manifesto?
11. What is the meaning of the "dialectic" in materialism, according to Marx?
12. What problem does the Communist theory regarding motion and matter run into when a "first mover" is sought to explain the origin or source of movement in the material world?
13. Explain why most treaties and negotiations with Communists have never been adhered to by the communists.
14. Why would the fall of Italy to communism be especially dangerous to the Catholic Church?
15. What have the various popes said about communism?
16. Summarize the intervention of heaven pertaining to events in Russia in 1917.
17. What significance can you see in the fact that between the dates when the Communist Revolution started in Russia and that great nation fell under the power of Communist forces, God's Mother was appearing at Fatima, where she mentioned Russia, the annihilation of nations, and the spread of the "errors of Russia" throughout the world?
18. It is often said that heaven gave us a peace plan at Fatima. How would you describe the Fatima message as a peace plan from heaven?

19. What does the "living" of the Fatima message require?
20. What has been the reaction of all the popes since 1917 to the Fatima message?
21. What happened to the Catholic Church on mainland China after the Communist takeover?

Chapter 18
Vatican Council II and the Church in the Modern World

1. Summarize the life of Pope John XXIII, who called Vatican Council II.

Angelo Roncalli was born November 25, 1881, at Sotte il Monte, Italy. He was educated in the seminary of the Bergamo diocese and at the Pontifical Seminary in Rome. He was ordained a priest on August 10, 1904. The first decade of his priesthood he served as secretary to the bishop of Bergamo, as an instructor in the seminary, and then as a medic and chaplain in the Italian army during World War I.

In 1921 Fr. Roncalli was given an assignment with the Society for the Propagation of the Faith. In 1925 he became apostolic visitor to Bulgaria. He also held such positions as apostolic delegate to Turkey and Greece, administrator of the Latin vicariate apostolic of Istanbul, and apostolic nuncio to France.

As Archbishop Roncalli, this great priest of the Church became an expert negotiator in delicate involvements with Roman, Eastern Rite, and Orthodox relationships. He represented the Church with people who suffered the consequences of World War II and he helped settle many suspicions that arose from wartime conditions.

On January 12, 1953, Archbishop Roncalli was named a cardinal by Pope Pius XII and then was appointed patriarch of Venice, the position he held when he was elected pope on October 28, 1958.

Already an old man when he was named pope, many thought he would be simply an "interregnum" pope, after the great pontifical reign of Pius XII. However, Pope John XXIII reigned for about 5½ years and his reign and decisions affected the history of the Catholic Church for present and future generations.

Pope John proved to be a strong, active pope and his influence was felt around the world, as he was loved by all men—by Christians of all persuasions and even by non-Christians. He became known in his own lifetime as "Good Pope John."

Pope John has often been misrepresented as responsible for radical elements within the Church (after Vatican Council II) which disturbed its peace, harmony, respect for authority, and loyalty to Church doctrine and discipline. Sometimes agitators and "reformers," who did not wish to follow the officially approved reforms of the Catholic Church, spoke of their motives and efforts as "in the spirit of Pope John" or "the spirit of Vatican Council II." In reality, the "spirit" of both was the opposite of theirs.

Since boyhood, as a young priest, a bishop, and then as pope, John XXIII was always loyal to the traditions of the Church, always stressing the necessity of undivided loyalty to Church doctrine and discipline and never advocating anything out of harmony with the faith and morals of the Catholic Church. His diary (kept since boyhood), titled *Journal of a Soul*, reveals how intensely loyal Pope John was until the moment of his death. He had intense loyalty to the rosary, praying all fifteen mysteries daily, even during his busy pontificate. His devotion to the Sacred Heart of Jesus and to the Real Presence of Jesus in the Blessed Sacrament, while at the same time being "progressive" enough to move the Church into the modern world so as to convert it, is a matter of documented history, edifying to any sincere Catholic.

Good Pope John issued eight encyclicals. Two are outstanding, and won immediate recognition in the world. *Mater et Magistra* (*Mother and Teacher* on Christianity and Social Progress) recapitulated in updated fashion and extended the social doctrine stated by Pope Leo XIII and Pope Pius XI. *Pacem in Terris* (Peace on Earth) concerned the natural principles of peace, and was the first encyclical ever formally issued by a pope to all men of good will as well as to Catholics.

On March 28, 1963, Pope John established a commission for revision of the Code of Canon Law, which performed its work for many years.

Pope John, who was beloved by all Christians, whether Catholic or not, assigned to the Second Vatican Council the task of promoting unity among all Christians, but he never called for any compromise of Catholic faith, for real unity can never be found in compromising the truth.

On January 25, 1959, Pope John XXIII announced his intention of calling the twenty-first ecumenical council of the Catholic Church.*

2. Why did Pope John XXIII convoke Vatican Council II?

His intention in convoking Vatican Council II as the twenty-first worldwide council (a council of the bishops of the entire Church) was to renew the life of

---

*For a more detailed life of Pope John XXIII, consult *Saints & Heroes Speak* (OSV Press).

the Church, to reform structures and institutions that needed updating, and to discover ways and means of promoting unity among all Christians.

Pope John used the Italian word *aggiornamento* in stating his purpose for Vatican Council II. Its general meaning is "to bring up to date," "to renew," "to revitalize." The word is descriptive of the processes of spiritual renewal and institutional reform and change in the Church judged necessary by Vatican Council II.

In his opening speech to the Ecumenical Council of Vatican II, Pope John said that the first need in calling the council was "to assert once again the Magisterium, which is unfailing and perdures until the end of time." The "magisterium" means the teaching authority of the Church. How unfortunate that, after this council, the magisterium, the teaching authority of the Church, was so often ignored even by some who said they spoke "in the spirit of Vatican II" or the "spirit of Pope John."

In calling the council, Pope John noted that he looked to the past, to listen to its voice. He declared that it was the principal duty of the council to defend and to advance the truth. The council was to be loyal to the sacred patrimony of truth, as received from the fathers, but to see ever new avenues by which to take the same, true faith of Christ to the world. He insisted that the Catholic Church would continue to oppose errors, but that its opposition must be treated with the medicine of mercy rather than that of severity. He sought ever greater unity in sanctity, and great joy in the eventual union of all the Christian churches of the world.

Thus the reform and change that Pope John sought in calling the council was in no way to change the faith and morals of the Catholic Church. His idea was to develop no new doctrine but a new way to make the constant unchangeable faith in Christ—as given the apostles in the sacred deposit of faith—ever more effective in the lives of people and for the evangelization of the entire world.

3. For how many sessions of the council was Pope John responsible?

Pope John called the council but he lived for only one of its four sessions. He opened the council on the Feast of the Divine Motherhood of Mary (October 11, 1962) after nearly four years of exhaustive preparation. The council's first work was the Constitution on the Sacred Liturgy, which brought about great changes in the structure and language of the Mass, without in any way changing its divine nature as sacrifice and sacrament, given us by the Lord Jesus Christ. That first session closed December 8, 1962, and Pope John died June 3, 1963.

Pope Paul VI reconvened the council for the remaining three sessions, which ran from September 29 to December 4, 1963; September 14 to November 21, 1964; and September 14 to December 8, 1965.

4. How many bishops participated in Vatican Council II?

A total of 2,860 council fathers (world bishops) participated in the Twenty-first Ecumenical Council of the Catholic Church. Attendance at council meetings varied from 2,000 to 2,500. For reasons such as health and the denial of exit visas from Communist-dominated countries, 274 bishops were not able to participate.

5. What documents were formulated and promulgated by Vatican II?

There was a total of sixteen, all of which represented the pastoral nature of Vatican Council II, directed to spiritual renewal and reform in the Church, without *in any way* changing the faith or morals of the Church.

The sixteen documents are as follows:

1. Dogmatic Constitution on the Church (*Lumen Gentium*), Nov. 21, 1964.
2. Dogmatic Constitution on Divine Revelation (*Dei Verbum*), Nov. 18, 1965.
3. Constitution on the Sacred Liturgy (*Sacrosanctum Concilium*), Dec. 4, 1963.
4. Pastoral Constitution on the Church in the Modern World (*Gaudium et Spes*), Dec. 7, 1965.
5. Decree on the Bishops' Pastoral Office in the Church (*Christus Dominus*), Oct. 28, 1965.
6. Decree on the Church's Missionary Activity (*Ad Gentes*), Dec. 7, 1965.
7. Decree on Ecumenism. (*Unitatis Redintegratio*), Nov. 21, 1964.
8. Decree on Eastern Catholic Church (*Orientalium Ecclesiarum*), Nov. 21, 1964.
9. Decree on the Ministry and Life of Priests (*Presbyterorum Ordinis*), Dec. 7, 1965.
10. Decree on Priestly Formation (*Optatam Totius*), Oct. 28, 1965.
11. Decree on the Appropriate Renewal of the Religious Life (*Perfectae Caritatis*), Oct. 28, 1965.
12. Decree on the Apostolate of the Laity (*Apostolicam Actuositatem*), Nov. 18, 1965.
13. Decree on the Instruments of Social Communication (*Inter Mirifica*), Dec. 4, 1963.
14. Declaration on Religious Freedom (*Dignitatis Humanae*), Dec. 7, 1965.
15. Declaration on the Relationship of the Church to Non-Christian Religions (*Nostra Aetate*), Oct. 28, 1965.
16. Declaration on Christian Education (*Gravissimum Educationis*), Oct. 28, 1965.

6. What did Vatican Council II say about the Blessed Virgin Mary?

Regarding the liturgy the council said: "In celebrating this annual cycle of Christ's mysteries, holy Church honors with special love the Blessed Mary, Mother of God, who is joined by an inseparable bond to the saving work of her Son. In Mary the Church holds up and admires the most excellent fruit of the redemption. In Mary the Church joyfully contemplates, as in a spotless model, that which the Church herself wholly desires and aspires to be."

The Vatican II council fathers devoted the entire eighth chapter of the Dogmatic Constitution on the Church to the Blessed Virgin Mary, Mother of God, in "The Mystery of Christ and the Church." The council also gave key statements about Mary in its Constitution on the Sacred Liturgy.

Pope Paul VI, in a speech to the council fathers, spoke as follows: "This year, the homage of our Council appears much more precious and significant. By the promulgation of today's constitution, which has as its crown and summit a whole chapter dedicated to our Lady, we can rightly affirm that the present session ends as an incomparable hymn of praise in honor of Mary.

"It is the first time, in fact, and saying it fills our souls with profound emotion, that an Ecumenical Council has presented such a vast synthesis of the Catholic doctrine regarding the place which the Blessed Mary occupies in the mystery of Christ and of the Church."

Vatican Council II was sensitive to the views of other Christians, as the council, at the request of Pope John XXIII, hoped to promote Christian unity, but knew there are different concepts about Mary among other Christians, especially Protestants. The council spoke of Mary as "Mediatrix," as strengthening—not lessening—confidence in Christ as the one essential Mediator.

The council, in speaking of Mary, used a biblical approach, with strong emphasis on her pilgrimage of faith. The council did not consider Mary as separate from its treatment of the Church, but discussed the mystery of Mary in the larger mystery of Christ and his Church.

After Vatican Council II, some misrepresented the council, claiming it had downgraded Catholic devotion to God's Mother. The council said "that the practices and exercises of devotion toward her, recommended by the teaching authority of the Church in the course of centuries, [are to be] highly esteemed." The council cautioned theologians and preachers of the word of God "to be careful to refrain as from all false exaggeration as from too summary an attitude in considering the special dignity of the Mother of God" (67, Dogmatic Constitution on the Church).

7. What other areas of Church life were misrepresented after Vatican Council II?

It is difficult to mention any area of Church life that did *not* experience misrepresentations. Misunderstandings created tendencies among many to "lose balance" on the Church and the modern world. Significant disturbances (which varied from area to area, with some areas experiencing little or no disturbance) were lack of respect for authority at all levels in the Church. There were disturbances in Catholic schools, colleges, and universities. Liturgical aberrations, as various individuals carried the reform of the liturgy further than authorized by the Church; ecumenism, where some experimented in circumstances that represented compromise of the true faith or pretended unity in areas where Christian unity did not exist; catechectics; loss by some priests and religious of the real sense of their vocation; seminaries where theologians taught a neo-Modernism in various forms; family life, when theologians attacked the position of the pope who reaffirmed the constant teaching of the Church which forbids artificial birth control. Such widespread disturbances also extended to a "vocation crisis," whereby fewer young men and women offered their lives to Christ in full service of the Church as priests and religious.

8. If such disturbances happened in the Church in the years immediately following Vatican II, how could they represent the renewal ("aggiornamento") called for by Pope John and the Council itself?

They did *not* represent authentic renewal in the Catholic Church. The history of the Church over its 2,000 years has been that, after various ecumenical councils, disturbances were experienced until the *authentic* renewal became thoroughly a part of Church life, reaching every aspect of Church life and its millions of members around the world. The Catholic Church is international, with millions of members of every nationality, culture, and background. The reforms of Vatican II brought more changes in the life of Catholics in a shorter time than had been experienced in its preceding 400 to 500 years.

The fact that the majority of the Church remained loyal and adapted to the changes (though sometimes with difficulty) is evidence of the divinity of the Church and the action of the Holy Spirit within Christ's Mystical Body. If the Church were only a natural body, such rapid changes as took place after the beginning of Vatican II (with its issuance of the Constitution on the Sacred Liturgy) would have torn a natural organization completely apart. But the Catholic Church is a *divine organism*, Christ's own Mystical Body, and at the same time that disturbances were felt, abundant signs of inner health and spiritual renewal were also taking place.

Unfortunately, some who lost their Catholic identity after Vatican II, or at least became confused, were not well informed in their faith and did not make proper distinctions. Some did not distinguish between *divine* law and *Church* law. Laws which come directly from God can never change. Laws which the Church has made in the course of centuries can change with time. Jesus gave the Church this power to bind and to loose (Mt 16:19).

With the rapid change of structures in the Catholic Church, stemming from

Vatican II (but which, in reality, Pope Pius XII had set in motion years before), some who had rightly been taught that the Catholic Church possesses the fullness of the true faith and can never be destroyed, and will be here until the end of the world, began to imagine that the inner nature (the faith and morals) of the Church was changing. Even some priests and religious found the changes difficult to adjust to, and sometimes the laity were scandalized by poor example in those to whom they looked for guidance.

Some said the Church was changing too fast. Others said the Church's changes were too little and too late. Because of such extreme accusations, one can rightly conclude that the Church, officially, was acting with balance, but all its members were not reacting with the same balance, which requires a spirit of obedience, humility, charity, and deep faith.

The 2,000-year history of the Catholic Church has given evidence, beginning with the twelve apostles, that not every priest, and certainly not every baptized member of the Church, remains loyal and faithful. However, no one is justified in becoming weak in the faith over the failure of a Judas. In fact, his sad history has strengthened members of the Church through the centuries, as they have encountered new Judases. Nor has the history of the Protestant Revolt of the sixteenth century disturbed Catholics of the last few centuries when they learned how Martin Luther, a priest (and other priests and religious) was the leader of a reformation and revolt *against* the Church.

Jesus, with sorrow, saw the dangers of disunity among his followers and, at the Last Supper, prayed that "all may be one" (Jn 17:21).

Christ Jesus established his Church with Peter as visible head, and the popes have been the successors of St. Peter. Every Catholic—lay, religious, priest, and bishop—has an obligation to listen to the pope, to obey him, and thus maintain the unity in faith and charity that Christ intended for his Church and for which he established the papacy.

9. Did all Catholic educators, theologians, priests, and religious remain obedient to the pope after Vatican Council II?

Many did, but others did not obey the pope, making subtle distinctions that the pope must be obeyed or listened to only when he speaks infallibly. Such has never been the teaching of the Church, and it was not the teaching of Vatican Council II.

For example, controversies broke out whereby the position of the pope was attacked on such matters as artificial birth control. Pope Paul VI, in his encyclical *Humanae Vitae* (July 29, 1968), restated the traditional teaching of the Church, by which Catholics, in the sacredness of matrimony, are told that "each and every marriage act must remain open to the transmission of life" (art. 11). A group of theologians took to the public media to protest the pope's restating of the Catholic position against artificial birth control, and their action was contrary "to the binding force of religious assent" which Pope Paul said his encyclical on marriage doctrine and morality required. As soon as it was announced that the pope was releasing the encyclical, restating the Church's traditional position, certain theologians even before they had read or studied the encyclical, took to the air waves, publicly denouncing the action of the pope.

The disrespect and disobedience shown the pope in reaction to his encyclical ("Of Human Life") was nothing less than scandalous. Such open protest and disobedience against the highest Church authority had sad repercussions in other areas of Church life, as it was followed by dissent in other matters during the years following the release of the encyclical. The scandalous dissent among Catholics aided the contraceptive mentality so widespread in America. This prepared the way to the abortion mentality, whereby five years later the Supreme Court of the United States legalized abortive murders of the unborn.

10. What did Vatican II say about the pope's speaking infallibly and about the obligation of Catholics to assent, even when he does not speak infallibly ("ex cathedra")?

"Bishops who teach in communion with the Roman Pontiff are to be revered by all as witnesses of divine Catholic truth; the faithful, for their part, are obliged to submit to their bishops' decision, made in the name of Christ, in matters of faith and morals, and to adhere to it with a ready and respectful allegiance of mind. This loyal submission of the will and intellect must be given, in a special way, to the authentic teaching authority of the Roman Pontiff, even when he does not speak *ex cathedra* in such wise, indeed, that his supreme teaching authority be acknowledged with respect, and sincere assent be given to decisions made by him, conformably with his manifest mind and intention, which is made known principally either by the character of the documents in question, or by the frequency with which a certain doctrine is proposed, or by the manner in which the doctrine is formulated.

"Although the bishops, taken individually, do not enjoy the privilege of infallibility, they do, however, proclaim infallibly the doctrine of Christ on the following conditions: namely, when, even though dispersed throughout the world but preserving for all that amongst themselves and with Peter's successor the bond of communion, in their authoritative teaching concerning matters of faith and morals, they are in agreement that a particular teaching is to be held definitively and absolutely. This is still more clearly the case when, assembled in an ecumenical council, they are, for the universal Church, teachers of and judges in matters of faith and morals, whose decisions must be adhered to with the loyal and obedient assent of faith.

"This infallibility, however, with which the divine Redeemer wished to endow his Church in defining doctrine pertaining to faith and morals, is coextensive with the deposit of revelation, which must be religiously guarded and loyally and courageously expounded. The Roman Pontiff, head of the college of bishops, enjoys this infallibility in virtue of his office, when, as supreme pastor and teacher of all the faithful—who confirms his brethren in the faith (cf. Lk 22:32)—he proclaims in an absolute decision a doctrine pertaining to faith or morals. For that reason his definitions are rightly said to be irreformable by their very nature and not by reason of the assent of the Church, in as much as they were made with the assistance of the Holy Spirit promised to him in the person of blessed Peter himself; and as a consequence they are in no way in need of the approval of others, and do not admit of appeal to any other tribunal. For in such a case the Roman Pontiff does not utter a pronouncement as a private person, but rather does he expound and defend the teaching of the Catholic faith as the supreme teacher of the universal Church, in whom the Church's charism of infallibility is present in a singular way" (*Lumen Gentium*, 25).*

11. What problem developed in catechetics after Vatican Council II?

Abundant sources of catechetical materials developed in the years immediately following Vatican II, together with various new methods of teaching the faith. While there were vast improvements in many tools for the communication of faith, extensive studies revealed—as in the case of the National Catechetical Consultation in 1974, in preparing a *National Catechetical Directory*—that there was great concern among Catholic parents and others about the *content* of religious education. The concern was that the *entire* content of the Christian message be taught, and not watered down. It was felt that many youths and young adults had not been properly formed in their Catholic faith because the fullness of Catholic faith had not been taught.

Monsignor Wilfrid H. Paradis, director of the *Directory* project for the United States, stated that the reaction of those suffering frustration and disappointment with regard to current religious educational content was well expressed by the statement that "doctrine seems blurred for many who are annoyed and upset by the uncertainty."

The confusion caused by *Modernistic* theologians' dissenting from authoritative papal positions and developing new theories in the interpretations of Catholic doctrines and the scriptures was felt by Catholic youth. Theological *opinions* were often expressed in religion textbooks and classrooms, in place of the authentic Catholic faith *in its fullness*.

12. How did the Vatican handle the catechetical crisis in the Church?

*From *Vatican Council II: The Conciliar and Post Conciliar Documents*, Liturgical Press, Collegeville, Minn.

The Vatican, through the Sacred Congregation for the Clergy, and with the authorization of the Supreme Pontiff, Paul VI, on March 18, 1971, issued a *General Catechetical Directory* to provide the basic principles of pastoral theology for pastoral action in the ministry of the word of God.

The *General Catechetical Directory* says its "course of action was adopted especially for the following reason: the errors which are not infrequently noted in catechetics today can be avoided only if one starts with the correct way of understanding the nature and purposes of catechesis and also the truths which are to be taught by it, with due account being taken of those to whom catechesis is directed and of the conditions in which they live."

It further stated: "The immediate purpose of the *Directory* is to provide assistance in the production of catechetical directories and catechisms."

It is obvious that the highest authorities in the Church recognized the catechetical crisis and that the fullness of true Catholic faith often was not adequately taught. This situation contributed to some youth never developing in or learning the fullness of the Catholic faith.

The Vatican also called catechetical synods at Rome for the purpose of improving the religious education of all people of all ages.

13. What did the American bishops do in response to the "General Catechetical Directory"?

In November 1972 the National Conference of Catholic Bishops issued a pastoral message on Catholic education, titled *To Teach as Jesus Did.* On January 11, 1973, reflecting the contents of the *General Catechetical Directory,* the United States bishops issued the document *Basic Teachings for Catholic Religious Education.* This latter document listed the essential elements of faith which must be stressed in the religious formation of Catholics of all ages. The bishops' document was approved by the Vatican.

The American bishops also spearheaded the development of a *National Catechetical Directory,* beginning in 1973 and consisting of three rounds of nationwide consultation of priests, religious, and lay persons, that would be a comprehensive United States-oriented guidebook for religious education. The general consultations continued until March 15, 1977, producing a Vatican-approved *National Catechetical Directory* which incorporates the basic features of the *General Catechetical Directory* approved by Pope Paul VI and the *Basic Teachings of Catholic Religious Education,* already approved by both the American bishops and the Vatican. On November 17, 1977, the bishops approved the *National Catechetical Directory* and sent it to the Holy See for final adjustments. It was approved by the Vatican's *Sacred Congregation for the Clergy* on October 30, 1978 and appeared in print in the spring of 1979, titled "Sharing the Light of Faith."

14. How did the Church react to nonofficial reports on the downplaying of devotion to the Mother of God which followed Vatican II?

On November 21, 1973, the United States Bishops issued a pastoral letter on the Blessed Virgin Mary, *Behold Your Mother, Woman of Faith.*

On February 2, 1974, Pope Paul VI issued a magnificent apostolic exhortation (*Marialis Cultus*) "for the right ordering and development of devotion to the Blessed Virgin Mary."

While documents in themselves do not solve problems unless they are implemented in the lives of people, the pope and the bishops clearly outlined the position of the Church on doctrine and true devotion concerning the Mother of God for men of good will.

15. Did the Church issue other documents after Vatican II to implement the Council and clarify the Church's teachings?

Yes, many documents. The Church issued postconciliar documents on such subjects as the proper celebration of the liturgy, administration of the sacraments, sacred music, first confession and First Communion, mixed marriages, ecumenical matters for christian unity, renewal of religious life, religious relations with Jews, the Church's missionary activity, etc.

16. How did the Church react to permissiveness and confusion in sexual ethics?

On December 29, 1975, the Church issued the *Vatican Declaration on Sexual Ethics* to clarify misunderstandings of the Church's position on human sexuality. The declaration said: "There are many people today who, being confronted with so many widespread opinions opposed to the teaching which they received from the Church, have come to wonder what they must now hold as true. The Church cannot remain indifferent to this confusion of minds and relaxation of morals."

The Church then reaffirmed its position, in harmony with God's word, requiring purity of thought and conduct, both personal and social, and total abstinence before marriage.

17. Was Vatican Council II responsible for the confusion in various aspects of Church life in the years which followed the issuance of its sixteen documents?

No. All the documents were in harmony with the deposit of faith entrusted to the original apostles by Jesus Christ. The confusion and misunderstandings resulted not from the official documents of Vatican II but from those who misinterpreted and misrepresented the ecumenical council.

Some put too great emphasis on *external* renewal, without sufficient emphasis on the *inner* spiritual renewal of souls. At first, emphasis on the change of the *structure* of the Mass—from Latin to the language of the people, with the priest now facing the people, and the assembly of God's people participating more actively by song and response—all this was thought by some to be the essential renewal to which Vatican Council II called all members of the Church. However, these were *externals*, intended merely as signs and expressions of the inner unity in Christ of all God's people in the common priesthood of the baptized.

The Catholic Church has always taught, as did Vatican Council II, that all the baptized participate in the priesthood of Christ. At the same time, priests ordained in holy orders participate in Christ's priesthood in a special way that differs in essence (not only in degree) from the priesthood of the faithful who are only baptized and confirmed. Perhaps because the council's special *Decree on the Apostolate of Lay People* emphasized laymen's duties and privileges as members of the Church, some began to fall into the same mistake that had been made by the Protestant reformers who denied the special powers of Christ's priesthood, reserved only to those who have received the sacrament of holy orders.

18. What superficial or false ecumenism developed after Vatican Council II?

Great progress was made in inter-Christian relations, both in understanding and appreciating other faiths, as well as cooperating in practical Christian works. Christians of various denominations met together, notably for a Week of Prayer for Christian Unity (each year, January 18 to 25), and prayed in common, which demonstrated that Christians have much in common—as well as differences.

All of this was well and good, and called for by Vatican II under the direction of bishops. Theologians of different persuasions met to discuss their faith, and often discovered they had more in common than they'd thought. Sometimes, however, theologians and various ecumenical commissions came to agreements that did not represent the official position of their respective churches. Publicity concerning such matters—often without full explanation or comprehension—led to confusion among the faithful.

Abuses consisted of inter-communion services which were not authorized and, at times, emphasis on other faiths when a full study and understanding of one's own faith had not first been accomplished. The Church had not approved "indiscriminate" common worship but only common prayer under certain conditions authorized by one's bishop. Among some, abuses in ecumenism led to religious indifference. Too often, Catholic youth, not well grounded and formed in the basics of their own faith, failed to understand and appreicate their Catholic identity and developed a religious indifference to their Church, as was also the case of many Protestants regarding organized churches.

Some youth turned to false religious cults, seeking mysticism in religion. Unfortunately for youthful Catholics thus deceived, they were unaware of the profound mystical tradition in the works and lives of the saints of the Catholic

Church from ancient days to the present time. They were unaware of the solid mystical theology of the Catholic Church available to those who study the "sources."

19. Did Vatican II authorize compromises of the Catholic faith?

No. It authorized just the opposite, as these quotations from the *Decree on Ecumenism* show:

"It is through Christ's Catholic Church alone, which is the universal help toward salvation, that the fullness of the means of salvation can be obtained. It was to the apostolic college alone, of which Peter is the head, that we believe that Our Lord entrusted all the blessings of the New Covenant, in order to establish on earth the one Body of Christ into which all those should be fully incorporated who belong in any way to the people of God. . . .

"For although the Catholic Church has been endowed with all divinely revealed truth and with all means of grace, yet its members fail to live by them with all the fervor that they should. As a result the radiance of the Church's face shines less brightly in the eyes of our separated brethren and of the world at large, and the growth of God's kingdom is retarded. Every Catholic must therefore aim at Christian perfection. . . .

"There can be no ecumenism worthy of the name without interior conversion. For it is from newness of attitudes of mind, from self-denial and unstinted love, that desires of unity take their rise and develop in a mature way. . . .

"In certain circumstances, such as in prayer services 'for unity' and during ecumenical gatherings, it is allowable, indeed desirable that Catholics should join in prayer with their separated brethren. Such prayers in common are certainly a very effective means of petitioning for the grace of unity, and they are a genuine expression of the ties which still bind Catholics to their separated brethren. . . .

"Yet worship in common (*communicatio in sacris*) is not to be considered as a means to be used indiscriminately for the restoration of unity among Christians. . . . The concrete course to be adopted, when all the circumstances of time, place and persons have been dully considered, is left to the prudent decision of the local episcopal authority, unless the bishops' conference according to its own statutes, or the Holy See, has determined otherwise."

The whole *Decree on Ecumenism opposed* any compromise of the true faith, but called for openness in charity and humility and for recognizing truth and goodness in our separated brethren, even though they do not possess the fullness of true faith. The unity Christ called for already exists in the Catholic Church, even though all her members do not fully live that faith, as they should.

20. Did Vatican II replace tradition and the teaching authority of the Church (magesterium) with the sole authority of God's word in sacred Scripture?

No. This is what Vatican II said in its *Dogmatic Constitution on Divine Revelation*:

"Sacred Tradition and sacred Scripture make up a single sacred deposit of the Word of God, which is entrusted to the Church. By adhering to it the entire holy people, united to its pastors, remains always faithful to the teaching of the apostles, to the brotherhood, to the breaking of bread and the prayers (cf. Acts 2:42). So, in maintaining, practicing and professing the faith that has been handed on there should be a remarkable harmony between the bishops and the faithful.

"But the task of giving an authentic interpretation of the Word of God, whether in its written form or in the form of Tradition, has been entrusted to the living teaching office of the Church alone. Its authority in this matter is exercised in the name of Jesus Christ. Yet this Magisterium is not superior to the Word of God, but is its servant. It teaches only what has been handed on to it. At the divine command and with the help of the Holy Spirit, it listens to this devotedly, guards it with dedication and expounds it faithfully. All that it proposes for belief as being divinely revealed is drawn from the single deposit of faith.

"It is clear, therefore, that, in the supremely wise arrangement of God, sacred Tradition, sacred Scripture and the Magisterium of the Church are so connected and associated that one of them cannot stand without the others. Working together, each in its own way under the action of the one Holy Spirit, they all contribute effectively to the salvation of souls" (11).

21. Was there a confusion of roles in the Church after Vatican II?

Yes. There can never be erosion of the Catholic faith in the Church as such. The Church is never in doubt as to what is true Christian faith. Individuals in the Church may become confused as to what is the Catholic faith, and *some* modern theologians assisted greatly in this. The Catholic faith in itself, as preserved by the Catholic Church, will always remain intact.

The chief attributes of the Catholic Church are authority, infallibility, and indefectibility. ("Indefectible" means the Church will last until the end of time.) The Catholic Church, and therefore the Catholic faith, cannot be destroyed, as our Lord has promised.

The introduction to the American bishops' document, *Basic Teachings for Catholic Religious Education* (January 11, 1973) states: "It is necessary that the authentic teachings of the Church, and those only be presented in religious instruction as official Catholic doctrine. Religion texts or classroom teachers should never present merely subjective theorizing as the Church's teaching.

"For this reason, a distinction must be borne in mind between, on the one hand, the area that is devoted to scientific investigation and, on the other, the area that concerns the teaching of the faithful. In the first, experts enjoy the freedom required by their work and are free to communicate to others, in books and commentaries, the fruits of their research. In the second, only those doctrines may be attributed to the Church which are declared to be such by her authentic Magisterium."

Archbishop Joseph Bernardin of Cincinnati summarized the confusion of roles after Vatican II in speaking of the distinct roles of bishop, teacher, and theologian: "Because he is the custodian of God's revelation, he [the bishop] also has the responsibility for cultivating an ever increasing understanding and penetration of that revelation. If he is a 20th century bishop, he cannot allow his people to be content with a 16th century understanding of their faith, or even a 19th century understanding of their faith."

The archbishop said that the basic role of teachers of religion is "to present, in their own concrete sphere of activity, the authentic teachings of the Church as proposed and guaranteed by the bishops. They are true collaborators, fellow workers, with the bishop in his teaching function. Without them, his work becomes impossible. . . . Their primary task is not to teach their own personal opinion or theological hypotheses."

About theologians, Archbishop Bernardin continued: "The bishop's task of encouraging further penetration of the meaning of revelation is directed toward the theologians. In the vast region of God's message to man, they are the explorers. Because they are explorers, they must have a certain amount of freedom. Because they are explorers, we must expect that their searches will not always be successful, and that there are going to be some mistakes. All this is part of the theologian's role. And in conducting these explorations, the theologian provides a great and necessary service to the Church.

"It is my opinion, that much of the confusion connected with Christian education could be avoided if we, and all God's people, kept clear and distinct in our minds these three areas of endeavor, each of which is unique.

"Nothing but frustration and confusion can arise in the minds of the Christian faithful if the theologian begins to think that he is a bishop and acts as the final arbiter of the content of religion.

"Or if the teacher of religion begins to act as theologian and thus gives his students the impression that he is teaching Catholic doctrine when he is really teaching personal opinions.

"Or, I might add, if a bishop refused to respect the competencies of his theologians and teachers of religion and insists that everthing be done in accord with his own private point of view."

Archbishop Bernardin succinctly states how *confusion of roles* became a major cause of trouble after Vatican Council II. The faith never changes, and is never added to, but doctrine can develop in the sense that our understanding of the faith develops through the ages without addition to or subtraction from the deposit of faith. It is the official position of the Catholic Church, reaffirmed by Vatican II, that the sacred deposit of faith will never be added to, because it was complete at the time of the death of the last apostle. Our *understanding* of the faith, as contained in the sacred deposit of faith, may develop, but not the deposit of faith itself, which contains the total truths revealed by Christ, taught infallibly by the Church and witnessed by scripture and tradition.

After Vatican II, *process theologians,* with ideas of "ongoing revelation," spread their false ideas of change and added to the confusion of the faithful. Some theologians imagined themselves another magisterium of the Church, whereas, in reality, theologians are in no way the authoritative teaching Church established by Christ.

22. What positive features of renewal were experiences as a result of Vatican Council II?

At least a hundred years will be needed to fully evaluate the fruit, value, and richness of the Vatican Council II renewal. The Catholic Church has been here for twenty centuries, and will still be here at the end of the world, and its effectiveness cannot be judged by any one period of time.

Vatican II "modernized" the Catholic Church without in any way compromising with the heresy of Modernism. Participation of the laity in the liturgy of the Church was made possible by Vatican II, and in a greater measure than was possible before the council. This "inner participation" was always possible and desirable, but the reforms of the liturgy brought the Mass and the sacraments closer to the people so that they can participate more intelligently.

Vatican Council II made members of the Church more aware that *all* baptized members (not simply the clergy and religious) are in fact the Church and share various functions and responsibilities in spreading the faith of Christ to the ends of the world. The nature of the Church as missionary was revealed to many Catholics.

Vatican II challenged the faith of millions of its members as to whether they were just drifting deadwood, merely part of an inherited culture, or whether their faith was living and deep and could be applied to the social issues of our times so as to Christianize the whole of society. While the faith of some was severely tested (and failed), millions of others came to a deeper involvement in the practical living of the true faith.

Vatican II stirred the consciences of all Christians, reminding them of their obligation to fulfill the will and the prayer of Jesus Christ that all his followers be one, even as he and the Father are one.

Vatican II, while calling for shared responsibility, in no way abdicated authority. It upheld all the teachings of all the preceding twenty councils of the Catholic Church and brought to light the doctrine of the priesthood of the laity, pointing out not only the dignity of all the baptized, but their duties before God and man in the Church.

Vatican II opened scripture more fully for the faithful in their participation in the Church year through the liturgy. It encouraged the laity (through councils) to assist their pastors in the work of the Church and priests (through synods or senates) to assist their bishops, without in any way confusing roles or usurping authority.

When the sixteen documents of Vatican II are fully digested and properly implemented into the life of the many millions of Catholic laity, religious, and priests, we can look to (as it were) a new Pentecost, for which Pope John XXIII called the council, and that "new springtime" of life in the Church, which Pope Pius XII predicted before his death.

Summary

How does one summarize an ecumenical council, such as Vatican II, that has been and is transforming Christian society and has brought more changes to the Church in a few years than during the preceding 400 to 500 years? Without harm to faith or morals, some of the changes of Vatican II would have been realized centuries earlier if it had not been for the Protestant Revolt (and its own reformation) in the sixteenth century.

At the time of the Protestant Revolt there were movements for the use of the vernacular (language of the people) in the liturgy. The "revolters" immediately put their services in the language of the people, and so Latin became identified with Christians who remained loyal to the pope in the unity of the ancient Catholic Church. Doubtlessly, the nonauthorized innovations, changes, and discard of doctrines which accompanied the religious upheaval of the sixteenth century necessitated that the Catholic Church, for the protection of her members and to save them from confusion, maintain its long-held position on such questions as use of the vernacular. Thus Latin became almost a fifth (though nonessential) mark of the true Church after the Protestant Revolt.

What does one say about those Catholics who, after Vatican II and during the implementation of the council documents, became confused about or disobedient to Church authority, striking out even against the Holy Father, the pope? Ultimately, only God judges souls. One can sympathize with the faithful who were led astray by some members of the clergy and religious, who themselves rebelled against or misrepresented the truth. And still we must remember that, for each and all, God's grace is always sufficient in every temptation, and once the gift of the fullness of the true faith has been bestowed by God upon a soul, our good, heavenly Father will not withdraw it, unless the person himself (or herself) rejects it.

After Vatican II, life in the Catholic Church became more challenging and more thrilling—more full of joy for those who engaged in the authentic renewal under and together with the magisterium. Confusion reigned only when educators, clergy, religious, and laity did not work in harmony with the Holy Father in interpreting and implementing the authentic renewal to which each Catholic is called.

Most who read and use this book of Church history are Catholic teenagers, tomorrow's adults and tomorrow's Church. But the Church of tomorrow will be the same as the Church of yesterday, of the last century, and of the first century. A newly conceived human life in its mother's womb, is a continuum, still the same life when it is born as it is one hour, one day, or fifty or eighty years later. So the Catholic Church, Christ's Mystical Body of today and the future, will always be the same Church Jesus Christ founded twenty centuries ago.

The cells of the human body change with the passage of years; still, it is the same human body. Individual members of the laity, religious, priests, bishops, and our Holy Father the pope change with the passage of years. Still, it is the same Church, "one Lord, one faith, one baptism." As sacred scripture says: "Jesus Christ is the same, yesterday, today, the same forever."

Our Catholic youth of today must become so strong in the faith—not beset by confusion or misunderstandings, but looking beyond the human failings of individual members of the Church and striving for personal perfection in Christ Jesus—that the reality and the sanctity of the Church, its true face, will truly be known and loved by all the world.

The Catholic Church is a divine organism. It is of Christ, the God-Man himself. It is human, and also divine. With the eyes of faith, each member must see beyond its human quality and witness the inner divine reality which is Christ's Mystical Body.

We have just studied its 2,000-year history, and as we look to the future we can know that, as in the past, Satan and the forces of evil will always be there, attempting to destroy the Church through its human quality. As Christ Jesus was tempted in the desert, the forces of evil, the spirit of wickedness, will never cease tempting the members of Christ. As the head of the Mystical Body did not and could not fail, for he is divine, so, through the indwelling of the Holy Spirit, the human quality will be strengthened and will prevail.

The history of the Catholic Church will always be full of pages of great and lesser saints who testify to that mark of the Church we call *holiness.* It will always retain its oneness, its catholicity (universality), and always remain apostolic: the only Church built upon the apostles and promised that "the gates of hell shall never prevail against it."

Questions for Discussion

1. Summarize the religious character of "Good Pope John."
2. What purpose did Pope John XXIII have in calling Vatican Council II?
3. Which pope presided over most of Vatican Council II?
4. What was the first work of the council which deeply affectd the religious practice of Catholics? Explain how it affected them.
5. How many documents did Vatican II issue and what was their main intent?
6. What did the council declare about Mary and why were the council fathers sensitive to Protestant concepts about Mary?
7. What are some of the disturbances which arose in the Church after Vatican II?

8. Did these disturbances truly reflect the reality of Vatican Council II? Explain.
9. Who especially questioned the official position of the Church and how did they react, thus causing confusion for many Catholic people?
10. What did Vatican Council II say about the obligation of Catholics toward the pronouncements of the pope, even when the Holy Father does not speak ex cathedra?
11. What was the catechetical problem that developed about the time of Vatican II and the years following?
12. How did the Vatican react to abuses that were not infrequent in the teaching of the faith?
13. Explain how our American bishops cooperated with the directives of the Vatican.
14. Did the Church make any official reaction to the false reports that it downplayed its former devotion to the Mother of God? Explain.
15. In summary, what did the Catholic Church say about the confusion in sexual ethics?
16. What is meant by superficial or false ecumenism?
17. Explain how Vatican II in no way called for a compromise of the Catholic faith.
18. Since Vatican II, some Catholics have acted as if scripture is the chief and *only* authority in the Church for our understanding in the faith of the word of God. How would you answer such a claim?
19. Explain what is meant by the confusion of roles which some Catholics were guilty of after Vatican Council II.
20. Name the positive features in Church life which resulted from the Second Vatican Council.
21. How did the Protestant Revolt of the sixteenth century in some respects cause the Catholic Church to remain "frozen" in updating features which *can* be changed?

Chapter 19
The Church in the World
to the Present Day
(Conclusion)

At 9:40 p.m. Rome time, August 6, 1978, Pope Paul VI died, 3 hours and 10 minutes after suffering a heart attack. As Cardinal Giovanni Montini, he had been elected Pope June 21, 1963, and took the name Paul VI as the 262d successor to St. Peter as bishop of Rome. He was crowned with the triple tiara (which he never wore again but donated for charitable purposes) on June 30, 1963, in St. Peter's Square at Vatican City.

On the day after his election to the papacy, Paul VI announced on Vatican Radio that he would continue the Church's renewal policy and the program of his predecessor, John XXIII. Pope Paul also said he would reconvene the Second Vatican Council, which had completed only one session before the death of Pope John.

During the last three sessions, Paul, like his preoecessor, seldom intervened, but on June 23, 1964, he announced that he was reserving to himself for study and decision a number of questions about birth control. During the third session, Paul took under personal advisement a number of questions related to mixed marriage and similar matters, at the request of a large majority of the council fathers. Several weeks after the fourth session began, Pope Paul VI terminated discussion of clerical celibacy because the matter affects the Church deeply and the communications media were treating the issue in an emotional manner. This action was hailed by the council fathers.

Paul brought the Second Vatican Council to a close on December 8, 1965, noting in a final address that the decisive phase of renewal had already been set in action. He declared a special jubilee of prayer, study, and work in the Church

221

to realize the objectives laid down in the sixteen documents of the council, and he implemented various enactments of the council. This 262d successor of St. Peter directed the Church in greater and farther reaching changes in the Church—while preserving its unity in faith and morals—than perhaps any other pontiff since St. Peter.

On August 6, 1964, Pope Paul issued his first encyclical, *Ecclesiam Suam*, in which he developed the four main themes related to Church renewal and the aims of Vatican Council II: awareness of the nature of the Church and the need to increase such awareness among its members; the internal renewal of the Church and the external expression of it; the dialogue the Church must engage in among its own members and with the total world; and the offer of his services to help the cause of world peace.

On April 29, 1965, Pope Paul issued *Mense Maio*, urging prayer, especially through the intercession of the Blessed Virgin Mary during the month of May, for the success of the Vatican Council.

On September 3, 1965, he issued *Mysterium Fidei*, a strong reaffirmation of the traditional doctrine of the Church concerning the holy Eucharist, which perpetuates the Sacrifice of the Cross and makes present the body, blood, soul and divinity of Jesus Christ in the Blessed Sacrament.

Christi Matri Rosarii, issued September 15, 1966, urged saying the rosary during the month of October as a special prayer for peace.

The Development of Peoples, March 16, 1967, extended the social doctrine of Pope John's *Peace on Earth* and was widely hailed. It was seen as having special application to the Third World and supplementing the council's *Pastoral Constitution on the Church in the Modern World*.

The traditional doctrine and practice of the Latin Church on clerical celibacy was restated in *Priestly Celibacy* (June 24, 1967). Although it was well documented in stating the tradition of the Church, many who had argued for a change of this discipline continued their debates openly, sometimes causing scandal.

Dissent against the Pope's Encyclical

Humanae Vitae (Of Human Life), dated July 25, 1968, restated the traditional doctrine of the Church, which prohibits artificial birth control. It too became an occasion for some theologians to take to the public media, defying the authority of the Pope. Dissent against papal authority, as expressed in this encyclical, became widespread and the resulting scandal brought great harm to unity among Catholics. A "contraceptive mentality" became widespread and contributed to the "abortion mentality" that soon followed. Whereas some had argued that the use of contraceptives would help many marriages, divorce statistics greatly increased, to the point that many feared the family as the basic unit of society was in grave jeopardy.

Pope Paul VI was active in directing the Church until his last days. Suddenly, while the world was beginning to celebrate the tenth anniversary of his controversial encyclical *Of Human Life,* he died. He had predicted for some months that his time upon earth was drawing to an end.

Shortly before his death (August 6, 1978), restudy of the encyclical *Of Human Life* caused many to realize that it contains divine wisdom as well as profound human insights into married love and responsible parenthood. By the time of the Pope's death, the world had begun to realize the grave social consequences of artificial birth control. Pope Paul VI showed prophetic vision in recognizing that use of contraceptives favors laxity in married behavior and disdain for human life at all stages of development. In countries where contraception is practiced, the number of abortions has increased.

Dialogue with Communist countries

The fifteen-year reign of Pope Paul VI (1963–1978) was marked with great successes as well as great tragedies for the Church. During his reign, the Church began to hold dialogue with the world. In his first encyclical, *Ecclesiam Suam,* Paul said he had no intention of excluding Communists from dialogue with the Church, even though it would probably be incomplete and very difficult. One purpose of the Secretariat for Non-Believers, which Pope Paul VI authorized and established April 8, 1965, is to study relations and initiate discussions with Communists and others on atheism.

The Vatican had limited success in negotiations with countries controlled by Communist governments. For example, negotiations with the Hungarian government led to an agreement in September 1964 that gives limited freedom to the Vatican in the appointment of bishops. However, Cardinal Mindszenty remained in seclusion in the American Embassy in Budapest until September 1971.

It took two years of diplomatic conversations before an agreement was signed between Yugoslavia and the Vatican. Full diplomatic relations were established in 1970.

For several years, negotiations with Czechoslovakia had little results, as did attempts to open diplomatic doors with other Communist countries. A measure of agreement was reached with the Communist Polish government in 1972, when Polish bishops were appointed to four jurisdictions in the Oder-Niesse territory formerly held by German prelates.

Pope Paul VI, a man of peace

When Pope Paul VI died in August 1978, the world recognized this pontiff as a man of peace. In 1963 he had spoken in favor of negotiations for a nuclear test ban agreement, which was signed by nearly 100 nations. At the beginning of 1964, when he went as a pilgrim to the Holy Places, he sent 220 peace messages from Jerusalem to heads of state and international leaders. Eleven months later, he appealed for peace and disarmament while attending the 38th International

Eucharistic Congress in Bombay. He also urged nations to spend the funds they would save through disarmament for useful and humanitarian purposes—to relieve hunger, misery, illness, and ignorance.

In 1965, Pope Paul VI had pleaded for peace in Vietnam, the Congo, the Dominican Republic, India, Pakistan, and Kashmir. He denounced terrorist guerrilla tactics under all circumstances.

On the twentieth anniversary of the atomic bombing of Japan, he prayed (only one of many such appeals): "May the world never again see a day of misfortune like that of Hiroshima."

On October 4, 1965, Paul VI visited United Nations headquarters in New York to plead: "No more war; never again war."

When the war intensified in Vietnam after 1965, Pope Paul VI increased his efforts for peace. In the fall of 1966 he sent a special fact-finding delegation to Vietnam to consult with the country's bishops.

Peace was the subject of many of his talks, especially his private talks with such persons as U.S. United Nations Ambassador Arthur Goldberg, U.S. Ambassador to Vietnam Henry Cabot Lodge, and Soviet Foreign Minister Andrei Gromyko.

In December 1965 he appealed for the relief of famine, particularly in India and Pakistan. By July 1966, almost $7.5 million had been raised in response.

Though peace was not achieved, throughout 1967 Pope Paul VI appealed again and again for peace and offered his services to achieve a peaceful resolution in Vietnam. Similar efforts were made regarding the Israeli-Arab conflict. The most the Pope could accomplish was the mobilization of Vatican relief forces to assist refugees. Beginning in July, he urged a peaceful settlement on leaders of the opposing factions in Nigeria, where tribal and political warfare was taking a terrible toll of human life.

Pope Paul VI continued his efforts as a Pope of peace in 1968 and 1969 in these same areas, and offered the Vatican as a site for Vietnam peace talks. With most other world leaders in 1968, the Pope spoke out against the Soviet invasion and occupation of Czechoslovakia.

From 1971 to 1975, Pope Paul VI often spoke against the war in Indochina and the Middle East. In 1971 he appealed for the end of the civil war in East Pakistan and called for international action to help the millions of refugees in India. Beginning in 1971, he also pleaded for peace in Northern Ireland. The Communist uprisings in Portugal in 1974 and 1975 brought new appeals from the Pope, and until the end of his life he sought peace in the Middle East, pleading especially for an end of violence in Lebanon.

Most traveled Pope in history

Pope Paul VI was the most traveled pope in the history of the papacy. Pope John XXIII had opened the post-war era by traveling outside the Vatican, the first time since 1870, but Pope Paul VI was the first pope to travel outside Italy since Pius VII was forced to flee by Napoleon (about 150 years earlier).

Pope Paul VI met the Ecumenical Patriarch Athenagoras I from January 4 to 6, 1964, when he went as a pilgrim to the Holy Places. Besides the Eucharistic Congress in Bombay in 1964 and the United Nations in New York in 1965, when he pleaded for peace before representatives of 116 countries, Paul VI traveled every year, until old age made it impossible.

In December 1966 he made a "pilgrimage" to the Florentine area of Italy, which had been devastated by a great flood. On May 13, 1967, he traveled to Fatima, to pray for peace in the Church and in the world, at the world-famous Marian shrine in Portugal.

On July 25, 1967, Pope Paul VI flew to Turkey to visit Patriarch Athenagoras I of Constantinople (great progress toward unity with Orthodox Christians was made during the pontificate of Pope Paul VI). On this same pilgrimage, he visited the ancient city of Ephesus, where, according to an ancient tradition (archeological evidence also points in that direction), the Virgin Mary lived at the end of her life and the ecumenical council which defined her title as *Theotokos* (Mother of God or God-bearer) met in 431. His pilgrimage was a combination of ecumenism and devotion to God's Mother.

In August 1968, Paul VI went to South America for the 39th International Eucharistic Congress in Bogota, Columbia. In 1969 he made two trips: to Geneva, where he addressed delegates at the headquarters of the International Labor Organization and the World Council of Churches (in June), and Kampala, to honor the martyrs of Uganda (July 31 to August 2). On April 24, 1970, Pope Paul VI went to Sardinia to join the islanders in their celebration in honor of their patroness, Our Lady of Bonaria.

His tenth and most extensive trip was also in 1970. The Pope stopped in Teheran (Nov. 26), Manila, the Philippines (Nov. 27 to 29), Samoa (Nov. 29), Sydney, Australia (Nov. 30 to Dec. 3), Djakarta, Indonesia (Dec. 3 and 4), Hong Kong (Dec. 4), Colombo, Sri Lauka (formerly Ceylon) (Dec. 4), and cyclone-ravaged Pakistan. A would-be-assassin atempted to stab the pope in Manila, and was forgiven.

Pope Paul VI visited Udine, Italy (Sept. 16, 1972) to take part in a eucharistic congress and stopped at Venice, where he met Cardinal Albino Luciani, and in St. Mark's Square, before thousands of spectators, removed his stole to place it temporarily on this cardinal-patriarch of Venice, who was to become his successor.

The papal reign was marked by striking changes in the structure of the Church as Pope Paul VI worked to implement the sixteen documents of Vatican Council II. Besides the dissent against his encyclical *Humanae Vitae,* Paul had to contend with a movement that urged the ordination of women, which he resisted as contrary to the tradition of the Church, and also with those who argued for a married clergy. He also met with such dissidents as Archbishop Marcel Lefebvre, who took rebellious stands against various enactments of the Second Vatican Council.

Archbishop Marcel Lefebvre gained worldwide attention in his resistance to the new rite of the Mass and in insisting on the Tridentine liturgy. He was suspended by the Pope from the exercise of holy orders but ignored the Pope and repeatedly ordained men for his society at his headquarters-seminary in Econe, Switzerland. Although Pope Paul VI made efforts at reconciliation with the archbishop, his efforts were not successful, and the archbishop's followers, desired a return to the Latin or Tridentine Mass.

During the years he was pope, Pope Paul VI canonized 84 saints, more than any other single pope.

The Pope who reigned 34 days

The death of Pope Paul VI, after a progressive but stormy reign, brought many speculations about which cardinal would succeed him. All widely publicized speculations proved wrong, and one of the "unknown" *papabili* (cardinals who were capable of being elected) was elected to replace Pope Paul VI. Patriarch Albino Luciani of Venice was elected on the fourth ballot.

The election of Cardinal Luciani (Aug. 26, 1978) caught the world by surprise, as did the name he chose: Pope John Paul I. He vowed to continue the policies of his two predecessors, implementing the documents of Vatican II.

Pope John Paul I immediately won the affection not only of the Catholic world but the world at large. Those who had hoped for a "pope of compromise" (as suggested by the media) were proved wrong. As bishop and as patriarch of Venice, Pope John Paul I stood firm on traditional Catholic doctrine and morality and promised to do so as the 263d successor of St. Peter. He warned against applying political labels to churchmen—labels of liberal or conservative or right or left, which he saw as crude and misleading descriptions of the Catholic approach to faith and morals which the Church must always protect and promote.

The new Pope, 65 years of age, came to the papacy with little experience in the Curia, the Church's central administrative agencies in the Vatican for the universal Church. (Pope John Paul had been made a cardinal a little more than five years earlier, on March 5, 1973.) The largest conclave in history, 111 cardinals, elected the new Pope on the first full day of balloting. He was invested as the new Pope on September 3, 1978, foregoing the traditional coronation with a triple crown (tiara), which to many symbolized temporal power.

John Paul I was quickly labeled "the smiling Pope." Although the Catholic world had been concerned about the type of man who would succeed the difficult reign of Pope Paul VI, it appeared that almost no one was disappointed. The cardinals had come from the conclave jubilant, and the new Pope greeted the world from the balcony of St. Peter's overlooking St. Peter's Square. Television cameras beamed the radiant smile and obvious deep love of the new Pope to the world within minutes after his election.

The world had called for a "pastoral" Pope and that is what it got. John Paul I had not spent his priesthood in high administrative offices of the universal Church. Rather, he had served as a priest and bishop among the people. He was a humble man, who took the word *humilitas* for his motto. His humility, warmth, and love for people (and children in particular) was obvious to all.

The world rejoiced, but in thirty-four days Pope John Paul I died of a heart attack in the late evening of September 28, about 11 p.m., while reading *The Imitation of Christ*. He did not appear for Mass early the next morning, and was found dead in bed about 5 a.m. on September 29.

Deprived of the "smiling Pope," who entered the papacy as a strong foe of communism and a defender of traditional doctrines of faith and morals, who would have been a strong pastoral pope, having immediately won everyone's confidence and affection, the world was shocked and acted with disbelief, then went into mourning.

Carlo Cardinal Confalonieri, dean of the College of Cardinals, gave the sermon at the funeral Mass, saying that Pope John Paul I "passed as a meteor which unexpectedly lights up the heavens and then disappears, leaving us amazed and astonished. We have scarcely had time to see the new Pope, yet one month was enough for him to conquer our hearts—and for us, it was a month to love him intensely." Hundreds of thousands of people stood in St. Peter's Square for the funeral, while millions watched the funeral Mass on television—as they had watched his installation Mass only a month earlier.

The world wanted another Papa Luciani

The world was so convinced that it needed a pope like the Pope who reigned for but thirty-four days, without naming a cardinal or issuing an encyclical, that the cardinals asked with the rest of the world: "Is there another like *Papa Luciani*?" All reports indicate the cardinals were determined to find one. Pope John Paul I's great gift to the world in his short reign was that he brought the papacy to the people.

Pope Paul VI, his immediate predecessor, had for fifteen years directed the Church during one of the stormiest periods of its history. It must be credited to Pope Paul VI that, under great pressures, he refused to bend on such issues as artificial birth control, priestly celibacy, and divorce and remarriage. On "closed" issues, men of faith said, the Holy Spirit could not permit the Pope to compromise. Pope Paul VI had therefore become a Pope of "controversy."

Some accused him of not being decisive enough, of delaying too long in making decisions, as on the issue of artificial birth control, thus waiting until things got out of hand (so that many expected the Church to reverse its traditional teachings) before he issued a reaffirmation of the Church's ban. Some also felt he permitted too many options in the liturgy of the Mass and the sacraments, in the manner of their celebration, thus losing in external appearances the sign of unity in the Church that was so evident when they were administered in Latin under tight and uniform rites. On the other hand, he was accused of being too rigid—not flexible enough. That he was a saintly man, fully dedicated to the love of God and souls, no one questioned.

In the last years of the reign of Pope Paul VI, some had felt that respect for the authority of the Pope had suffered. The Pope, who had moved the Church in renewal, implementing the sixteen documents of Vatican Council II, had met rebellion, dissent from not a few theologians, priests, and laity—even from a few bishops. The Church had experienced upsets after previous ecumenical councils, and it was the fate of Pope Paul VI to serve the Church during such a period.

The special charisma with which the successor of Pope Paul VI charmed the world was felt to be just what the universal Church needed to regain the confidence of all in its chief leader. Pope John Paul I, the "smiling Pope," was also called the "people's Pope." His infectious smile assisted in winning hearts. His love for children (he brought them to his side during general audiences' won the admiration of all. He advised American bishops: "Go to the children." Priests were told to remain at their posts. Pope John Paul I was quoted as saying that God is as much a mother as he is a father.

At the end of September 1978 the Church was mourning the death of its second pope in two months and by early October was looking for a third in as many months.

Three popes in three months

For three months, August through October, the public media of the world focused daily on the papacy. Again the public media advanced their *papabili* as they speculated on who the next pope might be. Again, the public media opined that the Catholic Church would have to solve its "questions" of a married clergy, whether women could be ordained, artificial birth control, and divorce and remarriage. All these matters had been settled under Pope Paul VI, but the world did not always like the answers. The possibility of a non-Italian pope was mentioned but not taken seriously.

Modern technology, in the form of communication satellites and television sets in millions of homes, helped to focus attention on the successors of St. Peter. It noted that the oldest continuous institution in the world is the Catholic Church, with its visible ruler, the pope, who according to Catholic faith reigns in the name of Jesus Christ.

Two conclaves in 1978 in less than two months for the election of a new pope was not the first time cardinals had to elect successors to St. Peter in rapid succession. In the sixteenth century, after the death of Pope Sixtus V (Aug. 27, 1590), the cardinals met in conclaves four times in eighteen months. Pope Urban VII reigned only twelve days. After his death (Sept. 27) a two-month conclave elected Pope Gregory XIV, who reigned a little more than ten months and died October 16, 1591. Thirteen days later Pope Innocent IX took the papal throne and reigned for only sixty-two days (he died Dec. 30, 1591). On January

30, 1592, the conclave elected 55-year-old Cardinal Ippolito Fano, who, as Pope Clement VIII, reigned for twelve years.

The first non-Italian Pope in 455 years

The sudden death of Pope John Paul I at 65 years of age raised the question of electing a younger man. On October 14, 1978, the cardinals (again numbering 111) went into secret conclave, conscious of their grave responsibility to select a successor to Pope John Paul I, and on October 16, Cardinal Pericle Felici appeared on the central balcony of St. Peter's Basilica to announce "We have a Pope." Hundreds of thousands had gathered to hear the news. As he announced the last words of the age-old formula, ". . . Wojtyla, who has chosen the name John Paul II," the crowd fell momentarily silent. Most did not recognize the name. Then the cheering began again, steadily gaining in volume, as those in St. Peter's Square realized the cardinals had elected Cardinal Karol Wojtyla of Kracow, Poland.

The television cameras of the world again focused on the balcony, waiting for the new Pope to appear. At 58 years of age, he radiated robust health, and the first words of Pope John Paul II to the world were these: "We salute Jesus Christ. We are still in profound sorrow after the death of the most beloved Pope, John Paul I, and the eminent cardinals have called for a new Bishop of Rome.

"They have called him from a country far away, distant, but ever close in the communion of the faith and the Chrisitan tradition.

"With fear I received this nomination, but I have accepted it in faithfulness to the spirit of obedience to which our Lord commands us, and like the obedience of his Blessed Mother, the Madonna.

"I am not sure I can express myself well in Italian; so correct me if I make mistakes.

"I present myself to you all, to confess our common faith, our hope, our confidence in the Mother of the Church, and also again to travel the passageways of the history of the Church with the aid of God and the aid of men."

The election of a cardinal from Poland surprised the world; it was the first time in 455 years that a non-Italian was elected. The last non-Italian had been Adrian VI, who served twenty months in 1522–23 while Martin Luther's rebellion raged.

Polish Pope well received

The election of a Polish cardinal was hailed by the world on many counts, for it reflected the universal nature of the Church, which is not intrinsically Italian. During the reign of Pope Paul VI, Catholicism in Africa grew 111 percent, to 52 million. Catholicism had shown signs of resurgence in Latin America and of reviving in Eastern, Communist-dominated Europe, with Poland the best example.

Cardinal Wojtyla was born in Wadowice, Poland, on May 18, 1920. He began studying philology in 1938 at Jagiellonium University in Krakow, with special interest in poetry and the theater, but his studies were interrupted with the outbreak of World War II. In 1940, during the Nazi occupation of his country, young Karol Wojtyla began working as a laborer, and in 1942 he entered an "underground" seminary in Krakow which was functioning secretly because of Nazi prohibitions. He was ordained a priest in 1946 and sent to Rome to further his studies in moral theology.

After finishing his doctorate with the Jagiellonian Theological faculty, Fr. Wojtyla was assigned as curate in a village parish. He also did pastoral work (chiefly among university students) when he was transferred back to Krakow. Fr. Wojtyla began teaching ethics at the Jagiellonian in 1953, and eventually held the chair of ethics at the Catholic University of Lublin.

He was only 38 when he was named a bishop, in 1958, and became auxiliary bishop of Krakow. He was put in charge of the Krakow diocese as *vicar capitular* when Bishop Eugeniusz Baziak died in 1962. He attended all the Second Vatican Council sessions in Rome from 1962 to 1965 and was particularly active in preparing the *Pastoral Constitution on the Church in the Modern World.*

In 1964 he was named archbishop of Krakow, an office that had been vacant since the death of Cardinal Adam Sapieha in 1951 because the Communist government refused to approve a successor. He was named a cardinal by Pope Paul VI in 1967, when he was only 47.

Pope John Paul II, unlike his short-reign predecessor, came to the papacy with experience in the Vatican's curial offices. He was a member of the Curia's Congregation of the Sacraments and Divine Worship, the Congregation for the Clergy, and the Congregation for Catholic Education. He made frequent visits to the Vatican, and the year before his election had given a retreat for Pope Paul VI and the Vatican staff.

When a non-Italian Pope had been announced 455 years earlier, the people in St. Peter's Square had booed the announcement. Not so with Pope John Paul II; excitement and enthusiasm were immediate when they learned that a cardinal from Poland was elected, and the same spirit quickly spread throughout the world. His command of the Italian language made him easily acceptable as the bishop of Rome, as well as Pope. Pope John Paul II has command of various languages, including German, French, Spanish, and his native language, Polish. He also speaks fluent English—the first Pope in history to be able to converse easily in the English language.

In his first general audience (Oct. 18, 1978), the new Pope spoke in the presence of the cardinals still assembled in Rome. He said: "It is difficult for me not to express deep gratitude to the Holy Father, Paul VI, for the fact that he gave the Sacred College such a wide, international, intercontinental dimension. Its members, in fact, come from the farthest ends of the earth. That makes it possible not only to accentuate the universality of the Church but also the universal aspect of Rome."

The Poland of Pope John Paul II

On September 17, 1978, the month before the election of the first pope from Poland, the Catholic bishops of Poland had called for the abolition of censorship in their Communist country, denouncing it a "weapon of totalitarian regimes." Their pastoral letter was read from pulpits throughout Poland on September 17. It was one of the strongest Church denunciations of Communist censorship in years, and among its signers were Cardinals Stefan Wyszynski and Karol Wojtyla. The bishops deplored "harassment of those who have the courage openly to express, orally or in writing, their opinions on public life." Restrictions on publication of Catholic periodicals in Poland, they said, kept the number of copies in circulation well below demand.

Poland is one of Europe's most religious nations and the Catholic Church is considered the most influential institution in the nation, aside from the Communist regime. Ninety percent of Poland's population is considered to be Catholic, and most of the Catholic people practice their faith through regular participation in holy Mass.

Poland has been different from other countries of the Eastern European Communist bloc in that most of its 35 million people are not only Catholic but strong in their practice of the faith. The government has feared to take extreme measures that might push the people to a popular uprising. However, many responsible jobs and positions are reserved exclusively for non-believers and non-practicing Catholics. At the time of the election of Pope John Paul II, several teaching institutes had reached the point of asking applicants to submit statements attesting to the fact that they were atheists.

Under the atheistic Communist government, parochial schools are not allowed to exist in Poland. Catholic youth and lay organizations are forbidden. The Church is almost entirely ignored by the news media and is given no access to state-controlled radio and television for broadcasting religious programs.

However, the election of Poland's first pope, which focused the world's attention on the reaction of its Communist government, caused the officials to permit the installation Mass of Pope John Paul II (Oct. 22, 1978) to be televised throughout Poland and their highest-ranking Communist official to attend the ceremony at Rome, namely, Poland's Communist president, Henryk Jablonski.

At the time of Pope John Paul's election, hundreds of thousands of Poles in the drab country's industrial suburbs had no alternative but to attend Mass outdoors, even in cold and rainy seasons, because the government would not permit the building of a sufficient number of churches. Communist authorities scheduled attractive outings for students and factory workers on Sundays to discourage attendance at Mass. In some fields, the government has made Sunday a day of work. Still, the people of Poland flock to churches on Sunday or to slap-dash shelters that protect the altar from the elements.

Polish Catholics have maintained a strong attachment to our Lady, especially honored as the "Black Madonna" of Czestochowa. Pope John Paul II has a large letter M for "Maria" on his coat of arms in the lower right-hand corner, with an off-center cross. His motto pertaining to the Blessed Virgin Mary is *Totus Tuus* (yours entirely).

The Communist regime of Poland has failed to separate the people from their bishops. Also, Poland's hierarchy has developed remarkable contact with the Church in other countries. In the early months of his pontificate, after a successful trip to Mexico where millions greeted the new Pope. John Paul II announced plans to visit his native land of Poland in June, 1979.

Pope Paul II is well known in the United States, having twice traveled to major U.S. cities. His first visit was in 1969; on his last visit, as Cardinal Karol Wojtyla, he participated in the 1976 International Eucharistic Congress in Philadelphia. At that time, he spent four weeks in the United States and visited Washington, D.C., where he spoke of how hardship had reinforced Polish Catholicism. He said: "The atheist character of the government forces people consciously to affirm their beliefs."

Absence of religious instruction in the schools requires young people (outside school hours) to go to churches or catechetical centers for religious instruction. He added: "We have vocations to the seminaries in sufficient numbers."

Pope John Paul II came to the papacy as "a servant." He prayed to Jesus Christ: "Make me be a servant—indeed, the servant of your servants." To Christians he pleaded: "Do not be afraid. Let Christ speak to man. He alone has words of life—yes, of eternal life." Pope John Paul II also chose not to be crowned with the tiara and was vested simply with a pallium of white sheep's wool (with black crosses) as a symbol of his spiritual authority in the universal Church.

Pope John Paul II, servant and friend of the working man and youth

John Paul II came to the papacy with the reputation of being a friend of the workingman—a reputation that is not appreciated by the Communist regime, whose history has been an attempt to separate the workingman from the Church. He is also a friend of youth, with a record of directing university students in Poland away from Communist ideology.

Pope John Paul II is also known as a hard worker, who works tirelessly to form souls in Jesus Christ. Even before his election, he had an international reputation as a defender of religious liberty at Vatican Council II. During numerous sessions he asked the council fathers to speak out clearly in defense of people who were denied religious freedom. In Poland, he defended the religious freedom of Jewish people.

In his first major address, Pope John Paul II pledged to promote applications of Vatican II "with action that is both prudent and stimulating." He reminded bishops and Catholics in general of the importance of fidelity to the Church's teaching authority, particularly in doctrine. He said that he intends to continue to work for Christian unity. Cardinals were reminded that their red robes mean the willingness to die, if necessary, for Jesus Christ.

Pope John Paul II immediately created the image of a pastoral pope, one who intensely loves people and will reach out to all men as the Vicar of Jesus Christ.

First encyclical—Redeemer of Man

On March 4, 1979 Pope John Paul II issued his first encyclical to the world, *Redemptor Hominis* (Redeemer of Man). In it the new Pope condemned the arms race and asked for changes in the world's social, political and economic life. He was critical of "consumer civilization" and totalitarian regimes restricting religious freedom. He did not mention communist governments by name but obviously meant them when he spoke of those which give "only atheism the right of citizenship in public and social life. . . ."

Pope John Paul II also spoke in his first encyclical of internal Church matters calling for a period of consolidation, stressing traditional Catholic values and the teachings of Vatican II. He praised Pope Paul VI for maintaining a "providential balance" in doctrinal matters during the controversies of the immediate post-council years.

Although the Church "has internal difficulties and tensions," the Pope added, "She is internally more strengthened against the excesses of self-criticism, she can be said to be more critical with regard to the various 'novelties,' more mature in her spirit of discerning."

The role of theologians in the Church

The Pope in "*Redemptor Hominis* spoke of theologicans as "servants of divine truth" and stressed the need for them to remain united to Church teachings. He said: "Theology has always had and continues to have great importance for the Church, the people of God, to be able to share creatively and fruitfully in Christ's mission as prophet. Therefore, when theologians, as servants of divine truth, dedicate their studies and labors to ever deeper understanding of that truth, they can never lose sight of the meaning of their service in the Church."

The Pope spoke about "a certain pluralism of methodology" in theology. "The work cannot however depart from the fundamental unity in the teaching of faith and morals which is that work's end. Accordingly, close collaboration by theology with the magisterium (official Teaching Church) is indispensable. Every theologian must be particularly aware of what Christ himself stated when he said: 'The word which you heard is not mine but the Father's who sent me.' Nobody, therefore, can make of theology as it were a simple collection of his own personal ideas, but everybody must be aware of being in close union with the mission of teaching truth for which the Church is responsible."

Pope John Paul II had an overall optimistic view of Church life. "In spite of all appearances the Church is now more united in the fellowship of service and in the awareness of apostolate."

Letter to Bishops and Priests of the world

Dated Holy Thursday, 1979, Pope John Paul II issued *A Letter To All The Priests of the Church* as well as *A Letter to the Bishops* of the world. The important need for priests in the Church today was stressed as well as the life-long commitment they make to Jesus Christ on the day of their ordination when they receive an "indelible character." The Pope upheld celibacy for those who accept the call to the Sacrament of Orders. In the same letter he entrusted the priesthood of every priest in the world to the Mother of Christ and asked each priest to do the same themselves.

Pope John Paul II made a triumphal return to Poland June 2–10, 1979. *Time* (June 18, 1979) reports: "It was like a carnival, a political campaign, a crusade and an enormous Polish wedding all in one... a performance unique in the annals of the papacy... John Paul made an astonishing three dozen public appearances... In Poland, the visible contrast between the Church and the ruling regime, even after it has been in power for more than 30 years, was devastating; he called himself history's 'first Slav Pope' whose succession to the Apostle Peter forms a bond of blood not only with Poles but with other Slavic peoples, including Czechs, Slovaks, Solvenes, Serbs, Croats, Bulgarians, Ukrainians and most dramatically, Russians—some 220 million Slavs in all... the Pope seemed to envision an eventual pan-European Christian alliance against the secular materialism of both East and West."

Summary

The passing of Pope Paul VI, who was rapidly succeeded by two popes within two months, not only focused the attention of the world on the importance of the papacy but indicated that the "style" of the papacy was changing. Paul VI had the image of a "suffering" pope; Pope John Paul I had a more relaxed image, as a "smiling" pope. When the latter's thirty-four-day reign ended abruptly, with his unexpected death, he was succeeded by Pope John Paul II from Poland, the first non-Italian pope in 455 years.

The changing style of the papacy seemed to be on the minds of most observers, not only as regards the personality and approach of those who sit on the chair of St. Peter but also by breaking the long tradition of Italian popes and selecting one from another country—from a country, moreover, under the control of an atheistic and Communistic government.

"The pope is universal, as is the Church," was the message projected to an anxious world. Pope John Paul II, only 58 at the time of his election, projects the image of a man who is strong, both physically and spiritually, who is full of vitality, who has suffered from the evils of the modern world but nonetheless lives an intense spiritual life and inspires millions in his homeland and in all the modern world to resist the forces of atheism.

That John Paul II would be a pastoral pope of the people, anxious to use modern technology to evangelize the world to Christ, was immediately evident. At the same time, he would uphold all the doctrinal and devotional traditions of the Church.

Though the world gives political considerations to what Pope John Paul II says and does, the glory of God and the salvation of souls are his real and ultimate motive. The second weekend after his election, he flew by helicopter to a Polish-run Marian shrine at Mantorella, about 35 miles from Rome, where he had spent four days in prayer before he entered the conclave which elected him pope. He said that the shrine had helped him pray and that *prayer* is the "first task and almost the first announcement of the Pope, as it is the first condition of his service in the Church and in the world."

The following weekend the Pope visited the tomb of St. Francis of Assisi. Shortly after his election, he also visited the tomb of St. Catherine of Sienna, in Rome. At a Sunday Angelus he said: "The rosary is my favorite prayer." The Vatican daily newspaper reported: "The visits are intended to put the Pope's reign under the patronage of those two holy protectors." Observers noted that his early actions signaled what might well become a hallmark of his papacy: new stress on popular devotion to Mary and the saints.

Pope John Paul II noted in his first address, however, that not even he could say exactly what his reign would be like. But he wanted to make it clear to all: he came to the papacy as the servant of the servants of God.

Questions for Discussion

1. Which subjects did Pope Paul VI reserve for himself, rather than have them dealt with by Vatican Council II?
2. Which encyclical letter of Pope Paul VI caused great controversy in the Church? Discuss it.
3. How did Pope Paul VI deal with countries under a Communist government?
4. For historical reasons, the popes had long been secluded to the Vatican. How did Pope Paul VI reverse that practice?
5. Do you agree with the opinion that Pope Paul VI was a hindrance to the Church's adjusting to the modern world? Explain.
6. Besides the resistance to the teaching of the Church forbidding artificial birth control, what other resistance did Pope Paul VI have to contend with?
7. How would you summarize the reign of Pope Paul VI? A success? A failure?
8. Describe the brief reign of Pope John Paul I.
9. What events caused the role of the papacy to be in the news of the world almost daily for three months during 1978?
10. What features in the election of Pope John Paul II surprised the world?
11. Describe the background of Pope John Paul II.
12. Would you say the reign of Pope John Paul II has been much like the early observers anticipated? Explain.

Addendum

List of Popes

(Source: *Annuario Pontificio*.)

Information includes the name of the pope, in many cases his name before becoming pope, his birthplace or country of origin, the date of accession to the papacy, and the date of the end of reign which, in all but a few cases, was the date of death. Double dates indicate times of election and coronation.

St. Peter (Simon Bar-Jona): Bethsaida in Galilee; d. c. 67.

St. Linus: Tuscany; 67–76.

St. Anacletus (Cletus): Rome; 76–88.

St. Clement: Rome; 88–97.

St. Evaristus: Greece; 97–105.

St. Alexander I: Rome; 105–115.

St. Sixtus I: Rome; 115–125.

St. Telesphorus: Greece; 125–136.

St. Hyginus: Greece; 136–140.

St. Pius I: Aquileia; 140–155.

St. Anicetus: Syria; 155–166.

St. Soter: Campania; 166–175.

St. Eleutherius: Nicopolis in Epirus; 175–189.

Up to the time of St. Eleutherius, the years indicated for the beginning and end of pontificates are not absolutely certain. Also, up to the middle of the 11th century, there are some doubts about the exact days and months given in chronological tables.

St. Victor I: Africa; 189–199.

St. Zephyrinus: Rome; 199–217.

St. Callistus I: Rome, 217–222.

St. Urban I: Rome; 222–230.

St. Pontian: Rome; July 21, 230, to Sept. 28, 235.

St. Anterus: Greece; Nov. 21, 235, to Jan. 3, 236.

St. Fabian: Rome; Jan. 10, 236, to Jan. 20, 250.

St. Cornelius: Rome: Mar., 251, to June, 253.

St. Lucius I: Rome; June 25, 253, to Mar. 5, 254.

St. Stephen I: Rome; May 12, 254, to Aug. 2, 257.

St. Sixtus II: Greece; Aug. 30, 257, to Aug, 6, 258.

St. Dionysius: July 22, 259, to Dec. 26, 268.

St. Felix I: Rome; Jan. 5, 269, to Dec. 30, 274.

St. Eutychian: Luni; Jan. 4, 275, to Dec. 7, 283.

St. Caius: Dalmatia; Dec. 17, 283, to Apr. 22, 296.

St. Marcellinus: Rome; June 30, 296, to Oct. 25, 304.

St. Marcellus I: Rome; May 27, 308, or June 26, 308, to Jan. 16, 309.

St. Eusebius: Greece; Apr. 18, 309 or 310, to Aug. 17, 309 or 310.

St. Melchiades (Miltiades): Africa; July 2, 311, to Jan. 11, 314.

St. Sylvester I: Rome; Jan. 31, 314, to Dec. 31, 335. (Most of the popes before St. Sylvester I were martyrs.)

St. Marcus: Rome; Jan. 18, 336, to Oct. 7, 336.

St. Julius I: Rome; Feb. 6, 337, to Apr. 12, 352.

Liberius: Rome; May 17, 352, to Sept. 24, 366.

St. Damasus I: Spain; Oct. 1, 366, to Dec. 11, 384.

St. Siricius: Rome; Dec. 15, or 22 or 29, 384, to Nov. 26, 399.

St. Anastasius I: Rome; Nov. 27, 399, to Dec. 19, 401.

St. Innocent I: Albano; Dec. 22, 401, to Mar. 12, 417.

St. Zozimus: Greece; Mar. 18, 417, to Dec. 26, 418.

St. Boniface I: Rome; Dec. 28 or 29, 418, to Sept. 4, 422.

St. Celestine I: Campania; Sept. 10, 422, to July 27, 432.

St. Sixtus III: Rome; July 31, 432, to Aug. 19, 440.

St. Leo I (the Great): Tuscany; Sept. 29, 440, to Nov. 10, 461.

St. Hilary: Sardinia; Nov. 19, 461, to Feb. 29, 468.

St. Simplicius: Tivoli; Mar. 3, 468, to Mar, 10, 483.

St. Felix III (II): Rome; Mar. 13, 483, to Mar. 1, 492.

He should be called Felix II, and his successors of the same name should be numbered accordingly. The discrepancy in the numerical designation of popes named Felix was caused by the erroneous insertion in some lists of the name of St. Felix of Rome, a martyr.

St. Gelasius I: Africa; Mar. 1, 492, to Nov. 21, 496.

Anastasius II: Rome; Nov. 24, 496, to Nov. 19, 498.

St. Symmachus: Sardinia; Nov. 22, 498, to July 19, 514.

St. Hormisdas: Frosinone; July 20, 514, to Aug. 6, 523.

St. John I, Martyr: Tuscany: Aug. 13, 523, to May 18, 526.

St. Felix IV (III): Samnium; July 12, 526, to Sept. 22, 530.

Boniface II: Rome; Sept. 22, 530, to Oct. 17, 532.

John II: Rome; Jan. 2, 533, to May 8, 535.

John II was the first pope to change his name, His given name was Mercury.

St. Agapitus I: Rome; May 13, 535, to Apr. 22, 536.

St. Silverius, Martyr: Campania; June 1 or 8, 536, to Nov. 11, 537 (d. Dec. 2, 537).

St. Silverius was violently deposed in March, 537, and abdicated Nov. 11, 537. His successor, Vigilius, was not recognized as pope by all the Roman clergy until his abdication.

Vigilius: Rome; Mar. 29, 537, to June 7, 555.

Pelagius I: Rome; Apr. 16, 556, to Mar. 4, 561.

John III: Rome; July 17, 561, to July 13, 574.

Benedict I: Rome; June 2, 575, to July 30, 579.

Pelagius II: Rome; Nov. 26, 579, to Feb. 7, 590.

St. Gregory I (the Great): Rome; Sept. 3, 590, to Mar. 12, 604.

Sabinian: Biera in Tuscany; Sept. 13, 604, to Feb. 22, 606.

Boniface III: Rome; Feb. 19, 607, to Nov. 12, 607.

St. Boniface IV: Abruzzi; Aug. 25, 608, to May 8, 615.

St. Deusdedit (Adeodatus I): Rome; Oct. 19, 615, to Nov. 8, 618.

Boniface V: Naples; Dec. 23, 619, to Oct. 25, 625.

Honorius I: Campania; Oct. 27, 625, to Oct. 12, 638.

Severinus: Rome; May 28, 640, to Aug. 2, 640.

John IV: Dalmatia; Dec. 24, 640, to Oct. 12, 642.

Theodore I: Greece; Nov. 24, 642, to May 14, 649.

St. Martin I, Martyr: Todi; July, 649, to Sept. 16, 655 (in exile from June 17, 653).

St. Eugene I: Rome; Aug. 10, 654, to June 2, 657.

St. Eugene I was elected during the exile of St. Martin I, who is believed to have endorsed him as pope.

St. Vitalian: Segni; July 30, 657, to Jan 27, 672.

Adeodatus II: Rome; Apr. 11, 672, to June 27, 676.

Donus: Rome; Nov. 2, 676, to Apr. 11, 678.

St. Agatho: Sicily; June 27, 678, to Jan 10, 681.

St. Leo II: Sicily; Aug. 17, 682, to July 3, 683.

St. Benedict II: Rome; June 26, 684, to May 8, 685.

John V: Syria; July 23, 685, to Aug. 2, 686.

Conon: birthplace unknown; Oct. 21, 686, to Sept. 21, 687.

St. Sergius I: Syria; Dec. 15, 687, to Sept. 8, 701.

John VI: Greece; Oct. 30, 701, to Jan. 11, 705.

John VII: Greece; Mar. 1, 705, to Oct. 18, 707.

Sisinnius: Syria; Jan. 15, 708, to Feb. 4, 708.

Constantine: Syria; Mar. 25, 708, to Apr. 9, 715.

St. Gregory II: Rome; May 19, 715, to Feb. 11, 731.

St. Gregory III: Syria; Mar. 18, 731, to Nov., 741.

St. Zachary: Greece; Dec. 10, 741, to Mar. 22, 752.

Stephen II (III): Rome; Mar. 26, 752, to Apr. 26, 757.

After the death of St. Zachary, a Roman priest named Stephen was elected but died (four days later) before his consecration as bishop of Rome, which would have marked the beginning of his pontificate. Another Stephen was elected to succeed Zachary as Stephen II. (The first pope with this name was St. Stephen I, 254–57.) The ordinal III appears in parentheses after the name of Stephen II because the name of the earlier elected but deceased priest was included in some lists. Other Stephens have double numbers.

St. Paul I: Rome; Apr. (May 29), 757, to June 28, 767.

Stephen III (IV): Sicily; Aug. 1 (7), 768, to Jan. 24, 772.

Adrian I: Rome; Feb. 1 (9), 772, to Dec. 25, 795.

St. Leo III: Rome; Dec. 26 (27), 795, to June 12, 816.

Stephen IV (V): Rome; June 22, 816, to Jan. 24, 817.

St. Paschal I: Rome; Jan. 25, 817, to Feb. 11, 824.

Eugene II: Rome; Feb. (May), 824, to Aug., 827.

Valentine: Rome; Aug. 827, to Sept., 827.

Gregory IV: Rome; 827, to Jan., 844.

Sergius II: Rome; Jan., 844, to Jan. 27, 847.

St. Leo IV: Rome; Jan. (Apr. 10), 847, to July 17, 855.

Benedict III: Rome; July (Sept. 29), 855, to Apr. 17, 858.

St. Nicholas I (the Great): Rome; Apr. 24, 858, to Nov. 13, 867.

Adrian II: Rome; Dec. 14, 867, to Dec. 14, 872.

John VIII: Rome; Dec. 14, 872, to Dec. 16, 882.

Marinus I: Gallese; Dec. 16, 882, to May 15, 884.

St. Adrian III: Rome; May 17, 884, to Sept., 885. Cult confirmed June 2, 1891.

Stephen V (VI): Rome; Sept., 885, to Sept. 14, 891.

Formosus: Portus; Oct. 6, 891, to Apr. 4, 896.

Boniface VI: Rome; Apr., 896, to Apr., 896.

Stephen VI (VII): Rome; May, 896, to Aug., 897.

Romanus: Gallese; Aug., 897, to Nov., 897.

Theodore II: Rome; Dec. 897, to Dec., 897.

John IX: Tivoli; Jan., 898, to Jan., 900.

Benedict IV: Rome; Jan. (Feb.), 900, to July, 903.

Leo V: Ardea; July, 903, to Sept., 903.

Sergius III: Rome; Jan. 29, 904, to Apr. 14, 911.

Anastasius III: Rome; Apr., 911, to June, 913.

Landus: Sabina; July, 913, to Feb., 914.

John X: Tossignano (Imola); Mar., 914, to May, 928.

Leo VI: Rome; May, 928, to Dec., 928.

Stephen VII (VIII): Rome; Dec., 928, to Feb., 931.

John XI: Rome; Feb. (Mar.), 931, to Dec., 935.

Leo VII: Rome; Jan. 3, 936, to July 13, 939.

Stephen VIII (IX): Rome; July 14, 939, to Oct., 942.

Marinus II: Rome; Oct. 30, 942, to May, 946.

Agapitus II: Rome; May 10, 946, to Dec., 955.

John XII (Octavius): Tusculum; Dec. 16, 955, to May 14, 964 (date of his death).

Leo VIII: Rome; Dec. 4 (6), 963, to Mar. 1, 965.

Benedict V: Rome; May 22, 964, to July 4, 966.

John XIII: Rome; Oct. 1, 965, to Sept. 6, 972.

Benedict VI: Rome; Jan. 19, 973, to June, 974.

Benedict VII: Rome; Oct., 974, to July 10, 983.

John XIV (Peter Campenora): Pavia; Dec., 983, to Aug. 20, 984.

John XV: Rome; Aug., 985, to Mar., 996.

Gregory V (Bruno of Carinthia): Saxony; May 3, 996, to Feb. 18, 999.

Sylvester II (Gerbert): Auvergne; Apr. 2, 999, to May 12, 1003.

John XVII (Siccone): Rome; June, 1003, to Dec., 1003.

John XVIII (Phasianus): Rome; Jan., 1004, to July, 1009.

Sergius IV (Peter): Rome; July 31, 1009, to May 12, 1012.

The custom of changing one's name on election to the papacy is generally considered to date from the time of Sergius IV. Before his time, several popes had changed their names. After his time, this became a regular practice, with few exceptions; e.g., Adrian VI and Marcellus II.

Benedict VIII (theophylactus): Tusculum; May 18, 1012, to Apr. 9, 1024.

John XIX (Romanus): Tusculum; Apr. (May), 1024, to 1032.

Benedict IX (Theophylactus): Tusculum; 1032, to 1044.

Sylvester III (John): Rome; Jan. 20, 1045, to Feb. 10, 1045.

Sylvester III was an antipope if the forcible removal of Benedict IX in 1044 was not legitimate.

Benedict IX (second time): Apr. 10, 1045, to May 1, 1045.

Gregory VI (John Gratian): Rome; May 5, 1045, to Dec. 20, 1046.

Clement II (Suitger, Lord of Morsleben and Hornburg): Saxony; Dec. 24 (25), 1046, to Oct. 9, 1047.

If the resignation of Benedict IX in 1045 and his removal at the December, 1046, synod were not legitimate, Gregory VI and Clement II were antipopes.

Benedict IX (third time): Nov. 8, 1047, to July 17, 1048 (d. c. 1055).

Damasus II (Poppo): Bavaria; July 17, 1048, to Aug. 9, 1048.

St. Leo IX (Bruno): Alsace; Feb. 12, 1049. to Apr. 19, 1054.

Victor II (Gebhard): Swabia; Apr. 16, 1055, to July 28, 1057.

Stephen IX (X) (Frederick): Lorraine; Aug. 3, 1057, to Mar. 29, 1058.

Nicholas II (Gerard): Burgundy; Jan. 24, 1059, to July 27, 1061.

Alexander II (Anselmo da Baggio): Milan; Oct. 1, 1061, to Apr. 21, 1073.

St. Gregory VII (Hildebrand): Tuscany; Apr. 22 (June 30), 1073, to May 25, 1085.

Bl. Victor III (Dauferius; Desiderius): Benevento; May 24, 1086, to Sept. 16, 1087. Cult confirmed July 23, 1887.

Bl. Urban II (Otto di Lagery): France; Mar. 12, 1088, to July 29, 1099. Cult confirmed July 14, 1881.

Paschal II (Raniero): Ravenna; Aug. 13 (14), 1099, to Jan. 21, 1118.

Gelasius II (Giovanni Caetani): Gaeta; Jan. 24 (Mar. 10), 1118, to Jan. 28, 1119.

Callistus II (Guido of Burgundy): Burgundy; Feb. 2 (9), 1119, to Dec. 13, 1124.

Hononius II (Lanberto(: Fiagnano (Imola); Dec. 15 (21), 1124, to Feb. 13, 1130.

Innocent II (Gregorio Papareschi):

Rome; Feb. 14 (23), 1130, to Sept. 24, 1143.

Celestine II (Guido): Citta di Castello; Sept. 26 (Oct. 3), 1143, to Mar. 8, 1144.

Lucius II (Gerardo Caccianemici): Bologna; Mar. 12, 1144, to Feb. 15, 1145.

Bl. Eugene III (Bernardo Paganelli di Montemagno): Pisa; Feb. 15 (18), 1145, to July 8, 1153. Cult confirmed Oct. 3, 1872.

Anastasius IV (Corrado): Rome; July 12, 1153, to Dec. 3, 1154.

Adrian IV (Nicholas Breakspear): England; Dec. 4 (5), 1154, to Sept. 1, 1159.

Alexander III (Rolando Bandinelli): Siena; Sept. 7 (20), 1159, to Aug. 30, 1181.

Lucius III (Ubaldo Allucingoli): Lucca; Sept. 1 (6), 1181, to Sept. 25, 1185.

Urban III (Uberto Crivelli): Milan; Nov. 25 (Dec. 1), 1185, to Oct. 20, 1187.

Gregory VIII (Alberto de Morra): Benevento; Oct. 21 (25), 1187, to Dec. 17, 1187.

Clement III (Paolo Scolari): Rome; Dec. 19 (20), 1187, to Mar., 1191.

Celestine III (Giacinto Bobone): Rome; Mar. 30 (Apr. 14), 1191, to Jan. 8, 1198.

Innocent III (Lotario dei Conti di Segni): Anagni; Jan. 8 (Feb. 22), 1198, to July 16, 1216.

Honorius III (Cencio Savelli): Rome; July 18 (24), 1216, to Mar. 18, 1227.

Gregory IX (Ugolino, Count of Segni): Anagni; Mar. 19 (21), 1227, to Aug. 22, 1241.

Celestine IV (Goffredo Castiglioni): Milan; Oct. 25 (28), 1241, to Nov. 10, 1241.

Innocent IV (Sinibaldo Fieschi): Genoa; June 25 (28), 1243, to Dec. 7, 1254.

Alexander IV (Rinaldo, Count of Segni): Anagni; Dec. 12 (20), 1254, to May 25, 1261.

Urban IV (Jacques Pantaléon): Troyes; Aug. 29 (Sept. 4), 1261, to Oct. 2, 1264.

Clement IV (Guy Foulques or Guido le Gros): France; Feb. 5 (15), 1265, to Nov. 29, 1268.

Bl. Gregory X (Teobaldo Visconti): Piacenza; Sept. 1, 1271 (Mar. 27, 1272),

to Jan. 10, 1276. Cult confirmed Sept. 12, 1713.

Bl. Innocent V (Peter of Tarentaise): Savoy; Jan. 21 (Feb. 22), 1276, to June 22, 1276. Cult confirmed Mar. 13, 1898.

Adrian V (Ottobono Fieschi): Genoa; July 11, 1276, to Aug. 18, 1276.

John XXI (Petrus Juliani or Petrus Hispanus): Portugal; Sept. 8 (20), 1276, to May 20, 1277.

Nicholas III (Giovanni Gaetano Orsini): Rome; Nov. 25 (Dec. 26), 1277, to Aug. 22, 1280.

Martin IV (Simon de Brie): France; Feb. 22 (Mar. 23), 1281, to Mar. 28, 1285.

The names of Marinus I (882–84) and Marinus II (942–46) were construed as Martin. In view of these two pontificates and the earlier reign of St. Martin I (649–55), this pope was called Martin IV.

Honorius IV (Giacomo Savelli): Rome; Apr. 2 (May 20), 1285, to Apr. 3, 1287.

Nicholas IV (Girolamo Masci): Ascoli; Feb. 22, 1288, to Apr. 4, 1292.

St. Celestine V (Pietro del Murrone): Isernia; July 5 (Aug. 29), 1294, to Dec. 13, 1294; d. 1296. Canonized May 5, 1313.

Boniface VIII (Benedetto Caetani): Anagni; Dec. 24, 1294 (Jan. 23, 1295), to Oct. 11, 1303.

Bl. Benedict XI (Niccolo Boccasini): Treviso; Oct. 22 (27), 1303, to July 7, 1304. Cult confirmed Apr. 24, 1736.

Clement V (Bertrand de Got): France; June 5 (Nov. 14), 1305, to Apr. 20, 1314. (First of Avignon popes.)

John XXII (Jacques d'Euse): Cahors; Aug. 7 (Sept. 5), 1316, to Dec. 4, 1334.

Benedict XII (Jacques Fournier): France; Dec. 20, 1334 (Jan. 8, 1335), to Apr. 25, 1342.

Clement VI (Pierre Roger): France; May 7 (19), 1342, to Dec. 6, 1352.

Innocent VI (Etienne Aubert): France; Dec. 18 (30), 1352, to Sept. 12, 1362.

Bl. Urban V (Guillaume de Grimoard): France; Sept. 28 (Nov. 6), 1362, to Dec. 19, 1370. Cult confirmed Mar. 10, 1870.

Gregory XI (Pierre Roger de Beaufort):

France; Dec. 30, 1370 (Jan. 5, 1371), to Mar. 26, 1378. (Last of Avignon popes.)

Urban VI (Bartolomeo Prignano): Naples; Apr. 8 (18), 1378, to Oct. 15, 1389.

Boniface IX (Pietro Tomacelli): Naples; Nov. 2 (9), 1389, to Oct. 1, 1404.

Innocent VII (Cosma Migliorati): Sulmona; Oct. 17 (Nov. 11), 1404, to Nov. 6, 1406.

Gregory XII (Angelo Correr): Venice; Nov. 30 (Dec. 19), 1406 to July 4, 1415, when he voluntarily resigned from the papacy to permit the election of his successor. He died Oct. 18, 1417. (See The Western Schism.)

Martin V (Oddone Colonna): Rome; Nov. 11 (21), 1417, to Feb. 20, 1431.

Eugene IV (Gabriele Condulmer): Venice; Mar. 3 (11), 1431, to Feb. 23, 1447.

Nicholas V (Tommaso Parentucelli): Sarzana; Mar. 6 (19), 1447, to Mar. 24, 1455.

Callistus III (Alfonso Borgia): Jativa (Valencia); Apr. 8 (20), 1455, to Aug. 6, 1458.

Pius II (Enea Silvio Piccolomini): Siena; Aug. 19 (Sept. 3), 1458, to Aug. 15, 1464.

Paul II (Pietro Barbo): Venice; Aug. 30 (Sept. 16), 1464, to July 26, 1471.

Sixtus IV (Francesco della Rovere): Savona; Aug. 9 (25), 1471, to Aug. 12, 1484.

Innocent VIII (Giovanni Battista Cibo): Genoa; Aug. 29 (Sept. 12), 1484, to July 25, 1492.

Alexander VI (Rodrigo Borgia): Jativa (Valencia): Aug. 22 (26), 1492, to Aug. 18, 1503.

Pius III (Francesco Todeschini-Picolomini): Siena; Sept. 22 (Oct. 1, 8), 1503, to Oct. 18, 1503.

Julius II (Giuliano della Rovere): Savona; Oct. 31 (Nov. 26), 1503, to Feb. 21, 1513.

Leo X (Giovanni de' Medici): Florence; Mar. 9 (19), 1513, to Dec. 1, 1521.

Adrian VI (Adrian Florensz): Utrecht; Jan. 9 (Aug. 31), 1522, to Sept. 14, 1523.

Clement VII (Giulio de' Medici): Florence; Nov. 19 (26), 1523, to Sept. 25, 1534.

Paul III (Alessandro Farnese): Rome; Oct. 13 (Nov. 3), 1534, to Nov. 10, 1549.

Julius III (Giovanni Maria Ciocchi del Monte): Rome; Feb. 7 (22), 1550, to Mar. 23, 1555.

Marcellus II (Marcello Cervini): Montepulciano; Apr. 9 (10), 1555, to May 1, 1555.

Paul IV (Gian Pietro Carafa): Naples; May 23 (26), 1555, to Aug. 18, 1559.

Pius IV (Giovan Angelo de' Medici): Milan; Dec. 25, 1559 (Jan. 6, 1560), to Dec. 9, 1565.

St. Pius V (Antonio-Michele Ghislieri): Bosco (Alexandria); Jan. 7 (17), 1566, to May 1, 1572. Canonized May 22, 1712.

Gregory XIII (Ugo Buoncompagni): Bologna; May 13 (25), 1572, to Apr. 10, 1585.

Sixtus V (Felice Peretti): Grootammare (Ripatransone); Apr. 24 (May 1), 1585, to Aug. 27, 1590.

Urban VII (Giovanni Battista Castagna): Rome; Sept. 15, 1590, to Sept. 27, 1590.

Gregory XIV (Niccolo Sfondrati): Cremona; Dec. 5 (8), 1590, to Oct. 16, 1591.

Innocent IX (Giovanni Antonio Facchinetti): Bologna; Oct. 29 (Nov. 3), 1591, to Dec. 30, 1591.

Clement VIII (Ippolito Aldobrandini): Florence; Jan. 30 (Feb. 9), 1592, to Mar. 3, 1605.

Leo XI (Alessandro de' Medici): Florence; Apr. 1 (10), 1605, to Apr. 26, 1605.

Paul V (Camillo Borghese): Rome; May 16 (29), 1605, to Jan. 28, 1621.

Gregory XV (Alessandro Ludovisi): Bologna; Feb. 9 (14), 1621, to July 8, 1623.

Urban VIII (Maffeo Barberini): Florence; Aug. 6 (Sept. 29), 1623, to July 29, 1644.

Innocent X (Giovanni Battista Pamfili): Rome; Sept. 15 (Oct. 4), 1644, to Jan. 7, 1655.

Alexander VII (Fabio Chigi): Siena; Apr. 7 (18), 1655, to May 22, 1667.

Clement IX (Giulio Rospigliosi): Pistoia; June 20 (26), 1667, to Dec. 9, 1669.

Clement X (Emilio Altieri): Rome; Apr. 29 (May 11), 1670, to July 22, 1676.

Bl. Innocent XI (Benedetto Odescalchi): Como; Sept. 21 (Oct. 4), 1676, to Aug. 12, 1689.

Alexander VIII (Pietro Ottoboni): Venice; Oct. 6 (16), 1689, to Feb. 1, 1691.

Innocent XII (Antonio Pignatelli): Spinazzola; July 12 (15), 1691, to Sept. 27, 1700.

Clement XI (Giovanni Francesco Albani): Urbino; Nov. 23, 30 (Dec. 8), 1700, to Mar. 19, 1721.

Innocent XIII (Michelangelo dei Conti): Rome; May 8 (18), 1721, to Mar. 7, 1724.

Benedict XIII (Pietro Francesco— Vincenzo Maria—Orsini); Gravina (Bari); May 29 (June 4), 1724, to Feb. 21, 1730.

Clement XII (Lorenzo Corsini): Florence; July 12 (16), 1730, to Feb. 6, 1740.

Benedict XIV (Prospero Lambertini): Bologna; Aug. 17 (22), 1740, to May 3, 1758.

Clement XIII (Carlo Rezzonico): Venice; July 6 (16), 1758, to Feb. 2, 1769.

Clement XIV (Giovanni Vincenzo Antonio—Lorenzo—Ganganelli): Rimini; May 19, 28 (June 4), 1769, to Sept. 22, 1774.

Pius VI (Giovanni Angelo Braschi): Cesena; Feb. 15 (22), 1775, to Aug. 29, 1799.

Pius VII (Barnaba—Gregorio— Chiaramonti): Cesena; Mar. 14 (21), 1800, to Aug. 20, 1823.

Leo XII (Annibale della Genga): Genga (Fabriano); Sept. 28 (Oct. 5), 1823, to Feb. 10, 1829.

Pius VIII (Francesco Saverio Castiglioni): Cingoli; Mar. 31 (Apr. 5), 1829, to Nov. 30, 1830.

Gregory XVI (Bartolomeo Alberto— Mauro—Cappellari): Belluno; Feb. 2 (6), 1831, to June 1, 1846.

Pius IX (Giovanni M. Mastai Ferretti): Senigallia; June 16 (21), 1846, to Feb. 7, 1878.

Leo XIII (Gioacchino Pecci): Car-pineto (Anagni); Feb. 20 (Mar. 3), 1878, to July 20, 1903.

St. Pius X (Giuseppe Sarto): Riese (Treviso); Aug. 4 (9), 1903, to Aug. 20, 1914. Canonized May 29, 1954.

Benedict XV (Giacomo della Chiesa): Genoa; Sept. 3 (6), 1914, to Jan. 22, 1922.

Pius XI (Achille Ratti): Desio (Milan); Feb. 6 (12), 1922, to Feb. 10, 1939.

Pius XII (Eugenio Pacelli): Rome; Mar. 2 (12), 1939, to Oct. 9, 1958.

John XXIII (Angelo Giuseppe Roncalli): Sotto il Monte (Bergamo); Oct. 28 (Nov. 4), 1958 to June 3, 1963.

Paul VI (Giovanni Battista Montini): Concessio (Brescia); June 21 (June 30), 1963 to 1978.

John Paul I (Albino Luciani); Aug. 26, 1978 to Sept. 29, 1978.

John Paul II (Karol Wojtyla); Oct. 16, 1978 to

Avignon Papacy

Avignon was the residence of a series of French popes from Clement V to Gregory XI (1309–77). Prominent in the period were power struggles over the mixed interests of Church and state with the rulers of France (Philip IV, John II), Bavaria (Lewis IV), England (Edward III); factionalism of French and Italian churchmen; political as well as ecclesiastical turmoil in Italy, a factor of significance in prolonging the stay of popes in Avignon. Despite some positive achievements, the Avignon papacy was a prologue to the Western Schism which began in 1378.

Western Schism

The Western Schism was a confused state of affairs which divided Christendom into two and then three papal obediences from 1378 to 1417.

It occurred some 50 years after Marsilius theorized that a general (not ecumenical) council of bishops and other persons was superior to a pope and nearly 30 years before the Council of Florence stated definitively that no kind of council had such authority.

It was a period of disaster preceding the even more disastrous period of the Reformation.

Urban VI, following transfer to Rome of the 70-year papal residence at Avignon, was elected pope Apr. 8, 1378, and reigned until his death in 1389. He was succeeoed by Boniface IX (1389–1404), Innocent VII (1404–1406) and Gregory XII (1406–1415). These four are considered the legitimate popes of the period.

Some of the cardinals who chose Urban pope, dissatisfied with his conduct of the office, declared that his election was invalid. They proceeded to elect Clement VII, who claimed the papacy from 1378 to 1394. He was succeeded by Benedict XIII.

Prelates seeking to end the state of divided papal loyalties convoked the Council of Pisa which, without authority, found Gregory XII and Benedict XIII, in absentia, guilty on 30-odd charges of schism and heresy, deposed them, and elected a third claimant to the papacy. Alexander V (1409–1410). He was succeeded by John XXIII (1410–1415).

The Schism was ended by the Council of Constance (1414–1418). This council, although originally called into session in an irregular manner, acquired authority after being convoked by Gregory XII in 1415. In its early irregular phase, it deposed John XXIII whose election to the papacy was uncanonical anyway. After being formally convoked, it accepted the abdication of Gregory in 1415 and dismissed the claims of Benedict XIII two years later, thus clearing the way for the election of Matin V on Nov. 11, 1417. The Council of Constance also rejected the theories of John Wycliff and condemned John Hus as a heretic.

20th Century Popes

Leo XIII

Leo XIII (Gioacchino Vincenzo Pecci) was born May 2, 1810, in Carpineto, Italy. Although all but three years of his life and pontificate were of the 19th century, his influence extended well into the 20th century.

He was educated at the Jesuit college in Viterbo, the Roman College, the Academy of Noble Ecclesiastics, and the University of the Sapienza. He was ordained to the priesthood in 1837.

He served as an apostolic delegate to two States of the Church, Benevento from 1838 to 1841 and Perugia in 1841 and 1842. Ordained titular archbishop of Damietta, he was papal nuncio to Belgium from January, 1843, until May, 1846; in the post, he had controversial relations with the government over education issues and acquired his first significant experience of industrialized society.

He was archbishop of Perugia from 1846 to 1878. He became a cardinal in 1853 and chamberlain of the Roman Curia in 1877. He was elected to the papacy Feb. 20, 1878. He died July 20, 1903.

Canonizations: He canonized 18 saints and beatified a group of English martyrs.

Church Administration: He established 300 new dioceses and vicariates; restored the hierarchy in Scotland, set up an English, as contrasted with the Portuguese, hierarchy in India; approved the action of the Congregation for the Propagation of the Faith in reorganizing missions in China.

Encyclicals: He issued 50 encyclicals, on subjects ranging from devotional to social. In the former category were *Annum Sacrum*, on the Sacred Heart, in 1899, and nine letters on Mary and the Rosary.

Interfaith Relations: He was unsuccessful in unity overtures made to Orthodox and Slavic Churches. He declared Anglican orders invalid in the apostolic bull *Apostolicae Curae* Sept. 13, 1896.

International Relations: Leo was frustrated in seeking solutions to the Roman Question arising from the seizure of church lands by the Kingdom of Italy in 1870. He also faced anticlerical situations in Belgium and France and in the Kulturkampf policies of Bismarck in Germany.

Social Questions: Much of Leo's influence stemmed from social doctrine stated in numerous encyclicals, concerning liberalism, liberty, the divine origin of authority; socialism, in *Quod Apostolici Muneris*, 1878; the Christian concept of the family, in *Arcanum*, 1880; socialism and economic liberalism, relations between capital and labor, in *Rerum Novarum*, 1891. Two of his social encyclicals were against the African slave trade.

Studies: In the encyclical *Aeterni Patris* of Aug. 4, 1879, he ordered a renewal of philosophy.

The Twenty-One Ecumenical Councils of the Church

The 21 ecumenical councils in the history of the Church are listed below, with indication of their names or titles (taken from the names of the places where they were held); the dates; the reigning and/or approving popes; the emperors who were instrumental in convoking the eight councils in the East; the number of bishops who attended, when available; the number of sessions; the most significant actions.

1. *Nicaea I.* 325: St. Sylvester I (Emperor Constantine I); attended by approximately 300 bishops; sessions held between May 20 or June 19 to near the end of August. Condemned Arianism, which denied the divinity of Christ; contributed to formulation of the Nicene Creed; fixed the date of Easter; passed regulations concerning clerical discipline; adopted the civil division of the Empire as the model for the organization of the Church.

2. *Constantinople I*, 381: St. Damasus I (Emperor Theodosius I); attended by approximately 150 bishops; sessions held from May to July. Condemned various brands of Arianism, and Macedonianism which denied the divinity of the Holy Spirit; contributed to formulation of the Nicene Creed; approved a canon which made the bishop of Constantinople the ranking prelate in the East, with primacy next to that of the pope. Doubt about the ecumenical character of this council was resolved by the ratification of its acts by popes and the Council of Chalcedon.

3. *Ephesus*, 431: St. Celestine I (Emperor Theodosius II); attended by 150 to 200 bishops; five sessions held between June 22 and July 17. Condemned Nestorianism, which denied the real unity of the divine and human natures in the Person of Christ; defined *Theotokos* ("Bearer of God") as the title of Mary, Mother of the Son of God made Man; condemned Pelagianism, which reduced the supernatural to the natural order of things.

4. *Chalcedon*, 451: St. Leo I (Emperor Marcian); attended by approximately 600 bishops; 17 sessions held between Oct. 8 and Nov. 1. Condemned: Monophysitism, also called Eutychianism, which denied the humanity of Christ by holding that he had only one, the divine, nature; and the Monophysite Robber Synod of Ephesus, of 449.

5. *Constantinople II*, 553: Vigilius (Emperor Justinian I): attended by 165 bishops; eight sessions held between May 5 and June 2. Condemned the *Three Chapters*, Nestorian-tainted writings of Theodore of Mopsuestia, Theodoret of Cyprus and Ibas of Edessa.

6. *Constantinople III*, 680–681; St. Agatho, St. Leo II (Emperor Constantine IV); attended by approximately 170 bishops; 16 sessions held between Nov. 7, 680, and Sept. 16, 681. Condemned Monothelitism, which held that there was only one will, the divine, in Christ; censured Pope Honorius I for a letter to Sergius, bishop of Constantinople, in which he made an ambiguous but not infallible statement about the unity of will and/or operation in Christ. Constantinople III is also called the Trullan Council because its sessions were held in the domed hall, Trullos, of the imperial palace.

7. *Nicaea II*, 787: Adrian I (Empress Irene); attended by approximately 300 bishops; eight sessions held between Sept. 24 and Oct. 23. Condemned: Iconoclasm, which held that the use of images was idolatry; and Adoptionism, which claimed that Christ was not the Son of God by nature but only by adoption. This was the last council regarded as ecumenical by Orthodox Churches.

8. *Constantinople IV*, 869–870: Adrian II (Emperor Basil I); attended by 102 bishops; six sessions held between Oct. 5, 869, and Feb. 28, 870. Condemned Iconoclasm; condemned and deposed Photius as patriarch of Constantinople: restored Ignatius to the patriarchate. This was the last ecumenical council held in the East. It was the first called ecumenical by canonists toward the end of the 11th century.

9. *Lateran I*, 1123: Callistus II; attended by approximately 300 bishops; sessions held between Mar. 18 and Apr. 6. Endorsed provisions of the Concordat of Worms concerning the investiture of prelates; approved reform measures in 25 canons.

10. *Lateran II*, 1139: Innocent II; attended by 900 to 1,000 bishops and abbots; three sessions held in April. Adopted measures against a schism organized by antipope Anacletus; approved 30 disciplinary measures and canons, one of which stated that holy orders is an invalidating impediment to marriage.

11. *Lateran III*, 1179: Alexander III; attended by at least 300 bishops; three sessions held between Mar. 5 and 19. Enacted measures against the Waldenses and Albigensians; approved reform decrees in 27 canons; provided that popes be elected by two-thirds vote of the cardinals.

12. *Lateran IV*, 1215: Innocent III; sessions held between Nov. 11 and 30. Ordered annual confession and Communion; defined and made first official use of the term "transubstantiation"; adopted measures to counteract the Cathari and Albigensians; approved 70 canons.

13. *Lyons I*, 1245: Innocent IV; attended by approximately 150 bishops; three sessions held between June 28 and July 17. Confirmed the deposition of Emperor Frederick II; approved 22 canons.

14. *Lyons II*, 1274: Gregory X; attended by approximately 500 bishops; six sessions held between May 7 and July 17. Accomplished a temporary reunion of separated Eastern Churches with the Roman Church; issued regulations concerning conclaves for papal elections; approved 31 canons.

15. *Vienne*, 1311–1312: Clement V; attended by 132 bishops; three sessions held between Oct. 16, 1311, and May 6, 1312. Suppressed the Knights Templar; enacted a number of reform decrees.

16. *Constance*, 1414–1418: Gregory XII, Martin V; attended by nearly 200 bishops, plus other prelates and many experts; 45 sessions held between Nov. 5, 1414, and Apr. 22, 1418. Took successful action to end the Western Schism; rejected the teachings of Wycliff; condemned Hus as a heretic. One decree, passed in the earlier stages of the council, asserted the superiority of an ecumenical council over the pope; this was later rejected.

17. *Florence* (also called Basel-Ferrara-Florence), 1438–1445: Eugene IV; attended by many Latin-Rite and Eastern-Rite bishops; preliminary sessions were held at Basel and Ferrara before definitive work was accomplished at Florence. Reaffirmed the primacy of the pope against the claims of Conciliarists that an ecumenical council is superior to the pope; formulated and approved decrees of union—with the Greeks, July 6, 1439; with the Armenians, Nov. 22, 1439; with the Jacobites, Feb. 4, 1442. These decrees failed to gain general or lasting acceptance in the East.

18. *Lateran V*, 1512–1517: Julius II, Leo X, 12 sessions held between May 3, 1512, and Mar. 16, 1517. Stated the relation and position of the pope with respect to an ecumenical council; acted to counteract the Pragmatic Sanction of Bourges and exaggerated claims of liberty by the French Church; condemned erroneous teachings concerning the nature of the human soul; stated doctrine concerning indulgences. The council reflected concern for abuses in the Church and the need for reforms but failed to take decisive action in the years immediately preceding the Reformation.

19. *Trent*, 1545–1563: Paul III, Julius III, Pius IV; 25 sessions held between Dec. 13,

1545, and Dec. 4, 1563. Issued a great number of decrees concerning doctrinal matters opposed by the Reformers, and mobilized the Counter-Reformation. Definitions covered the rule of faith, the nature of justification, grace, faith, original sin and its effects, the seven sacraments, the sacrificial nature of the Mass, the veneration of saints, use of sacred images, belief in purgatory, the doctrine of indulgences, the jurisdiction of the pope over the whole Church. Initiated many reforms for renewal in the liturgy and general discipline in the Church, the promotion of religious instruction, the education of the clergy through the foundation of seminaries, etc. Trent ranks with Vatican II as the greatest ecumenical council held in the West.

20. *Vatican I*, 1869–1870: Pius IX; attended by approximately 800 bishops and other prelates; four public sessions and 89 general meetings held between Dec. 8, 1869, and July 7, 1870. Defined papal primacy and infallibility in a dogmatic constitution on the Church; covered natural religion, revelation, faith, and the relations between faith and reason in a dogmatic constitution on the Catholic faith. The council suspended sessions Sept. 1 and was adjourned Oct. 20, 1870.

Vatican II

The Second Vatican Council which was forecast by Pope John XXIII Jan. 25, 1959, was held in four sessions in St. Peter's Basilica.

Pope John convoked it and opened the first session, which ran from Sept. 11 to Dec. 8, 1962. Following John's death June 3, 1963, Pope Paul VI reconvened the council for the other three sessions which ran from Sept. 29 to Dec. 4, 1963; Sept. 14 to Nov. 21, 1964; Sept. 14 to Dec. 8, 1965.

A total of 2,860 Fathers participated in council proceedings, and attendance at meetings varied between 2,000 and 2,500. For various reasons, including the denial of exit from Communist-dominated countries, 274 Fathers could not attend.

The council formulated and promulgated 16 documents—two dogmatic and two pastoral constitutions, nine decrees and three declarations—all of which reflect its basic pastoral orientation toward renewal and reform in the Church.